Blockchain for Smart Systems

Blockchain technology has been penetrating every aspect of Information and Communications Technology (ICT), and its use has been growing rapidly in recent years. The interest and development of this technology has primarily been driven by the enormous value growth of cryptocurrencies and large investments of venture capital in blockchain start-ups. *Blockchain for Smart Systems: Computing Technologies and Applications* is intended to clarify and define, in simple terms, the technology behind blockchain. It provides a deep dive into the core fundamentals of blockchain: hashing algorithm behind each block, distributed technology, smart contracts, and private vs. public blockchain.

Features

- Discusses fundamental theories of practical and sophisticated applications of blockchain technology
- Includes case studies
- Discusses the concepts with illustrations, appropriate figures, tables, and simple language

This book is primarily aimed at undergraduates, graduates, research scholars, academicians, and industry and technology enthusiasts working in various aspects of blockchain technology.

Chapman & Hall/CRC

**Blockchain for Smart and
Green Society: Promise, Practice and Application**

Series Editors
Vishal Bhatnagar and Vikram Bali

Blockchain for Smart Systems: Computing Technologies and Applications
Latesh Malik, Sandhya Arora, Urmila Shrawankar and Vivek Deshpande

Blockchain for Smart Systems
Computing Technologies and Applications

Edited by
Latesh Malik
Sandhya Arora
Urmila Shrawankar
Vivek Deshpande

CRC Press
Taylor & Francis Group
Boca Raton London New York

CRC Press is an imprint of the
Taylor & Francis Group, an **informa** business

A CHAPMAN & HALL BOOK

First Edition published 2022
by CRC Press
6000 Broken Sound Parkway NW, Suite 300, Boca Raton, FL 33487–2742

and by CRC Press
4 Park Square, Milton Park, Abingdon, Oxon, OX14 4RN

CRC Press is an imprint of Taylor & Francis Group, LLC

ISBN: 978-1-032-06804-6 (hbk)
ISBN: 978-1-032-06805-3 (pbk)
ISBN: 978-1-003-20393-3 (ebk)

DOI: 10.1201/9781003203933

Typeset in Palatino
by Apex CoVantage, LLC

Contents

Section I   Blockchain Fundamentals

Section II   Blockchain Algorithms & Security

Section III   Applications of Blockchain

Preface

The trend of digital technology advancement is changing many aspects of society including administration, industry, healthcare and personal life. New technologies such as Blockchain, the Internet of Things (IoT), Cloud Technology, Robotics, Artificial Intelligence, Machine Learning and Big Data can affect the course of a society and continue to progress. The ultimate aim of technological development is to benefit humankind. By doing so the society of the future will be one in which new values and services are created continuously, making people's lives more conformable and sustainable. Future society will be a people-centric super-smart society.

This book aims to cover the technological developments, concepts, case studies, research and solutions for societal benefit using the Internet of Things, Cloud Technology, Machine Learning and Data Science to handle societal challenges.

Blockchain technology has been penetrating every aspect of Information and Communications Technology (ICT) and its use has been growing rapidly in recent years. The interest and development of this technology has primarily been driven by the enormous value growth of cryptocurrencies and large investments of venture capital in blockchain start-ups.

Blockchain technology promotes transparency in a distributed and scalable way. It is a trustworthy way to share valuable data in a secure, tamperproof way. It uses distributed ledger technology that can be applied to track fraud in finance, securely share data in peer-to-peer communication and effectively handle legal documents in a distributed manner. This technology uses digital assets which are decentralized and accessible in real time, ensures integrity of the document and creates trust in the asset. It enables financial transactions to be both anonymous and secure through the distributed ledger.

Blockchain technology will immensely improve the delivery of expanding financial services and the safeguarding of personal identity information. Blockchain also has benefits for business contracts and the development of the Internet of Things. Major application areas include: secure sharing of medical data, music royalties tracking, cross-border payments, real-time IoT operating systems, personal identity security, anti-money laundering tracking systems, supply chain and logistics monitoring, voting mechanisms, advertising insights, original content creation, cryptocurrency exchange, real estate processing platforms, etc.

This book is divided in three sections, Blockchain Fundamentals, Blockchain Algorithms & Security and Applications of Blockchain, and is organized in 12 chapters.

Chapter 1 covers the basics of blockchain. It discusses the anatomy, attributes and types of blockchain. The chapter is organized according to need, introduction, background history and basic concepts of blockchain. At the end, a case study on blockchain is discussed.

Chapter 2 presents a deep dive into the block structure, use of Merkle trees for transactions and the blockchain structure. The power of decentralization, the built-in redundancy in the blockchain architectures and how it helps establish a trustless system is explained. It presents the challenges of distributed consensus and how they are dealt with via various consensus algorithms in the blockchain architecture. The chapter ends with a sample use case discussion of maintenance and service supply chain over a permissioned blockchain architecture using the Hyperledger framework.

Chapter 3 covers five Principles of Blockchain Technology and elements. It also covers a summary of the types of blockchain and discusses proof of work, the consensus mechanism used in Bitcoin. At the end of this chapter, use cases of blockchain in various sectors and industries are discussed.

Chapter 4 deals with hybrid services of Blockchain-Cloud. This hybrid combination provides more flexibility in storage with validation of data. Authorization of transactions is monitored and increases the network elasticity. Cloud technology is a well-known, very low-cost solution for resource availability. If blockchain technology is added to cloud data and services, the cloud data security will be improved significantly.

Chapter 5 discusses different consensus algorithms which can be used for this like Proof of Stake, Byzantine Fault Tolerance, Proof of Work, etc. These are the most widely used consensus algorithms. Algorithms like Proof of Contribution have also been introduced to secure digital content.

Chapter 6 converses the notion of blockchain technology and challenging security and privacy issues, along with available BT research solutions. In addition, it discusseshow to acclimatize security issues in blockchain security in detail concerning the Internet of Things and cloud computing.

Chapter 7 focuses on the use of blockchain and its underlying concepts for decentralization in identity management systems. The chapter begins with an introduction to blockchain and then sheds light on decentralization solution for identity management systems. The next part explains the concepts from self-sovereign identity, which are the base of decentralized identity management systems. A case study explores the distributed nature of blockchain for identity management.

Chapter 8 covers the constant threats to the current cryptographic systems of blockchain by the advancement of quantum computers. As the security and privacy of blockchain solely depends on hashing and digital signatures, the quantum algorithms like Shor's algorithm and Grover's algorithm can prove to be a real problem if developed in the coming future. ECDSA is used as a way to sign digitally; it uses the logarithmic problem as security, which cannot be solved by classical computers, making it secure. But this can be compromised by Shor's algorithm. Furthermore, the chapter discussed the Post-Quantum Cryptographic schemes which are considered as Quantum Resistant, i.e., secure from future quantum attacks.

Chapter 9 covers the use of blockchain for the digital economy. This chapter focuses on online transaction systems that make use of blockchain technology and its features, namely distributed database, Advanced Encryption Standard (AES) and Secure Hash Algorithm 256 (SHA-256) to make the cash-less payment system more robust to cyber security threats. As the outcome, a more secure and reliable model for a digital payment wallet service using blockchain technology has been developed.

Chapter 10 provides security and privacy preservation of important documents used as evidence in the police system. The proposed scheme provides an Ethereum-based decentralized application (DApp) to track a police complaint starting from First Information Report (FIR) until the complaint gets resolved. DApp also provides security to forensic reports as security, confidentiality and integrity are at the highest priority. The proposed application supports forensic investigation with authenticity, immutability, traceability, resilience and distributed trust between evidential entitles. Details of tracking police complaints, further investigation, forensic report preservation and analysis will be recorded in chains of blocks. The proposed system is validated through various experimental results for security, privacy and sensitivity of important documents used as evidence by the police department.

Chapter 11 describes the integration of blockchain technology in healthcare, the issues and challenges faced by the current traditional healthcare systems, the workflow, architecture and practical use cases of these systems, and some challenges to build these systems. A case study of a DApp for a blockchain-based medical data management system built using Ethereum Blockchain and IPFS (Interplanetary File System) is also explained.

Chapter 12 discusses the concept of blockchain technology in brief, features Microgrid or smart grid, some useful use cases of energy blockchain and benefits of application of blockchain technology to smart grid operations.

Acknowledgments

This book is the outcome of the initiation of an edited book series on "Blockchain For Smart and Green Society: Promise, Practice and Applications" by our series editors Dr. Vishal Bhatnagar and Dr. Vikram Bali.

It is considered that technology is enabling people so that they could access advances and could avail benefits of technology in day-to-day life. It is highly required that in a future smart and green society, any product or service will be optimally delivered to people and tailored to their needs. Blockchain technology has been penetrating every aspect of Information and Communications Technology (ICT) and its use has been growing rapidly in recent years. The interest and development of this technology has primarily been driven by the enormous value growth of cryptocurrencies and large investments of venture capital in blockchain start-ups.

Many professionals have contributed chapters in this book. The Taylor & Francis team, who initiated, designed, proofread and indexed the book. We offer them all our heartfelt thanks for their editorial and production support. We would like to thank all the reviewers of this book, who helped us through their critical comments and creative suggestions which eventually helped us to improve the text of the book. Many of the ideas in this book come from Blockchain Fundamentals, Blockchain Algorithms & Security, Applications of Blockchain in Digital Economy, Secure Evidence Management, Healthcare Systems And Smart Microgrid Based Energy Management. We thank all our professors who helped and taught us basic concepts of the subjects. Thanks to all contributors who completed all revisions and submitted chapters as per guidelines.

We owe an enormous debt of gratitude to our series editors who have given us the opportunity to contribute. We would like to take this opportunity to thank our mentors, teachers and friends for motivating us throughout this journey. We also thank all our college colleagues and principal who have given immense support for molding this work.

Finally, we would like to thank our family members for their support, good wishes, encouragement and understanding while we wrote this book.

Editor Biographies

Latesh Malik is working as Associate Professor & Head, Department of Computer Science & Engg, Government College of Engineering, Nagpur. She has completed a Ph.D. (Computer Science & Engineering) from Visvesyaraya National Institute of Technology in 2010, M.Tech. (Computer Science & Engineering) from Banasthali Vidyapith, Rajasthan, India and B.E. (Computer Engineering) from the University of Rajasthan, India. She is a gold medalist in B.E. and M.Tech. She has teaching experience of over 20 years. She is a life member of ISTE, CSI, ACM and has more than 160 papers published in international journals and conferences. She is a recipient of two RPS and one MODROBs by AICTE. She guided over 30 PG projects and eight students completed their Ph.D.s under her. She is the author of three books: *Practical Guide to Distributed Systems in MPI* and *Python for Data Analysis* on Amazon Kindle Direct Publishing, and *R Programming for Beginners* by University Press India.

Sandhya Arora is working as Professor, Department of Computer Engineering, MKSSS's Cummins College of Engineering for Women, Pune. She has completed her Ph.D. (Computer Science & Engineering) from Jadavpur University, Kolkata in 2012, M.Tech. (Computer Science & Engineering) from Banasthali Vidyapith, Rajasthan, India and B.E. (Computer Engineering) from the University of Rajasthan, India. She has a rich teaching experience of over 24 years. She is a life member of ISTE, CSI, ACM and has published papers in thoroughly acclaimed international journals and conferences. She is guiding PG and Ph.D. students. She has received prestigious awards in the field of Computer Science. She has authored three books: *Practical Guide to Distributed Systems in MPI* and *Python for Data Analysis* on Amazon Kindle Direct Publishing, and *R Programming for Beginners* by University Press India.

Urmila Shrawankar received her Ph.D. in Computer Sci & Engg from SGB Amravati University and M.Tech. degree in Computer Sci & Engg from RTM Nagpur University. She is the author of two books, six book chapters and more than 160 research papers in international journals and conferences of high repute. She has published 16 patents. Her biography was selected and published in the *Marquis Who's Who in the World*. She is a recipient of an international travel grant and UGC Minor Project Grant. She participated in many international conferences as a core organizing committee member, technical program committee member, special session chair and session chair. Dr. Urmila is a member of IEEE (SM), ACM, CSI (LM), ISTE(LM), IE(LM), IAENG, etc. At present, Dr. Shrawankar is working as a professor in the Department of Computer Science and Engineering, G H Raisoni College of Engineering, RTM Nagpur University, Nagpur (MS), India.

 **Vivek Deshpande** received his MBA from the University of Wisconsin, Madison. He completed a blockchain specialization from MIT, Cambridge, Massachusetts. He completed a Bachelor of Engineering, REC Kurukshetra and later transferred to IGGEC, Sagar, M.P. He holds leadership positions in managing the Enterprise Software Systems across 13 four-year institutions at the University of Wisconsin. He is the CEO of Arbudausa.com, a medical platform that advances healthcare by connecting local patients and their doctors in India to top cancer experts in the US. He earned three prestigious grants from the University of Wisconsin and is a Vice President of IDP, an Edtech start-up founded by four faculty members of the computer science department of the University of Wisconsin.

Contributors

Padma D. Adane
Department of Information Technology
Shri Ramdeobaba College of Engineering
    and Management
Nagpur, Maharashtra, India

Supriya Aras
School of Computer Science, MIT World
    Peace University
Pune, Maharashtra, India

Sachin Babar
Sinhgad Institute of Technology
Lonaval, Maharashtra, India

Mangesh Bedekar
School of Computer Science
    MIT World Peace University
Pune, Maharashtra, India

Prajwal Sameer Deshmukh
Sinhgad Academy Of Engineering
Pune, Maharashtra, India

Rashmi Jain
S. B. Jain Institute of Technology
    Management and Research
Nagpur, Maharashtra, India

Sachin Jain
Oklahoma State University
Stillwater, Oklahoma

Sanchit Jain
Vishwakarma Institute of Information
    Technology
Pune, Maharashtra, India

Gargi Kulkarni
Sinhgad Academy of Engineering
Pune, Maharashtra, India

Nupur Kulkarni
Pimpri Chinchwad College
    of Engineering
Pune, Maharashtra, India

Shailaja Nitin Lohar
Sinhgad Institute of Technology
Lonavala, Maharashtra, India

Maulik Hiten Pandya
Government College of Engineering
Nagpur, Maharashtra, India

Shreeya Patil
MKSSS's Cummins College of Engineering
    For Women
Pune, Maharashtra, India

Sonali Patil
Pimpri Chinchwad College Of
    Engineering
Pune, Maharashtra, India

Rohini Pise
Pimpri Chinchwad College
    Of Engineering
Pune, Maharashtra, India

M.A. Pund
Ram Meghe Institute of Technology &
    Research
Badnera, Maharashtra, India

Sonali Ridhorkar
G.H. Raisoni Institute of Engineering and
    Technology
Nagpur, Maharashtra, India

Chaitreya Shrawankar
RTM Nagpur University
Nagpur, Maharashtra India

Urmila Shrawankar
G.H. Raisoni College of Engineering
Nagpur, Maharashtra, India

Sheetal Thakare
Bharati Vidyapeeth College
    of Engineering
Navi Mumbai, Maharashtra, India

K.S. Thakre
Sinhgad Academy of Engineering
Pune, Maharashtra, India

Section I

Blockchain Fundamentals

1

Introduction to Blockchain and Terminologies

Sheetal Thakare and M.A. Pund

CONTENTS

DOI: 10.1201/9781003203933-2

3

Introduction

Internet and computing devices together made business and every aspect of life easier. The entire globe is reachable and available at our fingertips 24/7. Business transactions are made all over the globe with increasing velocity. So the need is for efficiency, cost-effectivity, reliability and trustworthiness in business transactions.

Currently, business transactions are going well, but not great. The scope of improvement is there regarding cashless facilities, redundant localized updates, transaction cost, transaction settlement time, monetary fraudulent and cyber-attacks. The possible architectures for business transactions required are decentralized, shared and at the same time distributed.

This requirement invented the concept of **Distributed Ledger Technology (DLT)**. Consider the analogy of a spreadsheet and a Google spreadsheet. In the case of spreadsheet use, each application has its own copy available for updates. In the end, all copies need to be referred to duplicate in a final version of the spreadsheet [1]. The process is definitely painful. Google saved time and effort with the Google spreadsheet solution. Google spreadsheet is shared amongst all users: everyone can simultaneously update the same shared copy in real time. At the same time, everyone can have their own copy made. Such is the technology requirement for today's growing business transactions [2].

In Figure 1.1, **Node** represents the User and **Transactions Record** is each User's individual copy of transactions done. The transactions are appended to a common copy of transactions record which can be accessed by all users on a network of nodes. The network in Figure 1.1 is implemented using P2P (peer-2-peer) architecture. In a P2P network, all nodes are at equal privilege, unlike in a client-server architecture. Each node is a computing machine representing a user participating in a transaction. A P2P network allows access to all other nodes from each and every node on the network. Such DLT architecture forms the base for **blockchain** technology [2, 4].

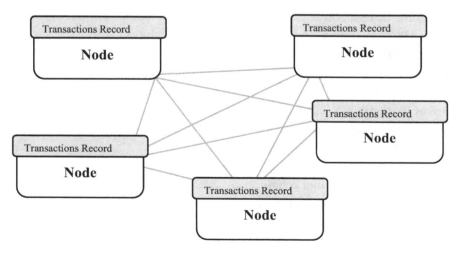

FIGURE 1.1
Distributed ledger architecture [3].

1.1 History of Blockchain

Blockchain technology is the byproduct of Bitcoin. Satoshi Nakamoto worked towards building the concept of electronic cash system **Bitcoin** in 2008. By November 2008, the thesis with electronic cash system concept was submitted and finalized with cryptographers from a US mailing team. By January 2009, Bitcoin was up with its first block. Since then, there has been no downtime in this chain of Bitcoin. It's growing day by day without any requirement of maintenance. Considering this feature of Bitcoin chain, people were curious about the technology behind this chain and its working. So from 2015, the technology on which Bitcoin chain is based came into the focus and it was known by the name of blockchain technology.[5, 6]

1.1.1 Why the Name "Blockchain"?

Block structure is used to store data related to a transaction. All blocks are chained as per time stamp ordering. So it forms a chain of blocks, referred as "blockchain". As all the users/nodes have access to each and every block, it is also referred as "Distributed Ledger".

Hashing is the concept which is used as the basis of chaining. Blocks are connected to each other using hash values. Each next block stores hash value of the previous block. Thus hashing forms a logical connection between blocks. This logical connection is termed as "chain". So in Figure 1.2 for visualization purposes of blockchain, it is given that blocks of data are actually connected with a physical chain. Chain is implemented using hashing [7].

1.2 Basic Concepts

1.2.1 What is inside the "Block"?

The blocks are of two categories, genesis block and transaction block.

I) **Genesis block:** It acts as the block zero, the origin of blockchain. There is no previous block hash field. A genesis block is not created every time upon transaction request; it is created only once when blockchain is ready to accept the very first transaction request. A genesis block also marks the end of blockchain when any transaction is traced back to its origin [8].

II) **Transaction block:** It has two sections, header and body, with information specified further in this chapter. Six common fields are generally there in the header section, as specified in Figure 1.3. Nonce stands for number only used once. The body section will have information about transactions and related data.

FIGURE 1.2
Blockchain visualization.

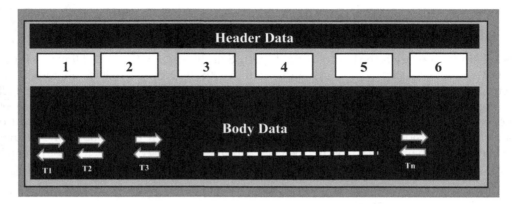

FIGURE 1.3
Block architecture [9].

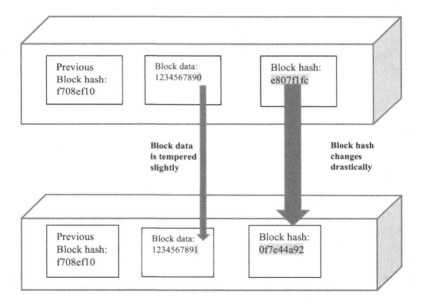

FIGURE 1.4
Block data tempering and block hash changes [7].

A parent block hash serves dual functionality. It's a linkage attribute and it also contributes to achieve the immutability feature of blockchain by not allowing block-update and in-between block insertion. Thus, blockchain is useful to store transactions with verified proof. Hash value plays an important role here [10]. Hash value of data written originally will always evaluate to the same number. Any update or tamper even to the slightest extent makes a huge difference to the hash values of data written originally (see Figure 1.4). This way, originality of data will be preserved, making blocks tamper proof [9].

1.3 Architecture

1.3.1 Data Layer

Physical storage represents the data layer of blockchain architecture (see Figure 1.5). Units of storage are in the form of blocks implemented using data structure concepts like linked list and trees. Hashing plays a very important role to secure block contents. Different data layer components are: block structure, Merkle tree [10], timestamp and hash.

1.3.2 Network Layer

P2P network represents the network layer of blockchain architecture (see Figure 1.5). This network provides a distributed and decentralized feature to blockchain. Each peer represents a node/user and all have rights to validate transaction, append the block and create their own local blockchain copy. A broadcast mechanism is required to send the requested transaction to all peers who will try to validate it. Only validated transaction can be structured into blocks, which are appended to blockchain [12].

1.3.3 Physical Layer

All the devices on a P2P network like various computing devices, IoT devices and servers represent the physical layer of blockchain architecture (see Figure 1.5). Each and every device has equal rights to validate transaction, append a block and create its own local blockchain copy. Examples of computing devices are phones, printing machines, mobile computing devices, computers or any electronic device with an IP address. These devices are considered nodes on a P2P network. Nodes are categorized into different types (see Figure 1.6) as represented in Table 1.1.

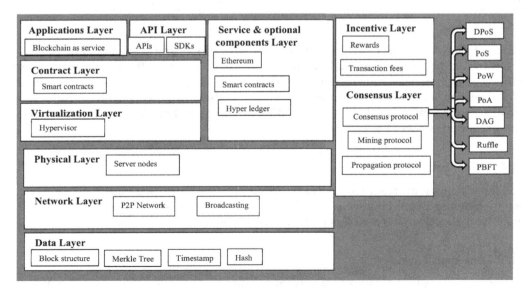

FIGURE 1.5
Blockchain architecture [11].

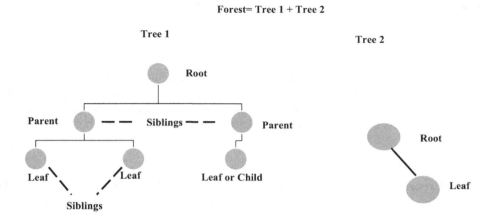

FIGURE 1.6
Categories of P2P nodes.

TABLE 1.1

P2P Network Node Categories

Node Category	Description
Child	Intermediate node, linked between parent node and leaf node
Forest	Collection of tree nodes
Leaf	Last level node, has no child nodes linked
Parent	Any extending node
Root	Topmost node, extending other nodes
Siblings	Child/leaf nodes, with same parent node
Tree	Collection of nodes extending from root node

Each of these nodes has to have a great amount of processing power. A node cannot be an electronic device with normal or average processing power. It needs to have a large amount of storage space also with very high computing speed. All nodes must follow some common set of rules for processing. This puts them in synchronization for carrying out all activities on the blockchain. Depending on the type of blockchain, some nodes may have extra powers over the other ones [3].

1.3.4 Virtualization Layer

This layer deals with resource allocation to virtual machines (see Figure 1.5). Resources also include hardware Hypervisor, a piece of virtualization software that can be used to implement allocation of resources to virtual machines [11].

1.3.5 Consensus Layer

All the nodes on a P2P network follow some common set of rules. The implementation and monitoring of those rules is the responsibility of the consensus layer [13] (see Figure 1.5). Consensus means supporting a certain proposed idea with the majority. In blockchain the proposed idea is about validity of a new transaction request; upon validation, a transaction request gets blocked and appended to the existing chain. Blockchain acts as storage structure only if the consensus protocol is not maintained. As the number of nodes in a P2P network increases, the time required to get consensus increases. The underlying algorithm also plays a role in reducing time. Algorithm generally works on following principles [9, 14]:

i. **Majority wins:** collect maximum possible agreements from all nodes.
ii. **Collaboration:** finding better agreement to benefit all.
iii. **Team spirit:** keeping aside self-gain working for benefit of all.
iv. **Equality:** each node's vote counts.
v. **Participation:** each node on network must vote.
vi. **Activeness:** each node has to be equally involved in network activities.

1.3.6 Contract Layer

This layer integrates a P2P network representing blockchain with external technologies required for implementing overall functionalities and activities on the blockchain (see Figure 1.5). Technologies integrated with blockchain include: E-wallets, smart contracts, multi-signatures, data-feeds, digital-IDs, etc. Integration is done with the help of algorithms and related scripts. So logic and scripts form the basis of the contract layer. All nodes taking part in transaction processing need to agree upon common a set of rules. This commonly agreed ground is a smart contract between participating parties. Token-systems, crop-insurance, saving-wallets etc. are some forms of a smart contract. Transaction will be cleared or settled in blockchain using a smart contract, eliminating the presence of third parties [15].

1.3.7 Incentive Layer

The name of layer itself suggests that more work by nodes will bring rewards for them. 100% nodes' participation is required in the consensus process to validate a requested transaction. But participation in blockchain activities requires a huge amount of processing power, storage and consumption of electricity. So nodes tend to be hesitant to participate. To encourage involvement of all nodes in blockchain network activities, incentives are rewarded. As all blockchain activities are in electronic forms, so are incentives. Virtual cash is the reward for intensive computation work done by nodes. Allocation of rewards/ incentives is done at this layer [5] (see Figure 1.5).

1.3.8 Service and Optional Component Layer

As the name suggests, this layer acts as service provider for application layer above it (see Figure 1.5). It also acts as communicator between lower layers and upper layers. Many companies are interested in developing this service provider platform for blockchain. Widely used service provider platforms are Hyperledger by Linux and Baas by IBM. Other companies who have developed this platform are included in Table 1.2.

1.3.9 API Layer

The application layer needs to interact with a smart contract and digital ledger. This interaction is done through programming interfaces included in the API layer. Software development kits and application programming interfaces are part of this layer (see Figure 1.5).

TABLE 1.2

Blockchain-Based Service Providers

Company Name	Location	Service Platforms Usage
Altoros	Sunnyvale, California	To automate workflow processes
Amazon AWS	Seattle, Washington	To manage business processes
Appinventiv	New York, New York	For almost all types of industries and related processes
BlockApps	New York, New York	For enterprise customers
Blockstream	Mountain View, California	To manage cryptocurrency
Bloq	Chicago, Illinois	For business security purposes
Clovyr	New York, New York	To deploy products
Cryptowerk	San Mateo, California	To manage important data
Dragonchain	Seattle, Washington	To secure critical business assets
Factom	Austin, Texas	For document management
Fluence	San Francisco, California	For smart contracts
Innominds	San Jose, California	For smart contracts and cryptocurrencies
Kaleido	Raleigh, North Carolina	For all types of enterprises
LeewayHertz	San Francisco, California	For all industry processes
PayStand	San Francisco, California	For payment and certificates security
Skuchain	Mountain View, California	For shipping and logistics industry
Symbiont	New York, New York	For financial institutes
tZERO	Midvale, Utah	For financial institutes with cryptocurrency transactions
VironIT	San Francisco, California	For mobile app development process

1.3.10 Application Layer

This layer contains all the applications and processes which need to explore blockchain functionality for their functioning (see Figure 1.5). These applications and processes belong to variety of domains such as academics, business, cryptocurrencies, finance, healthcare, gaming, mobiles, e-commerce, real estate, etc.

1.4 Characteristics

The characteristics of blockchain are included in Table 1.3. [8, 16].

1.5 Appending Transaction

1.5.1 ABCD of Transaction Getting into the Blockchain

Any transaction cannot be appended directly to the chain of blocks. All participants need to inspect the requested transaction block then authenticate it before appending (see Figure 1.7). The following steps should be carried out in order [17]:

- **A**uthentication of received transaction request
- **B**lock creation for authenticated transaction request
- **C**arrying created block to each network node
- **D**eep inspection of transaction block by each node to validate transaction

TABLE 1.3

Characteristics of Blockchain

Characteristic	Description
Anonymity	Anonymity is achieved through the use of an asymmetric encryption algorithm. This algorithm assigns a public-private key pair to each node. Participating nodes only broadcast the public key. The private key is not exposed. The information sender encrypts information using its own private key. The information receiver decrypts using its own private key. No central authority is present to check identity of node, blockchain being the decentralized network. The node can keep more than one address on blockchain to participate in activities. Encrypted addresses are used to perform transactions.
Auditability	Auditability is achieved through the use of timestamped transactions. Using digital timestamps backtracking of transactions is possible.
Consensus	Consensus is achieved through the rights given to every node to validate a requested transaction. The majority of nodes need to agree upon a decision to validate or invalidate a requested transaction. If the majority give consensus that the request is valid, the transaction is blocked and appended to the blockchain. This also maintains trust amongst nodes and reduces chances of wrong data appended to the blockchain.
Decentralization	Decentralization is achieved through the absence of central authority to validate blockchain activities. All nodes have a copy of the blockchain. All nodes have the right to validate a transaction. Data is not stored in a central location, so related maintenance costs are also saved.
Digitization of data	Digitization is achieved by no documentation policy related to every activity on blockchain. All data are recorded in digital form only.
Expandable	Expandability is achieved by allowing everyone to participate in blockchain activities and by not keeping any limitation on the number of blocks that can be added to the chain. Limitation is on block size and not on adding blocks to blockchain. Everyone can expand chain for each valid transaction.
Finality	Finality is achieved by keeping only one shared copy of the blockchain shared amongst nodes. Data appearing in the block of the blockchain is of valid and completed transaction, so ownership of data is certain and not questionable.
Immutable	Immutability is achieved by use of hashing. Even a bit-level data tampering makes a huge difference to its hash, calling for mismatched hash values between next block "previous hash field" and current block "hash field" values. Use a transaction to undo erroneous transaction. Blocks of both will be public.
Independence	Independence is achieved by giving each node the right to verify, validate and transfer data. No central authority is present to intervene in activities of node on blockchain.
Liveness	Liveness is achieved through the use of a consensus protocol. Validity of transaction must be agreed upon by all/majority nodes on blockchain. Protocol broadcasts messages related to the consensus. Nodes take their own required time to reply, but consensus is achieved. This reflects liveness of blockchain.
Openness	Openness is achieved by allowing all nodes on the blockchain to access, manage and store all blockchain-related data. Source code is kept open to be queried by any node. At the same time, a node not on the blockchain cannot gain access to data.
Persistency	Persistence is achieved through consensus in the blockchain. The authenticity of blockchain data also claims persistency of blockchain. Transaction can be backtracked for its authenticity and origin. Tampering of data is made impossible with use of hashing.
Safety	Safety is achieved by allowing each node to validate each requested transaction and keeping only one shared copy of finalized block data chained together.
Timestamped	Each newly appended block is timestamped and then added to chain. Tracing the origin of data is made easy with timestamping.
Transparency	Transparency is achieved through the openness feature, i.e. by allowing all nodes on blockchain to access, manage and store all blockchain-related data. The source code is kept open to be queried by any node.
Unforgeable	Once data is stored in appended block, it cannot be reversed. Block of data is broadcasted to each and every node on the blockchain network. Every node has visibility and accesses to the block data. Reversal of data needs a consensus of 51% of nodes. Unethical erase or tampering of data is also not possible.

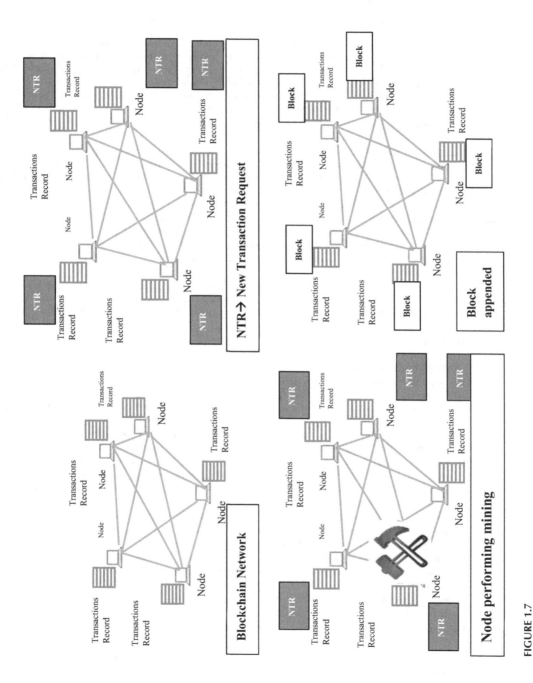

FIGURE 1.7
Block appended to blockchain [20].

- Encouragement of node validating transaction by rewarding with incentives
- Finally appending validated transaction block to existing chain
- Gathering data updates and distributing across network
- Heading towards new transaction request

1.6 Transaction Request Authentication

Rights to authenticate a transaction request belong to all participating nodes on blockchain network. Nodes are the computing devices used to validate a transaction. Validating a transaction requires finding a solution to a complex mathematical problem [18]. The work requires tremendous computing capacity and power. The time required to complete the work can be very much high on scale, so when one of the nodes comes up with the solution to a complex mathematical problem and will validate transaction at the earliest, the owner will be rewarded. This incentive is proof of the tremendously complex work done by the node. The process is called the proof of work. Such transaction validated and authenticated by most/all participants can be appended to the blockchain network [19]. Exercising such a huge computing power demands a great amount of electricity and infrastructural facilities, driving up the related cost. So the point to be noted here is that the incentive received should be able to recover the mount spent on acquiring computing power. Here, the term used for finding a solution to a complex mathematical problem is "mining". Owners of nodes are termed as "miners". The odds of earning incentives are against the miners, i.e. the chance of finding the correct solution to a complex mathematical problem is rare. Digital signature, hash function and public-private keys are the requirements for validation and append operation.

1.7 Consensus Algorithms

Permissioned and permission-less consensus algorithms are presented in Table 1.4.

TABLE 1.4

Different Types of Consensus Algorithms [20]

	Permissioned	Permission-less	Example
PoW		√	Bitcoin, Ethereum before Ethereum 2.0 Bitcoin Cash, Litecoin, Monero
PoS		√	NXT
DPoS	√		Bitshare, Gridcoin
PoA		√	Decred (DCR)
PoC		√	Storj, Chia, Burstcoin, SpaceMint
PoI		√	NEM
PoET	√		Hyperledger Sawtooth
PoB		√	Slim coin
DAG		√	Nano
LPoS		√	WAVES
PBFT	√		Stellar, Ripple, and Hyperledger
DBFT	√		NEO
Tendermint	√		Tendermint

1.8 Smart Contract

A contract between two parties is a legal document defining transaction terms. It is executed by a subject matter expert, a lawyer in this case. But as the transactions are digitized in a smart system, there is the need for a digitized contract, too. Nick Szabo came with a smart contract in the form of a computer program. Moreover, this program code is self-executing and so it is considered a smart contract.

A smart contract does not need any controlling authority to get executed. Solidity and Vyper are the computer programming languages to develop smart contracts. Any node can develop and execute a smart contract, but the cost of preparing and executing is high. As smart contracts work similar to APIs (application program interfaces), they can be called from within one another. Although there is no central authority executing and monitoring smart contracts, the transactions executed by smart contracts are trustworthy, visible to all, and can be backtracked and immutable. Bitcoin, Tezos, Cardano, Ethereum and EOS IO are the platforms supporting smart contracts. These contracts are not legal documents.

1.9 Types of Blockchain

The different types of blockchain are presented in Table 1.5.

TABLE 1.5

Types of Blockchain [20]

	Public Blockchain	Bitcoin Ethereum
Types of Blockchain	Private Blockchain	Monax Multichain
	Consortium Blockchain	R3 Corda

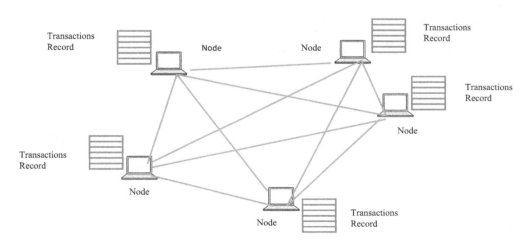

FIGURE 1.8
Public blockchain architecture [20].

1.9.1 Public Blockchain Network

This type of blockchain is open to all types of blockchain network. Every node has equal rights related to validating a requested transaction and appending block to blockchain. This type of blockchain works on a consensus principle in true sense. A public blockchain allows each node to store its own local copy, so transparency of data is maintained (see Figure 1.8). As no node has special rights, all nodes work at the same level, maintaining anonymity with each other. As every node participates in mining activity, the implementation of a strong consensus mechanism is very important. The decentralization principle is followed in this type of blockchain network rigorously [21].

1.9.2 Private Blockchain Network

This is a closed and tightly guarded blockchain network. Nodes do not have equal rights related to validating a requested transaction and appending block to a blockchain. Unlike a public blockchain, this network follows a non-democratic approach for activities. A private blockchain allows each node to store its own local copy with no edit rights (see Figure 1.9). The central authority represented by an organization controls all activities on this type of blockchain network. The central authority can grant special access rights to node/s, so nodes are not working at the same level in a private blockchain. The consensus mechanism is of least importance, but the presence of a central authority is the preferred feature of private blockchain to be used by private organizations. The decentralization feature of blockchain is not followed in a true sense in this type of blockchain.

1.9.3 Consortium Blockchain Network

This is a partially closed and partially open type of blockchain network. Nodes do not have equal rights related to validating a requested transaction and appending block to a blockchain (see Figure 1.10). This type of blockchain is available to all nodes with restricted data accessibility. Unlike a public blockchain network where a democratic approach is

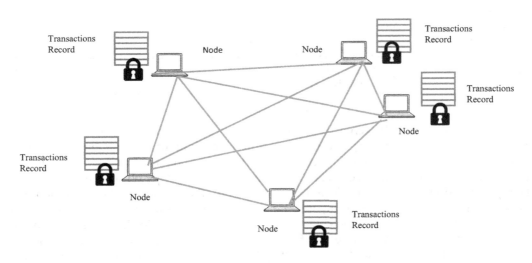

FIGURE 1.9
Private blockchain architecture [21].

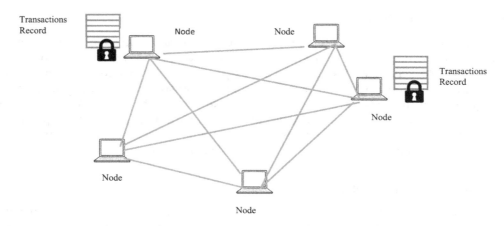

FIGURE 1.10
Consortium blockchain architecture [21].

TABLE 1.6

Summary of Blockchain Types [7]

Features	Public	Private	Consortium
Nature	Open	Controlled	Controlled
Centralized	No	Yes	Partially
Participants	Anonymous	Known	Known
Consensus determination	All nodes	One organization	Selected nodes
Decentralized	Yes	No	Partially
Read/write permission	Permission-less	Permissioned	Permissioned
Participant's trust	50%	100%	100%
Immutability	Nearly 100%	Not sure	Not sure
Efficiency	Less	More	More
Scalability	More	More	Less
Transaction approval time	More	Less	Less
Energy consumption	More	Less	Less
Transparency	Low	High	High
Observation	Costly, medium speed	Moderate cost, high speed	Moderate cost, high speed
Example	Bitcoin, Blockstream, Dash, Ethereum, Factor, Litecoin	Bankchain, Multistack, Blockstack	Hyperledger, Ripple, R3

followed, and a private blockchain network where a non-democratic approach is followed, for activities on a blockchain network, consortium blockchain networks follow a selective-democratic approach. A consortium blockchain does not allow each node to store its own local copy of the blockchain. Few selected nodes only have a copy with them. The authority represented by a cluster of selected nodes controls all activities on the blockchain network. So all nodes are not working at same level in a consortium blockchain as they are in a private blockchain. Selective consensus mechanism is practiced, but the presence of a clustered authority is the preferred feature of a consortium blockchain to be used by corporate organizations. The decentralization feature of blockchain is followed partially in this type of blockchain. Summary of blockchain types on various features are shown in Table 1.6.

1.10 Issues and Concerns of Blockchain

The issues and concerns of blockchain are outlined in Table 1.7.

1.11 Challenges of Blockchain Technology

The challenges of blockchain technology are discussed in Table 1.8.

1.12 Case Study

1.12.1 Digital Content Management Using Blockchain

Piracy is the biggest threat to creativity and creator. As the world is going digital in every sphere of life, creating pirated content has become the quickest and easiest task. But to find

TABLE 1.7

Issues and Concerns of Blockchain [22, 23]

Issues	Concerns
Scaling up problems	Comparatively processing is not faster, so scaling up presents limitations.
Trust	With expansion, more nodes are involved in mining; trust factor reduces with increasing number of miners.
Emerging technology	Comfort and trust level of people towards emerging technology rises very slowly.
Regulation policy	Decentralization feature does not work very well with government regarding financial matters. Government policies are not very supportive for blockchain technology.
Security	Security gets affected because of the centralized approach of power gain injected by selfish mining. A cluster of 51% nodes can compromise blockchain by forming a majority.
Selfish mining	Selfish mining injects a centralization approach in blockchain for acquiring more blocks as well as more rewards.
Cost of mining vs reward	Cost of mining tends to be higher than the reward received.
Energy consumption	Huge processing power calls for large amounts of electricity usage.
Privacy	User's identity can be tracked using an IP address.
Interoperability	Interoperability demands integration of various modules of different platforms. But being the emerging technology, standard convention still needs to be developed for adopting blockchain across all platforms.
Overtaking current databases	Blockchain introduced itself to the world with mainly cryptocurrency application, so compatibility and usability of blockchain as the database is under a scanner and needs to be validated thoroughly.
Larger hard drives	Mining calls for a large amount of hard drive space.
Consistency with the real world	Synchronizing blockchain timing and real world timing seems to be questionable and a tough task.
Policy for script and operational error	Immutability feature needs to be reworked for correcting script and operational errors/bugs.
Bandwidth consumption	Bandwidth consumption is higher.

TABLE 1.8

Challenges of Blockchain Technology [20, 24]

Challenges	Description
Technology adaption	Technology for current applications, systems and procedures goes back a few decades and is tried and tested. Blockchain technology is entirely a new concept challenging:
	— the role of a central authority to control activities in the network — the need to keep data hidden from users — the need to know the identity of users — the need for paperwork and documentation
	Considering these points, it is difficult to convince business veterans to adopt blockchain technology.
Governance and administration	Complete digitization of governance and administration is still a farfetched concept to achieve in India. Paperless activities are still not widely accepted.
Business related	Implementation and demonstration of blockchain technology for all types of businesses related to society still seems to be the far aim to achieve.
Electric power consumption	Mining activity on blockchain needs a large computational power and electric energy consumed is directly proportional to computing power required. Countries on the verge of development, under-developed countries and countries with moderate electricity generation will find it very difficult to cope up with electric power requirements of blockchain technology if technology is used widely.
Computational power	Need for huge amount of processing power for mining needs to be minimized to encourage more participation.
Participation in mining	Participation of users in mining depends on the requirement of large-scale infrastructure and powerful hardware. The majority of users cannot afford these costs, so the related cost needs to be cut down to be affordable.
Task scheduling	Synchronizing real-world time and blockchain time for task scheduling needs thorough research and testing.
Network security	Security testing for blockchain networks implemented in various domains needs in-depth research.

TABLE 1.9

Examples of Blockchain-Based Digital Content Management

Name	Use	Advantage
Dtube	Blockchain-based video-sharing platform	Works with a token system. Users enjoy ad-free contents. For every use, the creator gets monetary benefit.
Flixxo	Blockchain-based digital content sharing platform	Content creators are rewarded with tokens. Users sharing the content are also rewarded.
Snapparazzi	Blockchain-based photo- and video-trading platform	Trading platform allows creators to showcase and bid for photos and videos. News agencies bid for exclusive photos/videos. Creators (journalists) get maximum rewards of their work in the form of SnapCoin, which News agencies have to trade with fiat money.

the original creator of a piece of content is a very tough task, so digital content management using blockchain is the current need.

OMI (Open Music Initiative) has taken up the project to provide a blockchain-based platform to music creators. Now a days, music audio-videos are used across the globe without acknowledging the creator and copyright acts. OMI creates a depository of music inside a distributed register. The creator remains the true owner of the content, and each and every legal right is at the disposal of the owner and royalties are paid to the creator. Creator and owner can be the same, and a smart contract here consists of charges for use of music and royalty money calculations. Every time music is played anywhere in the globe, a smart contract gets executed. This automates the credit of charges to the owner account and royalties to the creator's account. On a similar track, other few examples of digital content management using blockchain are included in Table 1.9.

References

[1] Yu, F., Liu Jianming, et al. "Virtualization for distributed ledger technology (vDLT)." *IEEE Access*, vol. 6 (2018): 25019–25028.

[2] www.thesslstore.com/blog/what-is-blockchain-how-does-blockchain-work/.

[3] Gopane, Thabo J. "Blockchain Technology and Smart Universities." *Kalpa Publications in Computing*, vol. 12 (2019): 72–84 (Proceedings of 4th International Conference on the Internet, Cyber Security and Information Systems 2019).

[4] https://mlsdev.com/blog/156-how-to-build-your-own-blockchain-architecture.

[5] Wang, Hai, Yong Wang, et al. "An overview of blockchain security analysis." In: X. Yun et al. (eds.), *Cyber Security. CNCERT 2018. Communications in Computer and Information Science*, vol. 970, Springer, Singapore, 2019, https://doi.org/10.1007/978-981-13-6621-5_5.

[6] Wood, Gavin. *ETHEREUM: A Secure Decentralized Transaction Ledger*. Yellow Paper, 2014, http://cryptopapers.net/papers/ethereum-yellowpaper.pdf.

[7] Survey on Blockchain Technologies and Related Services. *FY2015 Report March 2016 Nomura Research Institute, Japan's Ministry of Economy, Trade and Industry (METI)*. https://www.meti.go.jp/english/press/2016/pdf/0531_01f.pdf.

[8] Saleh, Omar S., Osman Ghazali and Muhammad Ehsan Rana. "Blockchain based framework for educational certificates verification." *Journal of Critical Reviews*, vol. 7 (2020): 79–84, https://doi.org/10.31838/jcr.07.03.13.

[9] Zheng, Zibin, Shaoan Xie, et al. "Blockchain challenges and opportunities: A survey." *International Journal of Web and Grid Services*, vol. 14, no. 4 (2018): 352–375.

[10] Narayanan, Arvind, Joseph Bonneau, Edward Felten, Andrew Miller and Steven Goldfeder. *Bitcoin and Cryptocurrency Technologies: A Comprehensive Introduction*, Princeton University Press, Princeton, 19 July 2016.

[11] Gatton, Yang Lu. *Blockchain: A Survey on Functions, Applications and Open Issues*. College of Business and Economics University of Kentucky, Lexington, KY, College of Business, The University of Manchester, Manchester, ziiyuu@gmail.com.

[12] Gamage, H.T.M., H.D. Weerasinghe and N.G.J. Dias. "A survey on blockchain technology concepts, applications, and issues." *SN Computer Science*, vol. 1, no. 114 (2020), https://doi.org/10.1007/s42979-020-00123-0.

[13] Wattenhofer. *The Science of the Blockchain*, https://dl.acm.org/doi/10.5555/3002702.

[14] Hölbl, Turkanovi Muhamed, Khristjan Kosic, Marjan Hericko and Aida Kamisalic. "EduCTX: A blockchain-based higher education credit platform." *IEEE Access*, vol. 6 (2018): 5112–5127, https://doi.org/10.1109/ACCESS.2018.2789929.

[15] Atzei, Nicola, Massimo Bartoletti and Tiziana Cimoli. *A Survey of Attacks on Ethereum Smart Contracts*. https://link.springer.com/chapter/10.1007/978-3-662-54455-6_8.

[16] Zhang, Rui, Rui Xue and Ling Liu. "Security and privacy on blockchain." *ACM Computing Surveys*, vol. 1, no. 1, Article 1 (January 2019): 35, https://doi.org/10.1145/3316481.

[17] Monrat, A.A., O. Schelén and K. Andersson. "A survey of blockchain from the perspectives of applications, challenges, and opportunities." *IEEE Access*, vol. 7 (2019): 117134–117151, https://doi.org/10.1109/ACCESS.2019.2936094.

[18] Antonopoulos. *Mastering Bitcoin: Unlocking Digital Cryptocurrencies*, https://www.oreilly.com/library/view/mastering-bitcoin-2nd/9781491954379/.

[19] Nakamoto, Satoshi. *Bitcoin: A Peer-to-Peer Electronic Cash System*, https://www.ussc.gov/sites/default/files/pdf/training/annual-national-training-seminar/2018/Emerging_Tech_Bitcoin_Crypto.pdf.

[20] Mohanta, Bhabendu Kumar, Debasish Jena, Soumyashree S. Panda and Srichandan Sobhanayak. "Blockchain technology: A survey on applications and security privacy challenges." *Internet of Things*, vol. 8 (2019): 100107, ISSN 2542–6605, https://doi.org/10.1016/j.iot.2019.100107; www.sciencedirect.com/science/article/pii/S2542660518300702.

[21] Kumar, Sandeep, Abhay Kumar and Vanita Verma. "A survey paper on blockchain technology, challenges and opportunities." *International Journal of Computer Trends and Technology*, vol. 67, no. 4 (2019): 16–20.

[22] Dave, Dharmin, Shalin Parikh, Reema Patel and Nishant Doshi. "A survey on blockchain technology and its proposed solutions." *Procedia Computer Science*, vol. 160 (2019): 740–745, ISSN 1877-0509, https://doi.org/10.1016/j.procs.2019.11.017; www.sciencedirect.com/science/article/pii/S187705091931717X.

[23] Casino, Fran, Thomas K. Dasaklis and Constantinos Patsakis. "A systematic literature review of blockchain-based applications: Current status, classification and open issues." *Telematics and Informatics*, vol. 36 (2019): 55–81, ISSN 0736–5853, https://doi.org/10.1016/j.tele.2018.11.006; www.sciencedirect.com/science/article/pii/S0736585318306324.

[24] Blockchain Goes to School. *Cognizant 20–20 Insights Codex 3775.02*, March 2019, https://www.cognizant.com/us/en/whitepapers/documents/blockchain-goes-to-school-codex3775.pdf.

2

Basics of Blockchain Architecture

Supriya Aras and Mangesh Bedekar

CONTENTS

DOI: 10.1201/9781003203933-3

After a low-lying span of around five years, blockchain technology has picked up on adaptation and focus since 2014. The compelling reason which has made blockchain architecture popular is the level of security offered in spite of transparency of transaction data. The key facets of blockchain architecture are depicted in Figure 2.1.

We will explore each of these aspects in detail and understand how these aspects are built into the blockchain architecture, first proposed by Satoshi Nakamoto [1] in 2009. We will understand how blockchain is different from a regular distributed database and how it utilizes the Peer to Peer architecture. We will also see how hashing plays a very important role in making the blockchain secure and the data therein non-repudiable.

2.1 'Distributed' Ledger

Blockchain is well known as the distributed ledger and a comparison with the traditional distributed databases is obvious. In the case of traditional Distributed Databases, the database nodes (machines) trust each other and know each other (identities, permissions, etc.) A distributed database may have nodes, storing only part of the data and/or performing

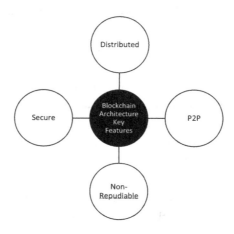

FIGURE 2.1
Blockchain architecture: key features.

part of the processing. The distributed database may be under the control of a master database or may be a part of network of peer databases. The overall state of the data is as maintained by all the databases together. The data shared by other node(s) is completely trusted by each node. A blockchain, on the other hand, is a network of trust-less nodes. The nodes of the blockchain need not (and typically do not, at least in public blockchains) know each other. All the nodes store the same copy of the ledger and perform the same operations, which make similar changes to the ledger state. Since the nodes are trustless (i.e. they do not need to trust each other), each node has its own validation protocol before it consumes and accepts the input data into its ledger.

2.2 Hash Functions and Hashing

The concept of hashing was proposed in 1976 by Diffie and Hellman, who proposed one way hashing for a digital signature scheme. Since then, multiple families of hash function have been proposed. The notable milestones have been MD5, RIPEMD, SHA-0, SHA-1, SHA-2 and SHA-3 family of algorithms. The SHA-3 algorithms standard is the latest one accepted by NIST in 2012 [2].

A Hash function is a mathematical function which converts data of any size into a fixed size output called a hash or a digest. Hash functions are used in cryptography, for secure storage of passwords, payments or user information, ensuring data integrity of file transfers, digital signatures, locating similar data via lookup, encrypted communication over the internet, etc. Typically, a d-bit hash function can generate 2^d different hashes. For example, SHA256 is a hashing function from the SHA-2 family which converts input data into 256-bit output. The SHA256 hash of the string '**Learning blockchain is fun!**' (without the single quote) is d28746855a1dab4adc93be99dbf2e9d55b57299d813f3a16970839ef2e452cda

2.2.1 Properties of Hashes

Hash functions are specifically designed to have the following properties. It is these properties that have led to their high impact usability in blockchains. These properties are:

1. Non-Reversibility: Hash functions are specifically designed to be one-way. Even for a simple 160 bit hash, the range is of 2^{160} possible values and it is very difficult to reverse the process and guess the original input, even if the hash value is known. This enables transparent logging of transactions in the blockchain ledger while protecting the content from un-intended recipients.

2. Avalanche Effect: A small change in input leads to a very large change in the digest. For the string in the earlier example—'**Learning blockchain is fun!**', a simple change of case for one alphabet (b to B) to make the string '**Learning Blockchain is fun!**' results in the following hash value:8f59bb6eceaa2da43d8496ae12d81ab0f68fd4b6 4c0c815cff0d0d79a87fe9d8, which is vastly different from the earlier hash value of d28746855a1dab4adc93be99dbf2e9d55b57299d813f3a16970839ef2e452cda. This property helps in verifying that the block/transaction is unchanged and not manipulated.

3. Determinism: This property of hash function ensures that a given input produces the same digest always. This property aids the integrity check of data/blocks by means of hash comparison.

4. Collision Resistance: It is not easy to find two strings which have the same hash output. This property aids use of hashing to ensure simple integrity checks in blockchain SPVs as we will see later in this chapter.

While vulnerabilities have been discovered in earlier hashing algorithms [3], SHA-3 and SHA-2 continue to be the recommended standards. The key applications of hash functions in the blockchain architecture are Generation of Addresses, Digital Signing of Transactions, and Transaction hashing into Merkle Trees and Block hashing for chaining blocks.

2.2.2 Generation of Addresses

In blockchains with cryptocurrencies, the digital currency is stored at a specified address. The hash functions are used to generate addresses with fixed bit-size to associate the cryptocurrency with the address. For example, let us see how Bitcoin [4], the first and most popular cryptocurrency, and Ethereum [5], the next popular one, use different hashing algorithms in their protocols.

In Bitcoin, SHA-256 and RIPEMD-160 are used together to generate bitcoin addresses.

$$Bitcoin\,Address = RIPEMD160\big(SHA-256\big(Public\,Key\,of\,User\big)\big)$$

In Ethereum, KECCAK-256 from SHA-3 family is used for generation of addresses.

$$Ethereum\,Address = First\,40\,bits\,of\big(KECCAK-256\big(Public\,Key\,of\,user\big)\big)$$

Thus, every unique public key will generate a unique address for its user in both these networks.

2.2.3 Digital Signing

In cryptocurrency transactions, the owner of the currency digitally signs the hash of the previous transaction (with the currency, which could be a currency generation transaction) and the public key of the next owner to whom the currency needs to be sent. A payee can verify the digital signatures to verify the chain of ownership [1].

Digital signatures are used in blockchain for message signing, signing digital legal smart contracts, signing consensus votes (in algorithms such as Practical Byzantine Fault Tolerance(PBFT)), etc. Digital signatures are also a means to ensure non-repudiation of data/information held in the blockchain transactions.

2.2.4 Transaction and Block Hashing

As seen later in this chapter, transaction content is hashed and successive hashing is used to form a Merkle tree (we will see this in detail in the sections ahead), which in turn facilitates simple, cost-effective transaction verification. As every transaction will generate a unique hash, a given set of transactions will generate a unique Merkle Root. Thus, this Merkle Root is a unique fixed length representation of the entire transactions data in the block.

The block hash itself (i.e. the hash of the header of a given block) is stored in the next block in the blockchain. For example, Bitcoin uses a double SHA-256 hash to generate the block hash.

$$BTCBlockHash = SHA256\big(SHA256\big(PrevBlockHeader\big)\big)$$

Ethereum uses Keccak256 hash of the previous blocks header.

$$ETHBlockHash = KECCAK256\big(PrevBlockHeader\big)$$

Due to the Determinism and Collision Resistance property of the hashing function, one can be sure that if the block hash is unaltered, the previous block is also unaltered. Any entity which modifies a given block in the blockchain must modify all subsequent blocks due to the inclusion of the parent hash in the next (child) block. This is a computationally infeasible task to achieve as there are more and more confirmations (i.e. blocks added after a given block).

2.3 The P2P Architecture

Blockchain uses a Peer to Peer (P2P) architecture. The concept of P2P architecture has existed much before the first blockchain came into being. A P2P network consists of multiple 'equal' and usually unspecialized nodes called 'peers' connected to each other. They are unspecialized in the sense that each node performs the same set of functions. The early music sharing network named Napster (which originated in 1999 and was active till around 2001) and the BitTorrent networks running BitTorrent P2P protocol (created in 2001) are examples of earliest P2P networks. Other famous users of P2P networks include Skype © messaging service and Content Based Mobile Edge Networking (CBMEN) and Mobile AdhocNETworks (MANETs). While BitTorrent Protocol was used for 'not so legal' distribution of copyrighted materials such as movies, the protocol had also been used for software distribution by OpenOffice.org.

The advantages of P2P networks compared to traditional client server networks are:

1. Horizontal scalability: The P2P networks can scale out horizontally endlessly. As of the writing of this book, the Bitcoin P2P network (the oldest blockchain network) has nearly ~10,000 full nodes. There are also claims that this number is actually ~100,000 and was once as high as 140,000 [6].

2. Fault Tolerance: Absence of a single point of failure and built-in redundancy due to multiple network paths makes the P2P networks fault tolerant.

3. Decentralized and Distributed Nature: No central server. Each node can act as a client or as a server depending on the function it is performing at a given instance.

Satoshi used a P2P network in his original blockchain concept [1] obviously for the not-so-legal reasons mentioned earlier. The main goal of Bitcoin was to implement a peer-to-peer electronic cash system without the involvement of intermediaries or a Central Authority. With the adoption of Bitcoin and the spread of the bitcoin network, the fault tolerance has certainly improved to make it the strongest P2P network so far. Figure 2.2 depicts a typical P2P blockchain network.

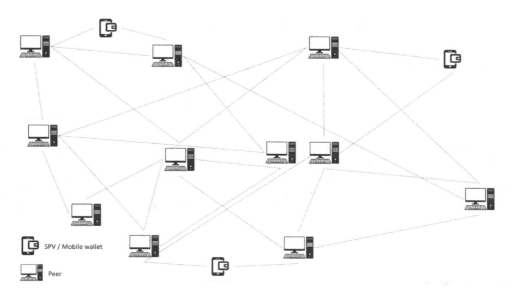

SPV / Mobile wallet

Peer

FIGURE 2.2
Typical Blockchain network.

Note that there may be a diversification in the peers in the blockchain network, depending on their function in the blockchain. For example, in the Bitcoin blockchain, one may have Full Nodes (which run the Bitcoin Core Client and store the entire Bitcoin blockchain ledger) or Simple Payment Verification Clients (SPVs, which only perform block and transaction validations). Each of the blockchain full nodes runs the same code and has the same copy of the ledger. As we will see in later sections, permissioned architectures may allow further diversification of peers into specialized roles to allow data compartmentalization.

2.3.1 The 'Chain' of Blocks

In this section, we will have a look at the architecture of the ledger stored in each of the peers. The blockchain is a chain of blocks which are chronologically linked to one another, so much so that the contents in the block (called transactions) are also chronologically linked. Every peer on the network has the same ledger copy. The blockchain protocol independently builds the ledger on each peer by accepting the next valid block onto the current ledger height. In the event that a certain peer does not receive a block due to network latency, or any other reason, they are eventually expected to catch up and the blockchain protocol has a built-in capability to do so. Also, as each peer on the network works independently of the other, it is possible in certain blockchain architectures that two peers generate different blocks at the same block height in parallel. In this case, both the blocks get relayed into the network. Based on the respective blockchain protocol, forks may or may not be allowed in the blockchain. In Section 2.4, we will see how different protocols deal with this scenario.

A unique property of the 'chain' of blocks is the presence of the previous block hash in the next block as shown in the Figure 2.3. This mechanism contributes to the finality aspect of the blockchain and makes changes to committed blocks extremely difficult.

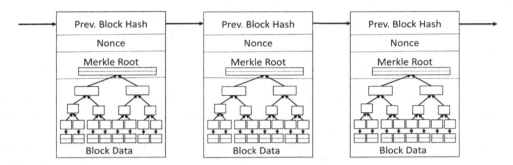

FIGURE 2.3
Typical Blockchain ledger.

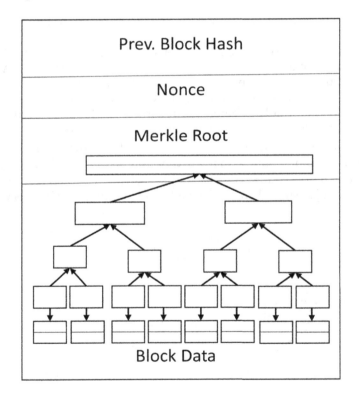

FIGURE 2.4
Typical block structure.

2.3.2 Typical Block Structure

The basic block design as proposed by Satoshi [1] has not undergone any significant change over a period of time. An individual block is designed to make efficient use of the Merkle Tree structure. As shown in Figure 2.4, a typical block consists of the Block Data and Block Header. The block header itself contains the Merkle Root, Previous Block hash, Nonce, Timestamp and protocol version number at a minimum.

Let us try to understand the Merkle Tree Structure. This concept was patented by Ralph Merkle in 1979 [7]. However, the patent had expired when Satoshi built the Bitcoin blockchain, and so he and future researchers and users of the Merkle Tree have been able to use the structure extensively. The Merkle Tree is a data structure which is implemented as a binary tree of hashes, i.e. a tree where every non-leaf node has a branching factor of 2. Every leaf node in the Merkle Tree represents the transaction to be included in the block. Every non-leaf node is a hash of its 2 child nodes. In case the number of transactions or leaf nodes are odd, the last transaction is duplicated to create a balanced tree. Some protocols may choose to use empty or default values rather than duplicating the transaction. See Figure 2.5 for a representation of the Merkle Tree. Thus, a set of 16 transactions will lead to a Merkle Tree of height 4 (i.e. $\log_2 4$). The top level hash of the Merkle Tree structure is called the Merkle Root. The Merkle Root is stored in the corresponding blocks header. The Merkle Root along with the other block contents is together hashed to get the block hash. This block hash is stored in the next block's header section as shown in Figure 2.4.

The Merkle Tree structure offers distinct advantages to the blockchain structure such as:

1. Data Integrity: The Merkle Tree is a tree of successive hashes. A matching Merkle Tree hash is a proof of the integrity of all the transactions beneath it. As we saw in Section 2.2.1, the hashing function showed an 'Avalanche Effect.' Any change in the data (or constituent transactions) of a block will result in a change in hashes for all levels above and finally a change in the Merkle Root. This in turn has a cascading effect on the block hash and hashes of all further blocks.

2. Low-cost transaction validation: With the Merkle Tree structure, transaction search becomes much simpler with worst-case time complexity of $O(\log_2(n))$ as against the $O(n)$ search time complexity of a simple hash list. The search of a transaction is performed along a path called Merkle Path, which is the set of hashes which enable

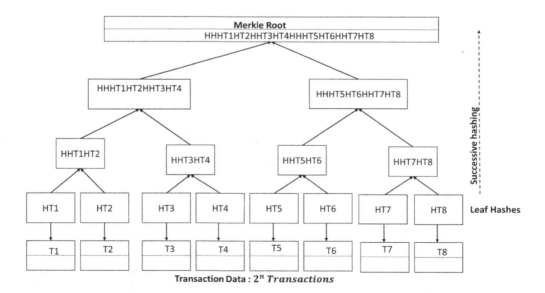

FIGURE 2.5
Merkle Tree.

the retrieval of the Merkle Root using the transactions. For example, consider the block at height 686346 in the Bitcoin blockchain [8]. This block has 2,332 transactions. In order to find a given transaction in this block, the Merkle Path will be only 12 hashes of 384 Bytes only as compared to the whole block of 1,302,648 bytes.

3. Simplified Payment Verification: The Merkle Path enables having Simple Payment Verification (SPV) nodes on the blockchain, which do not store the full blockchain but only the block headers. They can nevertheless participate in transaction validation. SPVs are usually wallet nodes which are not interested in all transactions, but only in specific transactions. Such SPV clients are lighter and can run on low resource devices such as mobile phones and tablets.

2.3.3 Blockchain Transactions

A blockchain transaction in the simplest of terms is a data structure that stores a piece of information along with a timestamp. The information may be a record of transfer of a currency (fiat currency or cryptocurrency), record of ownership of a tangible or an intangible asset, record of state of a process, record of an event, etc. The nature of digital information stored in a blockchain transaction depends on the goal of the network itself. For example, a cryptocurrency blockchains transactions will store a log of generation and transfer of cryptocurrency, a banking blockchain shall store monetary transactions between parties, a supply chain blockchain may store temperatures of a storage van, a blockchain to track intellectual property may store idea ownership, and so on.

In the block, transactions are arranged in chronological order. Typically, due to the usage of Merkle Trees, a block stores up to 2^n transactions where n is the number of levels in the Merkle Tree. The actual number of transactions may also be governed by the permitted block size for the given blockchain framework. For example, in Bitcoin blockchain the block size is 1 MB, while a later fork called Bitcoin Cash (BCH) has a larger block size of 32 MB to accommodate more transactions per block. In Hyperledger Fabric framework, block size is a configurable value.

In the blockchain ledger on each node in the network, blocks at the same height have the same set of transactions. A transaction record gets reinforced as more and more blocks are added over the block containing the given transaction. Blockchain transactions can lead to conditions or events that further trigger execution of smart contracts.

2.3.4 Flavors of Blockchain Architecture

Though the original Bitcoin Blockchain architecture was proposed to be a public architecture, over a period of time and in order to support the needs of the enterprise systems, private blockchain and consortium blockchain architectures have evolved. A public blockchain is a network that can be joined by any node, usually anonymously and is likely to provide an incentive (usually in the form of native currency) to those nodes which join as full nodes and take part in transaction validation and block generation. Private or permissioned blockchains have the nodes which are permitted to join the network by a controlling entity and are usually goal-oriented and aim to achieve a specific data-sharing goal within the network. (E.g. Hyperledger Fabric, R3 Corda [9, 10]). Organizations who share a common objective or participate in a set of workflows form a consortium, which participates in the consortium blockchain network. Recent architectures like Hyperledger, R3 and Corda allow for significant flexibility to implement a consortium blockchain architecture.

2.4 The Distributed Consensus Challenge

The blockchain architecture can be well appreciated only if we understand how this architecture achieves distributed consensus.

2.4.1 What is Distributed Consensus?

A unanimous agreement by a group of systems or processors on a given proposal is called Distributed Consensus. Each of the processors process inputs independently and are physically separated (the separation may even be in form of different Docker containers on the same server). Due to the physical separation, the medium of communication, i.e. the network, comes into the picture. The processors in a distributed system therefore have two challenges in arriving at consensus: presence of faulty communication channel and presence of faulty processors.

In the context of blockchain, which we consider a trustless network, our goal is to address any problem which leads to a breach of trust or malicious behavior by a given node. We will therefore define two basic problems associated with distributed consensus: the Two-Army Problem and the Byzantine General's Problem.

2.4.2 The Two-Army Problem

The Two-Army Problem is a representative problem which denotes the fact that it may not be possible for even two non-faulty processors to successfully come to a consensus in a distributed environment. An analogy is drawn here from a situation wherein two loyal army generals try to communicate with each other via potentially unreliable messengers. Such problems at processor level can be addressed by using upper bound on time limits to receive communication.

2.4.3 Byzantine General's Problem

A more complex problem is the Byzantine General's problem. In this problem, a set of army generals have surrounded a castle (in the city of Byzantine) for an attack. Only a synchronous attack can lead to victory over the castle. However, the army generals need to communicate with each other for the time of the attack. The problem here is the fact that one or more generals may be traitors who may pass on incorrect messages to the messenger, leading to an overall attack failure due to a lack of consensus. This problem is the Byzantine General's Problem, first elaborated and solved by Lamport et al [11].

A Byzantine fault in a multi-processor system is thus a fault wherein the faulty processor(s) continue to communicate and send messages to their peers. This is unlike the 'fail stop' scenario wherein the faulty processor stops communicating and ceases to be a part of the network.

Let us see how the Byzantine General's Problem related to a blockchain network. A typical blockchain network can be considered analogous to a distributed multi-processor system with default communication upper bounds (in order to take care of the faulty channel problem). Malicious nodes in the blockchain network can be likened to faulty processors who stay online and try to add malicious transactions to the block (or add malicious blocks to the blockchain). There are multiple algorithms which have been proposed to solve the Byzantine fault and achieve consensus in distributed systems. In the next sections, we will see how Bitcoin and other popular blockchains solves the distributed consensus problem.

Note that we are not worried about those nodes which fall 'failsilent' or go off the network, as they will not take part in current consensus. When such nodes come online and sync their blockchain to current level, the hash-based chained structure of the blockchain makes it difficult for them to act malicious.

2.4.4 Proof of Work—Bitcoin's Way to Solve the Byzantine General's Problem

Various blockchain networks have come up with innovative solutions, some based on distributed consensus algorithms proposed earlier and some using their own novel solutions. The Bitcoin blockchain uses a consensus algorithm called 'Proof of Work' (POW) [1]. In the Bitcoin blockchain, in order to add a block to the blockchain, the node must perform the following steps:

1. Create a block by gathering unconfirmed transactions from the transaction pool.
2. Solve the cryptographic puzzle to generate a hash which is lesser than a certain pre-defined value or has a certain number of leading zeroes.

The number of leading zeroes required for the block hash is called the 'difficulty level.' In order to solve this puzzle using a fixed set of transactions selected in Step 1, the node has to change the nonce value, which is the only dynamic part of the block at this stage. There is no algorithm to obtain the required hash. Solving this puzzle takes work that increases proportionally with the difficulty level (The verification of the solution, however, requires computation of a single hash). Thus, each block added to the Bitcoin blockchain is a result of 'work' done by the winning node which has solved the puzzle. The work done (hashing energy spent) by other nodes who competed to solve the puzzle is wasted. As more and more blocks get added to the blockchain, the earlier blocks become increasingly secured and final. This is because, in order to change any existing block or its contents, the malicious node has to change all subsequent blocks as well by performing the work for each of the blocks 'successfully.' And this is a probabilistically nearly impossible task. Since the node has to expend a significant amount of energy in terms of computational power, this method of ensuring consensus is called 'Proof of Work.' The nodes which compete in the race to solve the puzzle are called 'Miners.' In addition, the difficulty of the mining puzzle is adjusted by the Bitcoin protocol roughly every 2,016 blocks in order to maintain the average time of block creation close to 10 minutes.

2.4.4.1 The 'Unpopular' POW

Bitcoin's POW is the reason behind the strength of the Bitcoin protocol. Growing faith into the Bitcoin network has resulted in increase in the number of miners and technological advances in terms of Graphics Processing Units (GPUs), Field Programmable Gate Arrays (FGPAs) and Application Specific Integrated Circuits (ASICs) being used for mining. The current average hashing power spent on Bitcoin mining is more than 150 million Terra Hashes/sec [8]. As per a study conducted by Mora et al.[12], Bitcoin mining alone may lead to over 2°C rise in global temperatures within 16–22 years. Needless to say, the POW is infamous and being considered as a threat to the environment.

2.4.4.2 Taming the POW for Double Spending

Double Spending is considered fraud wherein the same currency is spent more than once. For example, if the same Bitcoin address is used in multiple transactions and both transactions are accepted in the blockchain blocks, we can say that double spending has been achieved. In a normal scenario, such transactions will be rejected by non-malicious nodes. As a result, blocks with such transactions will result in dead forks, even if they are added to the blockchain.

In order to achieve double spending, the malicious nodes must win the puzzles successively at a rate faster than the non-malicious nodes in the network, thus building the longest chain with malicious transactions in malicious blocks. Since the probability of generating the winning hash is proportional to the hash rate of the node, a majority hash rate of 51% hash rate is required to be maintained 'consistently' by the set of malicious nodes to attempt double spend. There have been few cryptocurrency networks such as Krypton, Shift and Bitcoin GOLD which are much smaller than the Bitcoin network which have been thus attacked [13].

2.4.5 Other Distributed Consensus Algorithms

Many less energy-intensive alternatives when compared to Proof of Work for distributed consensus have been developed and used in blockchains that emerged post Bitcoin. We discuss some of the most popular consensus algorithms used in blockchain networks. Proof of Work, Proof of Stake and its Variants are more popular in the cryptocurrency blockchains. The permissioned blockchains have their own consensus mechanisms which take into account the permission-based limited participation of members in the blockchain network. New algorithms continue to be added to the list as newer blockchains networks emerge.

2.4.5.1 Proof of Stake

Proof of Stake (POS) is the next most popular algorithm that is much more energy-friendly as compared to POW as it does not require specialized hardware investments on part of the nodes. In this algorithm, there is no mining or race for block creation. Instead, nodes put up a part of their holdings as 'stake' to become block forgers. While Peer Coin introduced POS in 2012 [14], there are other popular blockchains such as Tezos, Dash [15, 16] and now Ethereum which are also using variants of POS. Nodes may lose parts or whole of their stake if they indulge in malicious forging, colluding, etc. This ensures integrity of the nodes as possible penalties are proportional to the stake. There are many variants of POS algorithm.

2.4.5.2 Coin Age-Based POS

Peercoin uses a variant of POS wherein higher the stake and longer the coins are at stake, higher are the chances for a node to mint or forge a block. Once a node uses its stake to forge a block, the coin age for holdings is set to zero. Also, many a time this variant requires a locking period for coins before the node becomes eligible for forging a block.

2.4.5.3 Random Node Selection-Based POS

In Ethereum, nodes have to pay a fixed stake to become Validator nodes. Nodes are selected at random based on their stake. Those validator nodes that are not selected have to perform validation of the created blocks.

2.4.5.4 Delegated Proof of Stake

In some blockchain, the stake amount can be variable and voluntary, thus leading rich nodes to stake higher and win block-forging incentive more frequently. In order to address this, a more 'democratic' algorithm—Distributed Proof of Stake (DPOS) was developed in 2014 by Daniel Larimer [17]. A set of nodes are selected (on rotation) as Witnesses. Other nodes vote for their representative among Witnesses. In case the delegate fails to forge block or forges an invalid block, they may be voted out by their voters. The block reward is shared among the voters of the Witness forging the block. DPOS is faster than POS or POW due to lesser number of nodes responsible for consensus.

2.4.5.5 Proof of Burn

Proof of Burn (POB) is a consensus algorithm that tests the commitment of the node to the blockchain network. A node that wishes to mine blocks is expected to 'burn' or destroy some of its currency by sending it to an 'eater address.' The currency cannot be ever recovered from this address. A blockchain protocol may require nodes to burn their native currency or may require burning of Bitcoins. An example of POB consensus can be found in Slimcoin [18].

2.4.5.6 Proof of Authority

We now move on to consensus in permissioned scenarios. In a permissioned network, where members know each other and have earned a membership in the network, Proof of Authority (POA) consensus is used. Selected nodes perform the role of validators and have their reputation at stake. For example, in a national level banking blockchain, the main regulatory bank can maintain the Validator nodes. The selected consensus members are known to be reputable and are expected to take full responsibility of the transactions approved for inclusion. Validators of POA usually run multiple nodes to ensure redundancy. There may be more than one validator and it is expected that they exercise their authority in rejecting any malicious transactions approved by other validators. POA is usually recommended for permissioned networks, as it brings about a certain degree of centralization which is permissible in private or consortium networks such as supply chains, banking or trade finance networks, etc. POA gives a higher throughput as lesser number of parties participate in consensus. For example: Ethereum Proof of Authority on Azure [19] offering and VeChain, which is a blockchain platform designed to enhance supply chain management and business processes, use POA.

2.4.5.7 Proof of Elapsed Time

Proof of Elapsed Time (PoET) is an algorithm used in permissioned blockchain. It uses a fair lottery system. Usually, a random wait time is assigned to nodes. Occasionally, the wait time may be proportional to resources (such as processors) contributed, such as in Hyperledger Sawtooth [20]. The node which completes its assigned wait time forges the next block. It is also an energy-saving alternative as the processes can sleep until their wait time is completed.

2.4.5.8 Practical Byzantine Fault Tolerance

The Practical Byzantine Fault Tolerance (PBFT) algorithm was proposed by Castro and Liskov in 1999 [21]. Leading blockchain offerings like Hyperledger Sawtooth, Ripple and

Stellar use PBFT consensus. PBFT is a voting-based consensus. This algorithm is Byzantine Fault tolerant as long as the number of faulty nodes $f = \dfrac{n-1}{3}$ where

$n = total\ number\ of\ nodes\ in\ the\ network$ and $f = maximum\ 'number\ of\ faulty\ nodes$.

This is a leader-based algorithm where there are primary nodes and backup or secondary nodes. The primary or leader nodes are responsible for producing candidate blocks. The secondary nodes vote for the blocks produced by the primary. The client awaits $f + 1$ replies from different nodes with the same result, where f represents the maximum number of potentially faulty nodes. This is again used for permissioned blockchains and provides a higher throughput.

2.4.5.9 More Miscellaneous Distributed Consensus Protocols

So far, we have covered the major consensus protocols used in blockchain networks. For the sake of completeness, we list here a few more lesser-known protocols which are used in one or more blockchain offerings that currently exist.

1. Proof of Capacity—Probability of a node forging a block increases with capacity or storage space committed by the node: E.g. BurstCoin [22]
2. Leased POS—Nodes lease their stake to mining nodes: E.g. Waves [23]
3. Hybrid POS-POW—POW miners create blocks and POS validators vote and approve them: E.g. Decred [24]
4. Proof of Importance (POI)—Use balance as well as user activity is given weightage in determining the probability of mining next block: E.g. NEM [25]
5. Ouroboros Proof-of-stake (O-POS): POS with security guarantees: E.g. Cardano [26]

2.5 Sample Use Case Discussion with Proposed Blockchain Architecture

To complete our architecture description, let us discuss a real-life use case for blockchain—Maintenance and Service Supply Chain over blockchain.

2.5.1 Use Case Description

Consider a hypothetical Original Equipment Manufacturer (OEM) manufacturing heavy equipment such as elevators (or ships or industrial equipment). The Business as Usual (BAU) activities for this manufacturer include tracking demand and supply, tracking maintenance needs of equipment after sale or lease, providing support in terms of personnel, parts for replacement, insurance, etc. Clearly, this is a typical trust-based environment, wherein the buyer and the seller have to trust each other (and possibly middlemen) for quantity and quality of supply. The customer, manufacturer, service provider vendors, insurance vendor and banks (or financers) have to trust each other for smooth functioning of this ecosystem. A breach of trust can happen at any interface with multiple implications, e.g. the buyer cancelling the order and not paying for the penalty, the supplier delaying the order and not paying the cancellation refund/penalty, no reimbursement for parts quality issues, delay in maintenance initiation, non-availability of parts, non-availability of personnel for service, non-payment of damages due to parts issues, usage of duplicate parts and more.

2.5.2 Proposed Blockchain Architecture

We propose a consortium blockchain architecture using a popular open source blockchain offering—the Hyperledger Fabric. At the time of writing, the latest version of Hyperledger Fabric is v 2.2 [9].

NOTE: In case you plan to use this reference architecture, make sure you check the latest version available and its associated documentation. Hyperledger Fabric is a permissioned blockchain architecture and an ideal one for consortium scenarios. It does not support native currency, but a currency may be created using code. Since our use case does not require a specialized currency ecosystem, we will refrain from creating one.

2.5.2.1 Merits of Blockchain in the Use Case

We first identify the merits of blockchain in our use case. As we can see, since this is a trust-based network, there is a dependency on the players in the network to behave correctly. Blockchain will certainly help us in making this network trustless and instill more confidence in the parties. OEMs can plan their business better, manage scale of demand and service, diverting resources reliably where required. Payments for quality and penalties for lack thereof can be guaranteed via smart contracts.

2.5.2.2 Role Players

Next, we identify the roles participating in the blockchain network. Table 2.1 lists the participating roles in the blockchain network and the data they handle. The use case can further be elaborated for an actual implementation to add more roles and data under its umbrella.

2.5.2.3 Network Participants

The OEM can be the network initiator or network controller of this blockchain network. The various OEM departments, equipment and part dealers, service management agencies (if servicing is outsourced), bank, transport agencies (if external to OEM) and insurance agencies will be added to the network in a permissioned manner by the OEM.

TABLE 2.1

Blockchain Participant Roles and Data Handled

Participant Role	Types of Data and Type of Access—Read/Write			
	Parts/Equipment	Demand/Order	Maintenance Data	Service Personnel
OEM	Yes (R,W)	Yes (R,W)	Yes (R,W)	Yes (R)
Part Dealers	Yes (R)	Yes (R,W)	Yes (R,W)	Yes (R,W)
Service Agencies	Yes (R)	–	Yes (R,W)	Yes (R,W)
Insurance	Yes (R)	–	Yes (R)	–
Bank/Financer	–	Yes (R)	Yes (R)	–
Transporters	Yes (R,W)	Yes (R,W)	–	–
Customers	Yes (R)	–	–	Yes (R)

2.5.2.4 Channels

The Hyperledger Fabric network allows a data compartmentalization using a feature called channels. Access to channels can be controlled using channel API. Given the different types of data that flows in this network, and the fact that all players need not have complete access to all the data, we can define multiple channels in our Hyperledger Fabric network. This will ensure privacy of the data. As per Table 2.1, we can define four different channels—Eqpmt_Data, Order_Data, Maintenance_Data andPersonnel_Data.

2.5.2.5 Network Diagram

Figure 2.6 represents the network diagram for our proposed solution for the Original Equipment Supply Maintenance Tracking use case. The Hyperledger Fabric offering v 2.2 has been considered for this design. Hyperledger Fabric also has other components such as the Orderer to order blocks as a part of consensus process and the Network Controller and Certification Authority for providing membership certificates for the network participants.
The various components in the diagram are as follows.

Network Participants (Peer):

R0: OEM (P0), R1: Dealer (P1), R2: Service Vendor (P2), R3: Insurance, R4: Bank, R5: Transporter

Channels: C1: Eqpmt_Data, C2: Order_Data, C3: Maintenance_Data, C4: Personnel_Data

Network Initiator/Orderer: O1: OEM

Network Controller: NC1: OEM

Applications: A0: OEM, Dealer, Service Vendor, Transporter, A1: Insurance, A2: Bank, A3: Customer

Certificate Authority: C0 to Cn

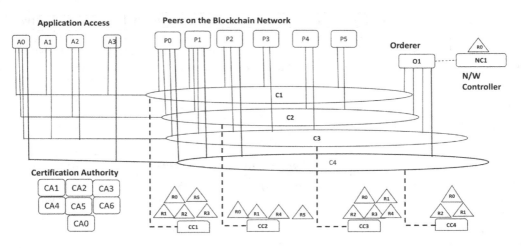

FIGURE 2.6
Blockchain network for OEM Supply Chain maintenance use case.

2.5.2.6 *Transactions and Smart Contracts*

The list of transactions and smart contracts which may be considered for this network are given in Table 2.2 and Table 2.3, respectively. Note that these lists are not exhaustive and more transactions and smart contracts can be included.

TABLE 2.2

List of Transactions

Transaction Code	Transaction Name	Transaction Function	Triggered By Role	Associated Smart Contract
T1:	Add_Equipment	Add details of available/newly manufactured equipment to blockchain	OEM	
T2:	Create_Order	Request equipment or parts by placing an order	Dealer	
T3:	Accept_Order	Accept order and plan for delivery or manufacturing as needed	OEM	Plan_manufacture
T4:	Assign_Equipment_ To_Order	Assign equipment to an order	OEM	
T5:	Dispatch_Order	Send out a packaged order	OEM/Dealer	
T6:	Update_Order_ Location	Tracking of order enroute	Transporter	
T7:	Deliver_Order	Deliver order after final quality checks	Transporter	
T8:	Accept_Order	Accept order and confirm quality checks before accepting	Dealer/Customer	Start_Warrranty Plan_maintenance Assign_Personnel
T9:	Request_Maintenance	Request non-scheduled maintenance	Dealer/Customer	Assign_Personnel
T10:	Assign_Maintenance_ Personnel	Assign personnel for maintenance work	OEM/Vendor	
T11:	Accept_Maintenance_ Asgmt	Accept maintenance work	OEM/Vendor	
T12:	Update_ Maintenance_Asgmt	Tracking maintenance of Equipment/Part	OEM/Vendor	
T13:	Complete_ Maintenance_Asgmt	Mark work completion	OEM/Vendor	Update_EndOf_Life_ Date
T14:	Confirm_ Maintenance_ Completion	Give work feedback and confirm maintenance is completed	Dealer/Customer	Make_Maintenance_ payment
T15:	Update_Payment_ Info	Log the payment or penalty paid details	Bank	

TABLE 2.3

List of Smart Contracts

Smart Contract Code	Smart Contract Name	Smart Contract Function
SC1	Plan_manufacture	This smart contract will plan/trigger the manufacturing process cycle based on new orders and/or order projections based on historic data.
SC2	Start_Warrranty	This smart contract will trigger warranty-based depreciation calculation maintenance planning as soon as the delivery of the equipment/part is accepted by the dealer/customer.
SC3	Plan_maintenance	For every equipment produced, this smart contract will plan for maintenance checks at regular intervals (before or after delivery to end customers). Accordingly, this contract will trigger the Assign_personnel smart contract.
SC4	Make_Delivery_payment	Delivery payments will be automated by this smart contract once the delivery is confirmed by the dealer/end customer.
SC5	Make_Maintenance_payment	Service request or maintenance payments (routine or requested) will be automated by this smart contract.
SC6	Assign_Personnel	This smart contract will assign personnel to perform service requests.
SC7	Update_End_Of_Life_Date	This smart contract will be used to update the end-of-life date for the equipment or part based on the service personnel's report of the service performed on the actual equipment/part.

2.6 Conclusion

In this chapter, various aspects of the blockchain architecture have been explained. The chapter also details how various distributed consensus algorithms are being used by blockchain architectures developed so far. The OEM Supply chain use case with a blockchain-based solution indicates how the blockchain concepts can be put into practice to build a trustless network for solutions to real-life problems.

References

[1] Nakamoto, Satoshi. *Bitcoin: A Peer-to-Peer Electronic Cash System*, 2008, https://bitcoin.org/bitcoin.pdf (accessed 21 September 2021).

[2] National Institute of Standards and Technology (US Department of Commerce). Cryptographic Standards and Guidelines, 2021, https://csrc.nist.gov/Projects/cryptographic-standards-and-guidelines (accessed 21 September 2021).

[3] National Institute of Standards and Technology (US Department of Commerce). *Research Results on SHA-1 Collisions*, 2017, https://csrc.nist.gov/News/2017/Research-Results-on-SHA-1-Collisions (accessed 21 September 2021).

[4] Bitcoin Project, 2021, https://bitcoin.org/ (accessed 21 September 2021).

[5] Ethereum Blockchain, 2021, https://ethereum.org/en/ (accessed 21 September 2021).

[6] Voell, Zach. *Bitcoin Node Count Falls to 3-Year Low Despite Price Surge*, May 2020, www.coindesk.com/bitcoin-node-count-falls-to-3-year-low-despite-price-surge (accessed 21 September 2021).

[7] Merkle, Ralph. *Method of Providing Digital Signatures*, 1979, https://patents.google.com/patent/US4309569A/en.

[8] Blockchain Explorer/ Total Hash Rate, 2021, www.blockchain.com/explorer /www.blockchain.com/charts/hash-rate (accessed 21 September 2021).

[9] Hyperledger Fabric v2.2 Documentation, 2021, https://hyperledger-fabric.readthedocs.io/en/release-2.2/ (accessed 21 September 2021).

[10] R3 Corda—Enterprise Blockchain Solution, 2021, www.r3.com/corda-platform/ (accessed21 September 2021).

[11] Leslie, Lamport, Robert Shostak and Marshall Pease. "The Byzantine generals problem." *ACM Transactions on Programming Languages and Systems*, vol. 4, no. 3 (July 1982): 382–401.

[12] Mora, C., R.L. Rollins, K. Taladay, et al. "Bitcoin emissions alone could push global warming above 2°C."*Nature Climate Change*, vol. 8 (2018): 931–933, https://doi.org/10.1038/s41558-018-0321-8.

[13] Redman, Jamie. *Small Ethereum Clones Getting Attacked by Mysterious'51 Crew'*, 2016, https://news.bitcoin.com/ethereum-clones-susceptible-51-attacks/ (accessed 21 September 2021).

[14] Peercoin—Proof of Stake, 2012, www.peercoin.net/(accessed 21 September 2021).

[15] Tezos—Open Source Platform for Assets and Application, https://tezos.com/ (accessed 21 September 2021).

[16] Dash—Digital Cash, www.dash.org/ (accessed 21 September 2021).

[17] Larimer, D. "Delegated proof-of-stake (dpos)."*A Peerto Peer Polymorphic Digital Asset Exchange-Bitshares*, 2013, www.the-blockchain.com/docs/BitShares%20A%20Peer-to-Peer%20Polymorphic%20Digital%20Asset%20Exchange.pdf (accessed 21 September 2021).

[18] Ethereum Proof of Authority on Azure, https://azure.microsoft.com/en-in/blog/ethereum-proof-of-authority-on-azure/ (accessed 21 September 2021).

[19] Slimcoin White Paper, 2014, https://github.com/slimcoin-project/slimcoin-project.github.io/raw/master/whitepaperSLM.pdf (accessed21 September 2021).

[20] Hyperledger Sawtooth Documentation, June 2021, https://sawtooth.hyperledger.org/docs/core/nightly/0-8/introduction.html#consensus (accessed 21 September 2021).

[21] Castro, Miguel and Barbara Liskov. "Practical byzantine fault tolerance."*OSDI'99: Proceedings of the Third Symposium on Operating Systems Design and Implementation* (February 1999): 173–186, http://pmg.csail.mit.edu/papers/osdi99.pdf (accessed 21 September 2021).

[22] Burstcoin, 2021, www.burst-coin.org/index.html (accessed21 September 2021).

[23] Waves Blockchain Documentation, https://docs.waves.tech/en/ (accessed 21 September 2021).

[24] Decred Cryptocurrency, 2021, https://decred.org/ (accessed 21 September 2021).

[25] NEM Blockchain, 2021, https://nem.io/ (accessed 21 September 2021).

[26] CardanoBlockchain, 2021, https://cardano.org/ (accessed 21 September 2021).

3

Unblocking the Blockchain: Concept and Use Cases

Padma D. Adane

CONTENTS

3.1 Definition

As defined in [1], Blockchain is an open distributed ledger that can record transactions between two parties efficiently and in a verifiable and permanent way. The technology is built upon five principles:

- **Distributed Ledger:** No single node in the network controls the ledger/information recorded in the ledger. The information in the ledger is accessible by every user of the Blockchain network.

- **Peer-to-Peer Transmission:** There is no central authority involved in the communication. The information is broadcasted between peers. Every node that receives the broadcast checks the validity of the transactions in the block before broadcasting it to its neighbor.

- **Transparency with Pseudonymity:** Each user in the network has a pair of keys: one public key and its associated private key. The hash of the public key, which is a long string of alphanumeric characters, is used as the address of the user. Thus, instead of the user-ID or user name, hashes of their respective public keys are used as addresses of the sender and receiver of the transaction providing pseudonymity

DOI: 10.1201/9781003203933-4

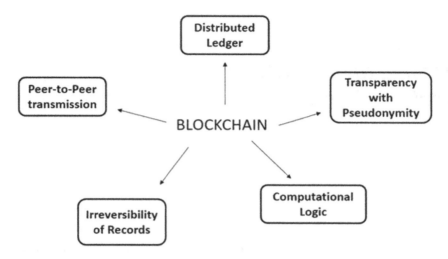

FIGURE 3.1
Five principles of Blockchain technology.

to the peers involved in the transaction. Each user of the network has access to the transactions and its related values, providing total transparency to the system.

- **Irreversibility of Records:** A group of transactions, whose validity has been verified, are collected to form a "block", which is then attached or linked to the existing Blockchain after a consensus is reached among the nodes regarding its inclusion in the Blockchain. Once a transaction gets recorded, it is practically infeasible, because of the underlying cryptographic algorithms, to revert back or undo the transactions. This provides immutability to the information stored in the Blockchain.

- **Computational Logic:** The information recorded in the Blockchain need not be a mere set of transactions. It is possible to embed logic in it with the help of programming languages like Solidity, Serpent, Vyper, etc., which gets executed when certain conditions are met. This is extremely beneficial for cooperating organizations using Blockchain for their business with the rules of business or "Smart Contract" getting automatically executed on attainment of the desired condition(s).

Figure 3.1 illustrates these five principles.

3.2 Elements of a Blockchain

A Blockchain includes four important components or elements to provide all the features of a secure distributed ledger [2]. Figure 3.2 shows these four elements. A brief description of these elements is as follows:

- **Protocol for Commitment:** Every transaction that is broadcasted in the network must be verified and get included in one of the blocks. The newly formed block is linked or included in the existing chain by certain designated nodes. These

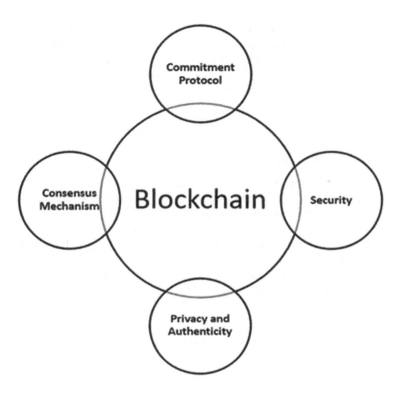

FIGURE 3.2
Elements of a Blockchain.

designated nodes must ensure that any transaction that has already been broadcasted but left out in the newly created block must get included in the next block.
This process must be completed in a finite time.

- **Consensus Mechanism:** The process of adding a newly created block in the
  Blockchain is based on certain rules known as the consensus mechanism, i.e. all
  the concerned nodes must agree upon the inclusion of the block in the Blockchain.
  This mechanism ensures that all the local copies of the chain are consistent
  and updated. The type of consensus mechanism used is based on the type of
  the Blockchain. A permission-less Blockchain uses a Challenge-Response-based
  consensus mechanism while a Permissioned Blockchain uses a State Machine
  Replication-based consensus mechanism.

- **Security:** Blockchain provides immutability or a tamper-proof property through
  the use of cryptographic hash algorithms. Hash of all the transactions in a block
  is included in the header of the block, which in turn is linked to the hash of all
  subsequent blocks that get added in the chain. A single change in any of the transactions already recorded in the Blockchain means change in all the subsequent
  blocks. This is practically almost impossible to achieve. Thus, any information that
  once gets recorded in the Blockchain is immune from any modifications.

- **Privacy and Authenticity:** Every transaction included in the chain is cryptograph-
  ically signed by the originator of the transaction, which is verified by every node/
  user in the network. This ensures that the sender cannot deny the transaction later

on. Moreover, the identity of the persons involved in the transaction is hidden because pseudo addresses are used for the sender and receiver of the transaction. Transactions occur between Blockchain addresses. Users can choose to remain anonymous or provide proof of their identity to others.

3.3 Classification of Blockchain

The type of Blockchain one should use depends on the need of the application that will run on top of it. For example, for an application like cryptocurrency, where any one is free to join or leave the network, a Permission-Less Blockchain is used, which is open to public. However, if an organization's need is a restricted network where only authorized employees can have access to the confidential information, a permissioned Blockchain is the right choice. It is a closed private network and nobody from the outside has access to it. Thus, there can be various combinations of the type of the Blockchain to be used depending on the requirements of the application. The Blockchain can be classified broadly in two ways [3]: based on the access of the information stored in it and based on the management of the network.

3.3.1 Classification Based on the Access of Information

- Permission-Less: An open access to the ledger, i.e. the Blockchain, is available to everyone with no restrictions on who can access and validate the transactions. The identity of the nodes is anonymous/pseudonymous.

- Permissioned: A closed environment suitable for control-free financial applications like cryptocurrency. The nodes have open read/write network access suitable for business applications like a smart contract. The nodes have a permissioned read/write access to the ledger, i.e. the access to the Blockchain is restricted. The identity of nodes is known, but the transaction identities can be private, anonymous, or pseudonymous.

3.3.2 Classification Based on the Management of Network

- Public Blockchain: As the name suggests, these Blockchain are public, i.e. accessible by anyone. The transactions are public: no one is given any special privileges or can control the network. No one trusts anyone in the network, the nodes must reach a consensus to add any new block (set of transactions) into the existing chain. The nodes are anonymous to each other and the one who gets to add the new block is incentivized. Public Blockchain can be permission-less, e.g. Bitcoin, or permissioned e.g. Ethereum.

  Among all the types of Blockchains, public Blockchains offer the highest level of decentralization. They are resilient to malicious attacks. However, scalability is an issue with this type of Blockchain.

- Private Blockchain: In a private Blockchain, participants identify each other. The network is controlled by one entity and has the power to decide who gets read/write access and permission to validate the transactions. Transaction processing is faster when compared to the Public Blockchains and efficiency is better. It is easier to remove malicious nodes trying to pollute the network. However, compared to public blockchains they are less decentralized and more centralized in nature, and hence less resilient to attacks.

- Consortium Blockchain: This type of Blockchain is semi-decentralized in nature and is controlled by a group rather than a single entity or organization. The participants know each other. A few selected nodes control the consensus process and the read/write access to the ledger. Consortium Blockchains are typically used by banks and government organizations.

- Hybrid Blockchain: A hybrid Blockchain [4] offers lots of flexibility as it is an amalgamation of private and public Blockchain. The access to the secure data is controlled and only a section of the data stored in the ledger is made public.

The type of Blockchain to be used for storing data in the ledger depends entirely on the requirements of the underlying application and the sought-after level of decentralization and security. Table 3.1 [5] summarizes the characteristics of the various types of Blockchain.

3.4 Consensus Mechanism

This protocol is crucial in ensuring that all the nodes have a consistent copy of the ledger and every new block that is added to the Blockchain is agreed upon by all responsible for the decision. Without a good consensus mechanism, Blockchains are at risk of various attacks [6]. A comprehensive survey of various consensus mechanisms for distributed systems and its impact on the applications is provided by [7]. A good consensus mechanism is vital for the stable operation of any Blockchain [8], and continuous improvements in theses consensus mechanisms have led to the evolution of Blockchain technology to Blockchain 3.0. The number of consensus mechanisms available in literature is extremely large and continuously evolving. An ideal consensus mechanism must handle the typical faults that can occur in a distributed system:

- Crash Fault: The node crashes or becomes unavailable
- Network or Partitioned Fault: A network/link failure causes network partition
- Byzantine Fault: Node starts behaving maliciously

The following section discusses Proof of work, the consensus mechanism used in Bitcoin.

3.4.1 Proof of Work (PoW)

Proof of Work is an incentive-based protocol that falls in the category of pure computation-based protocol [9]. This mechanism was proposed by [10] and is used in Bitcoin—permission less Blockchain. To understand the working of this consensus mechanism one must first understand the structure of a block in a Bitcoin Blockchain. There are two important components of a block:

1. A header
2. List of transactions

TABLE 3.1

Summary of Types of Blockchain

Parameters	Public		Consortium		Private
	Permission-less	Permissioned	Permission-less	Permissioned	Permissioned
Access	Open read/open validation of transactions	Open read/permissioned validation of transactions	Open read/permissioned validation of transactions	Permissioned or open read/permissioned validation of transactions	Permissioned read/validation of transactions
Participants	Anonymous/pseudonymous	Anonymous/pseudonymous	Usually identified	Identified	Identified
Validation based on consensus protocol	Open to every participant in the network	Open to every participant in the network, subject to certain conditions	Depending on the consensus mechanism chosen for the platform	By pre-approved participants (across organizations involved)	By pre-approved participants (within the single entity)
Speed of validation	Slow	Quicker	Quick	Quick	Quick
User's level of privacy	None	None	Tailored to the needs of the participants	Tailored to the needs of the participants	Tailored to the needs of the participants
Computation power required	High, variable depending on the consensus mechanism	Intermediate, variable depending on the consensus mechanism	Lower	Lower	Lower
Transaction fees	Yes	Slightly higher	Optional—depending on the rules of the Blockchain	Optional—depending on the rules of the Blockchain	Optional—depending on the rules of the Blockchain
Scalability	Low	Slightly higher	Higher	Higher	Higher

Source: Ganne, E (2018)

The header of a block stores the metadata of the block. The prominent information recorded in the header of a block includes [11]:

- Previous Block Hash: The hash of the block that is the immediate predecessor of the current block. Inclusion of this in the current block helps in linking it to the existing Blockchain and forms the chain.
- Timestamp: The date and time when the block is added into the Blockchain.
- Number of transactions in the block: The designated node (miner) collects the transactions broadcasted in the network that are yet to be included in the Blockchain. Each transaction is signed by the originator of the transaction using his/her private key. The transaction can be verified by anyone in the network using the corresponding public key of the originator.
- Merkle Root: The transactions are organized in a Merkle Tree structure. The root of the Merkle Tree is the verification of all the transactions and is an important component in calculating the hash of the current block. Any change in a single transaction changes the hash of that transaction, which changes the subsequent hashes until it changes the Merkle Root. This, in turn, requires a change in the block hash of all the preceding blocks. Thus, it is extremely difficult to make any change in a transaction that gets committed in the Blockchain, providing it the required immutability or tamper proofness. Figure 3.3 illustrates the construction of the Merkle Root.
- Nonce: This is the random number which the miner needs to compute the current block hash so that it satisfies the current specified difficulty level (leading number of zeros).
- Difficulty: This parameter is a measure of how difficult it is to find a hash below a given target. It is computed after 2,016 blocks have been generated or every two weeks (one block every 10 minutes). It is changed using the following mathematical formulation:

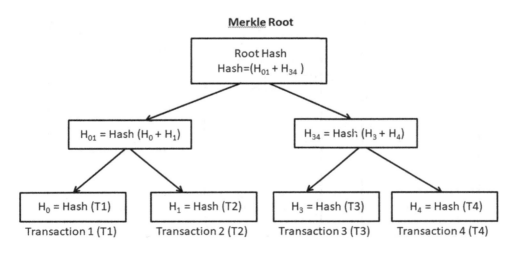

Merkle Root

Root Hash
Hash=(H_{01} + H_{34})

H_{01} = Hash (H_0 + H_1)

H_{34} = Hash (H_3 + H_4)

H_0 = Hash (T1)

H_1 = Hash (T2)

H_3 = Hash (T3)

H_4 = Hash (T4)

Transaction 1 (T1) Transaction 2 (T2) Transaction 3 (T3) Transaction 4 (T4)

FIGURE 3.3
Construction of Merkle Root.

current difficulty = previous difficulty*(2 weeks in ms*)/ms to mine last 2,016 blocks)

ms*: milliseconds

- Current Block Hash: This is calculated as

$H_k = Hash(H_{k-1} \,||\, Merkle\ Root \,||Timestamp \,||\, Nonce)$
where H_{k-1} is the previous Block hash

Finding the nonce with the required number of leading zeros is computationally intensive. This discourages the attackers from proposing the block or making changes in the existing blocks. The miners collect the transactions approximately for 10 minutes and start mining using PoW. It is difficult to predict which miner will be able to solve the challenge. Thus, no miner can control the network. The miner who successfully adds the new block is given an incentive, i.e. the Block reward. This amount is also included in the block header. Figure 3.4 illustrates the structure of a block.

In the event that two miners solve the mathematical puzzle simultaneously, i.e. find the required nonce satisfying the given difficulty level, both of them add their own block into the existing chain. This results in a fork or bifurcation in the existing Blockchain. Any subsequent new block can be added in either prong of the forked chain. In Bitcoin, as per the longest chain rule [12], only one of the forked chain continues while all the blocks in the other forked path are declared orphaned and discarded.

As illustrated in Figure 3.5, Block 3 and Block 4 are mined and added to Block 2 at the same time; similarly, Block 6 and Block 7 are mined simultaneously. However, in due course, Block 3, Block 7, and Block 9 are declared orphaned and the longest chain prevails.

There are several shortcomings of this consensus mechanism.

- Huge computation power: Finding the nonce with the desired level of difficulty, also referred to as solving the puzzle, is computationally intensive. Given the fact that it is practically infeasible to crack SHA-256, the hash algorithm used by Bitcoin, miners have to adopt a brute force approach trying with different random

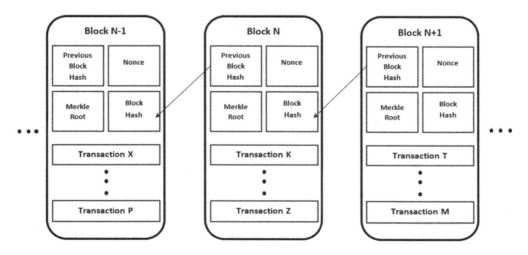

FIGURE 3.4
Structure of a Blockchain.

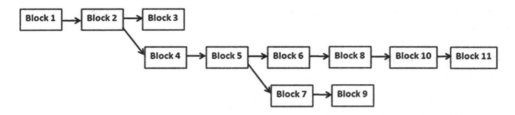

FIGURE 3.5
Forking of Blockchain.

values to find the nonce that satisfies the criteria, i.e. a value with the required number of leading zeros. This requires huge computation power and consumes a lot of electricity. The chance of being the first to come up with a solution is proportional to the fraction of the total computing power [12].

- Sybil Attack: A malicious user or attacker can include a large number of nodes, under its control, into the network. These controlled nodes then follow the instructions of the attacker. They may deny broadcast of valid blocks or broadcast only the blocks generated by the attacker, which can lead to double spending. Thus, these nodes collectively can compromise the operation of the consensus mechanism. Although this attack can be addressed by diversifying the connections, it does not completely remove the possibility of the attack.

- Denial of Service Attack: In this type of attack, the attacker storms the nodes with lots of data, making them busy with processing that data. This not only consumes lots of computation power of the nodes, but also delays the whole mining process of the network. Bitcoin has adopted certain measures like restricting the block size, limiting the script size, disconnecting the node which broadcast too many messages, etc. to limit this attack.

Implementation of PoW consensus mechanism in Bitcoin is discussed in [13].

Over the years, researchers have proposed many consensus mechanisms. Prominent among them are Proof of Stake (PoS) [14], Delegated Proof of Stake (DPoS) [15], Proof of Burn (PoB) [16], PAXOS [17] and Practical Byzantine Fault Tolerance (PBFT) [18].

3.5 Use Cases

Though this technology was made known to the world through its usage by Bitcoin, the technology has lot of potential beyond cryptocurrencies. Governments are drafting new laws to promote the use of Blockchain to support Blockchain applications [19]. Researchers are exploring the avenues that can benefit from this technology. [20] Presents the classification of Blockchain applications as financial and non-financial. Classification of Blockchain applications according to its versions (1.0, 2.0 and 3.0) is presented by [21, 22]. A comprehensive and in-depth classification of Blockchain-based applications is presented by [23].

As published in an article by NASSCOM [24], the following are the top promising Blockchain use cases:

- Banking and finance
- Digital identity
- Energy and sustainability
- Government and the public sector
- Healthcare and the life sciences
- International trade and commodities
- Law
- Media and entertainment
- Real estate
- Sports and e-sports
- ·Supply chain

In PwC's 2018 survey [25] of 600 executives from 15 territories, 84% said that their organizations have at least some involvement with Blockchain technology. Figure 3.6 shows the involvement of Blockchain technology across various sectors of industries. A graph illustrating the use of this technology by various countries and its projected usage is shown in Figure 3.7.

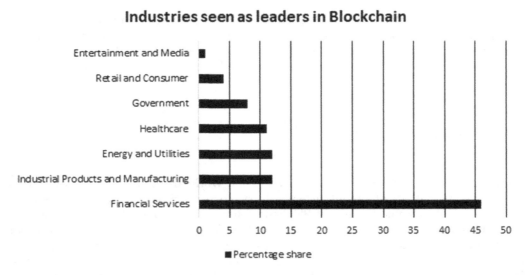

FIGURE 3.6
Industries seen as leaders in Blockchain.
Source: PwC Global Blockchain survey, 2018

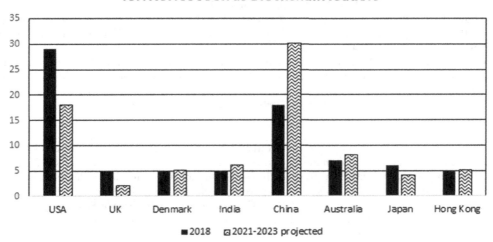

FIGURE 3.7
Territories seen as Blockchain leaders.
Source: PwC Global Blockchain survey, 2018

3.6 Conclusion

Blockchain is suitable not only for cryptocurrencies or the financial sector, but also has a great potential to transform the non-financial sectors. Although there are many issues to be addressed in this domain, it is widely being deployed in many diversified applications. It is an amalgamation of many features known for years, driving it to be adopted by more and more industries in their products and applications. As the technology matures, it is going to see a surge in its acceptance by the industry.

References

1. Marco, Iansiti and Karim R. Lakhani. "The truth about blockchain." *Harvard Business Review*, vol. 95 (January 2017).
2. Chakraborty, Sandip and Praveen Jayachandran. *Blockchains: Architecture, Design and Use Cases*. NPTEL Online Certification Course. https://onlinecourses.nptel.ac.in/noc19_cs63/preview.
3. Tanskinsoy, J. "Blockchain: A Misunderstood Digital Revolution. Things You Need to Know about Blockchain." *SSRN Electronic Journal* (October 2019), https://www.semanticscholar.org/paper/Blockchain%3A-A-Misunderstood-Digital-Revolution.-You-Taskinsoy/5d6796f0881c9c7d8f12c50e77aeae1c37f24fa7.
4. https://data-flair.training/blogs/types-of-blockchain/.
5. Ganne, E. *Can Blockchain Revolutionize International Trade?*. World Trade Organization, 2018, https://www.wto.org/, Print ISBN 978-92-870-4760-1, Web ISBN 978-92-870-4761-8.
6. Blockgenic. *Different Blockchain Consensus Mechanisms*, 2018, https://hackernoon.com/different-blockchain-consensus-mechanisms-d19ea6c3bcd6.

7. Wang Wenbo, et al. "A survey on consensus mechanisms and mining strategy management in blockchain networks." *IEEE Access*, vol. 7 (January 2019).

8. Zhang, C., C. Wu and X. Wang. 2020. *Overview of Blockchain Consensus Mechanism*. Proceedings of the 2nd International Conference on Big Data Engineering, https://dl.acm.org/doi/abs/10.1145/3404512.3404522.

9. Dinh, T.T.A., R. Liu, M. Zhang, G. Chen, B.C. Ooi and J. Wang. "Untangling blockchain: A data processing view of blockchain systems." *IEEE Transactions on Knowledge and Data Engineering*, vol. 30, no. 7 (2018): 1366–1385.

10. Nakamoto, S. *Bitcoin: A Peer-to-Peer Electronic Cash System*. Self-published Paper, May 2008, https://bitcoin.org/bitcoin.pdf.

11. www.blockchain.com/.

12. Tschorsch, F. and B. Scheuermann. "Bitcoin and beyond: A technical survey on decentralized digital currencies." *IEEE Communications Surveys Tutorials*, vol. 18. no. 3 (2016): 2084–2123.

13. Zhu, Xingxiong. "Research on blockchain consensus mechanism and implementation." *IOP Conference Series: Materials Science and Engineering*, vol. 569 (2019): 042058.

14. King, S. and S. Nadal. *Ppcoin: Peer-to-Peer Crypto-Currency with Proof-of-Stake*. Self-published Paper, August 2012, https://peercoin.net/assets/paper/peercoin-paper.pdf.

15. Larimer, D. "Delegated proof-of-stake (dpos): Bitshare whitepaper. Technical report." *IEEE Access*, vol. 99 (2014).

16. Slimcoin: A peer-to-peer crypto-currency with proof-ofburn. *Technical Report*, May 2014, www.slimcoin.org; https://github.com/slimcoin-project/slimcoin-project.github.io/blob/master/whitepaperSLM.pdf.

17. Cachin, C. *Yet Another Visit to Paxos*. Technical Report RZ3754, IBM Research, Zurich, Switzerland, 2009.

18. Castro, M. and B. Liskov. "Practical byzantine fault tolerance and proactive recovery." *ACM Transactions on Computer Systems*, vol. 20, no. 4 (2020): 398–461.

19. https://research.aimultiple.com/blockchain-applications/.

20. Crosby, M., P. Pattanayak, S. Verma and V. Kalyanaraman. "Blockchain technology: Beyond bitcoin." *Applied Innovation*, vol. 2 (2016): 6–10.

21. Swan, M. *Blockchain Blueprint for a New Economy*. O'Reilly Media Inc., Sebastopol, CA, 2015.

22. Zhao, J.L., S. Fan and J. Yan. "Overview of business innovations and research opportunities in blockchain and introduction to the special issue." *Financial Innovation*, vol. 2, no. 1 (2016): 28.

23. Casino, Fran, et al. "A systematic literature review of blockchain-based applications: Current status, classification and open issues." *Telematics and Informatics*, vol. 36 (2019): 55–81.

24. https://community.nasscom.in/communities/emerging-tech/blockchain/top-promising-blockchain-use-cases.html#.

25. www.pwc.com/gx/en/industries/technology/blockchain/blockchain-in-business.html.

4

BlockCloud: Blockchain as a Cloud Service

Urmila Shrawankar and Chaitreya Shrawankar

CONTENTS

4.1 Introduction

Cloud Computing uses a centralized approach but when data is available on public cloud, there is a serious issue with security [1, 2]. Therefore many companies have started using blockchain technology for storing data and performing transactions.

The earlier hybrid (cloud and blockchain) approach, as shown in Figure 4.1, uses to incorporate blockchain technology into cloud computing on public as well as private cloud for storing data [3]. Blockchain takes care of the information and ensures that security is present.

Blockchain uses a fully decentralized approach [4] to store data on multiple nodes all over the world. It provides improved protection and security of data. It is accessible and

DOI: 10.1201/9781003203933-5

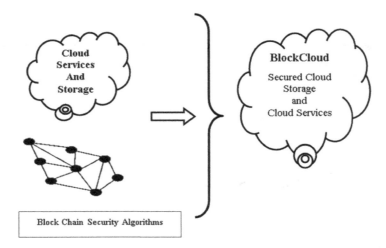

FIGURE 4.1
BlockCloud architecture.

controlled to multiple vendors. Every vendor uses a public and private key to open and save encrypted files. If anyone tries to access other files, a part of the file will be available to them instead of complete file.

A BlockCloud storage takes costumer data and divides it into small parts. It then uses some algorithms like hash functions and encryption methods to enforce additional security [5]. After adding the additional security layers, it distributes over the network, providing secure cloud storage.

4.2 Cloud Computing

Cloud Computing is a services oriented, pay-per-use model. Services include infrastructure, servers, networking, platform, operating system, storage, database, software, analytics, intelligence and many more. These services are easily accessible through the internet, and service providers perform the management and maintenance of these services [6]. These services are ubiquitous with reasonable cost. The security issue is also handled by the provider, not by

FIGURE 4.2
Cloud Technology features.

the user. Major features of cloud technology as shown in Figure 4.2 include demand-based services, wide network access, resource sharing, pay-per-user service, elastic scalability, etc.

4.2.1 Cloud Computing Architecture

Cloud technology focuses mainly on its different category of deployment models and service models [7]. The deployment model explains the architectural setup and use of cloud architecture as shown in Table 4.1 and Figure 4.3, whereas cloud service models give the idea about how cloud services are offered for users are shown in Table 4.2 and Figure 4.4.

4.3 Cloud Deployment Model

TABLE 4.1

Cloud Deployment Model

Cloud Deployment Model	Purpose	Example
Public Cloud	This cloud architecture is available to the public. Anyone can connect to the cloud, pay of the service and use it.	Microsoft Azure and Google App Engine
Private Cloud	It is restricted for organizations only. This facility is available to the person connected to that organization.	Eucalyptus System
Hybrid Cloud	It is a combination of cloud models.	Amazon Web Services
Community Cloud	It is devolved for a specific group of people have the same interest.	Facebook

FIGURE 4.3
Cloud deployment model.

TABLE 4.2

Cloud Service Model

Cloud Service Model	Purpose	Example
IaaS: Infrastructure as a Service	Cloud customers get virtualized infrastructure, hardware, storage, computing facilities, network. A completely virtualized machine.	Amazon EC2 GoGrid
PaaS: Platform as a Service	Cloud customers get complete software development platform with programing languages interface.	Microsoft Azure
SaaS: Software as a Service	Ready web-based applications connected over the internet.	Amazon web services Google Mail

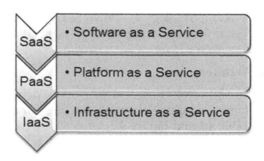

FIGURE 4.4
Cloud Service Model.

4.3.1 Cloud Major Challenges

Now a days, cloud technology has become very popular and useful, but still it faces some challenges, as listed in Table 4.3.

TABLE 4.3

Cloud Major Challenges

Challenges	Description
Security of Data	Cloud providers offer security mechanisms for data security; it is a challenge to prevent data leakage.
Downtimes	Services are available 24/7 [6], but for scheduled maintenance some services are unavailable for a limited time.
Limited Control	User works on virtual machines and has limited control. Provider maintains and manages the services.
Network Dependency	Services available through Web only. Internet service and speed is a major issue to access cloud services.

4.4 Blockchain Technology

Blockchain is the technology of keeping information about particular data available to the public in such a way that others cannot change it. The information is stored in a chain of blocks as per the category of data.

Transactions are stored in a database, where it is further repeated and distributed over the network [8].

Transaction records of the database are immutable. Further security algorithms (like hash) are implemented on these blocks. Since it is in decentralized nature, blocks are stored in a distributed network, called nodes. All these transactions are stored in an encrypted form with a proper private and public key, and multiple-party verification is required to access the transaction. The complete working of Blockchain Technology is shown in Figure 4.5.

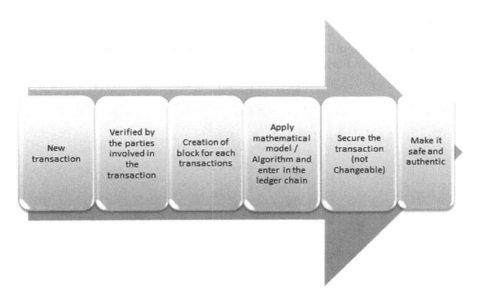

FIGURE 4.5
Working model of blockchain technology.

4.4.1 Blockchain Ecosystem's Major Components

A blockchain ecosystem's major components are i. Node Application ii. Shared Ledger iii. Consensus Algorithm iv. Virtual Machine. A pictorial look is given in Figure 4.6.

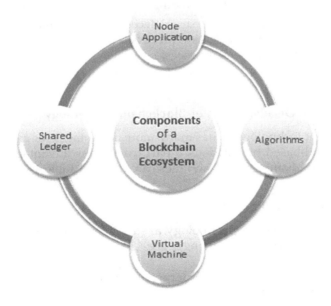

FIGURE 4.6
Major components of a blockchain ecosystem.

4.4.2 Blockchain Models

Based on the users' accessibility and availability, a blockchain is divided into four major categories [9], as shown in Figure 4.7.

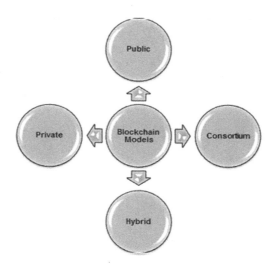

FIGURE 4.7
Blockchain models.

    i. **Public Blockchain:** It is a fully decentralized model. Any new node can take part in the network and can be involved in the computing storage and validation activities using a consensus mechanism.

    ii. **Private Blockchain:** It is developed for a particular organization or industry.

    iii. **Consortium Blockchain:** It uses a partial decentralization chain approach. On the basis of service access, node selection process is implemented prior. Other nodes do not take part in the consensus process.

    iv. **Hybrid Blockchain:** It is simply a combination of two or more blockchain models.

4.4.3 Advantages and Disadvantages of Blockchain Technology

Blockchain is a recent technology; it has many more advantages for secured transactions as compared to cloud-based transactions. Apart from many advantages, the technology suffers from some disadvantages [10], and these are listed in Table 4.4.

4.4.4 Major Challenges in Blockchain

Blockchain is a new and emerging technology, as such it has many good features and some challenges [11]. Some of the major challenges are:

    i. **Scalability:** Block size is limited for large number of transactions and creation of new blocks takes more time.

    ii. **Privacy Leakage:** Transactions' public key is shared by multiple companies in a distributed environment, therefore no guarantee for complete privacy.

TABLE 4.4

Advantages and Disadvantages of Blockchain Technology

Advantages/Benefits	Disadvantages/Limitations
• Decentralization	• Not a Distributed Computing System
• Autonomous	• Scalability is an issue
• Distributed Ledgers	• Some solutions consume too much energy
• Immutability	• Transaction cannot go back; data is immutable
• Faster Settlement	• Blockchains are sometimes inefficient
• Integrity	• Not completely secure
• Persistency	• Users are their own private keys
• Anonymity	• Costly
• Transparency	• Implementation difficult
• Traceability	• Expert knowledge required
• Enhanced Security	• Interoperability
• Consensus	• Legacy systems
• Auditability	• Maturity

iii. **Regulations and Laws:** Blockchain technology is still very new and becoming accepted by society. Legal issues and law are in a developmental stage.

iv. **Governance:** Blockchain uses a distributed network, therefore governance of multiple public and private organizations is difficult.

4.4.5 Blockchain vs. Cloud Computing

The major difference of Cloud technology and blockchain are listed in Table 4.5.

TABLE 4.5

Blockchain vs. Cloud Computing

Issue/Parameter	Cloud Computing	Blockchain
Architecture type	Extremely centralized model	Fully decentralized model
Service architecture	Computing services are available through the internet under pay-per-user model	Currently, blockchain services are costly; useful for larger organizations
Service Models	Provides services through different category of services: • SaaS: Software as a Service • PaaS: Platform as a Service • IaaS: Infrastructure as a Service	Does not provide any service directly. Blockchain and blockchain networks may offer services through a cloud computing service
Data Store and Access Method	Changeable online through the internet	Immutable/not changeable Uses encryption algorithms and hash techniques Store in decentralized manner
Database structure	Uses traditional database structure; data is stored in data centers [12]	Uses online database registry
Data visibility and transparency	In public cloud data is visible In private cloud data is hidden from other users	It maintains data transparency

TABLE 4.5 Continued

Blockchain vs. Cloud Computing

Issue/Parameter	Cloud Computing	Blockchain
Integrity of data	Not assured	Assured
Support for corporate software development	Cloud helps to develop software for blockchain	For developing corporate software for blockchain, it demands data security and transparency
Some major service providers	• Amazon Web Services (AWS) • IBM • Microsoft • Google • Oracle • Alibaba • Salesforce	• Amazon • IBM • Microsoft • Ethereum • Bitcoin • Hyperledger Fabric • Quorum

4.4.6 BlockCloud: Cloud with Blockchains

After gaining popularity of virtualization technology for cloud and Bitcoin in blockchain separately, there is a need for technology for secure transactions with high availability and minimum cost. A hybrid model of Cloud and blockchain, i.e. BlockCloud [13], a blockchain-based cloud, will prove the perfect solution for the requirement. Blockchain ensures the protected and secured data storage [14], whereas the cloud ensures the availability of computing resources at a low cost [15, 16], ensuring that users will get secure data storage and high performance computing facility together with pay-per-use.

4.4.7 BaaS: Blockchain as a Service

Blockchain as a Service (BaaS) [17] is a new concept. It is a cloud-based blockchain service offered and managed by a third-party. BaaS is a web host that runs back-end operations of blockchain solutions. BaaS is a solution for large organizations and businesses as they get a solution at a reasonable cost.

Many companies including Linux Foundation (an open-source initiative) are trying to build blockchain solutions, frameworks, tools, APIs and many more. Some popular BaaS providers include Microsoft with Azure, Amazon Managed Blockchain, using Ethereum and Hyperledger Fabric.2, R3 Corda service, SAP Leonardo, PayStand, etc.

4.4.8 BaaS: Key Features

Some of the most common features offered in blockchain-as-a-Service platforms are as follows:

• Management of platforms
• Infrastructure and networks
• Workflow setup management
• App development and administration
• Dashboards for checking and analyzing chaincode
• Transaction auditing
• Customer support

4.4.9 System Model of BlockCloud for BaaS

The complete working of BaaS is given in the block diagram in Figure 4.8.

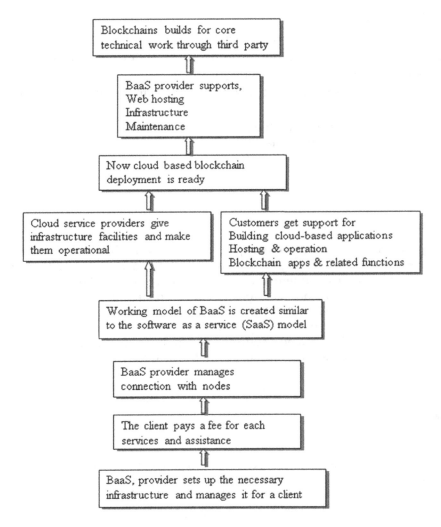

FIGURE 4.8
System model of BlockCloud for Blockchain as a Service (BaaS).

4.4.10 Blockchain Applications

In real day-to-day lives, there are many applications that are coming-up [18, 19]. Some of the prominent application are as follows:

  i. **Finance Sector Applications:** Crypto currency, global payments, insurance claims and processing
 ii. **Smart Property Applications:** Asset management, money lending
iii. **Healthcare Industry:** Healthcare system management, patients health history management, diagnosis, treatment and prescriptions records

iv. **Data Provenance:** Data storage, access and processing

v. **Network Services:** Network capacity, resource management, network virtualization

vi. **Aviation Systems:** Travel services

vii. **E-passport:** Secured passport for customers

viii. **Supply Chain Systems:** Collection of information, maintenance of large amounts of data and its analysis, like food supply chain

ix. **Smart Home Applications:** With the help of the Internet-of-Things (IoT), home appliance operations and safety

x. **Smart Cars and Devices:** with the help of well-authenticated algorithms, devices can be protected on behalf of the owner

4.5 Conclusion

Cloud computing is a proven, useful ubiquitous architecture that provides services anywhere at a reasonable cost. Though it has many more benefits, it struggles with some challenges like data security, interoperability and management. Blockchain is a rising, up-coming technology with more security and improved authenticity. An integrated combined model of blockchain with cloud computing is a trusted, secure service model. This model inherits properties of both cloud and blockchain, therefore overcomes the limitations of both models, and gives a new future model in the form of cloud-based Blockchain as a Service (BaaS). It will be helpful to society in the near future.

References

[1] Harshavardhan, Achampet, T. Vijayakumar and S. Mugunthan. "Blockchain Technology in Cloud Computing to Overcome Security Vulnerabilities." *2018 2nd International Conference on I-SMAC (IoT in Social, Mobile, Analytics and Cloud)* (2018): 408–414.

[2] Park, J.H. and J. Park. "Blockchain security in cloud computing: Use cases, challenges, and solutions." *Symmetry*, vol. 9 (2017): 164.

[3] Westerlund, M. and Nane Kratzke. "Towards distributed clouds: A review about the evolution of centralized cloud computing, distributed ledger technologies, and a foresight on unifying opportunities and security implications." *2018 International Conference on High Performance Computing & Simulation (HPCS)* (2018): 655–663.

[4] Barenji, A.V., Hanyang Guo, Z. Tian, Zhi Li, Wai Ming Wang and George Q. Huang. "Blockchain-based cloud manufacturing: Decentralization." *Transdisciplinary Engineering Methods for Social Innovation of Industry 4.0* (2019), ArXiv abs/1901.10403, https://doi.org/10.3233/978-1-61499-898-3-1003.

[5] Gorkhali, Anjee, Ling Li and Asim Shrestha. "Blockchain: A literature review." *Journal of Management Analytics*, vol. 7, no. 3 (2020): 321–343.

[6] Ghutke, B. and U. Shrawankar. "Pros and cons of load balancing algorithms for cloud computing." *2014 International Conference on Information Systems and Computer Networks (ISCON)* (2014): 123–127, https://doi.org/10.1109/ICISCON.2014.6965231.

[7] Surianarayanan, Chellammal and P. Chelliah. *Essentials of Cloud Computing: A Holistic Perspective*. Springer, Cham, 2019.

[8] Namasudra, S., G. Deka, P. Johri, Mohammad Hosseinpour and A. Gandomi. "The revolution of blockchain: State-of-the-art and research challenges." *Archives of Computational Methods in Engineering*, vol. 28 (2020): 1497–1515.

[9] Nguyen, Q. and Q.V. Dang. "Blockchain technology for the advancement of the future." *2018 4th International Conference on Green Technology and Sustainable Development (GTSD)* (2018): 483–486.

[10] Zheng, Zibin, Shaoan Xie, Hongning Dai, Xiangping Chen and Huaimin Wang. "Blockchain challenges and opportunities: A survey." *International Journal of Web and Grid Services*, vol. 14 (2018): 352–375.

[11] Niranjanamurthy, M., B. Nithya and S. Jagannatha. "Analysis of blockchain technology: Pros, cons and SWOT." *Cluster Computing* (2018): 1–15.

[12] Dhule, Chetan and U. Shrawankar. "Energy efficient green consolidator for cloud data centers." *2019 6th International Conference on Computing for Sustainable Global Development (INDIACom)* (2019): 405–409.

[13] Sanghi, Nikita, Rupali Bhatnagar, Gaganjot Kaur and Vinay Jain. "BlockCloud: Blockchain with cloud computing." *2018 International Conference on Advances in Computing, Communication Control and Networking (ICACCCN)* (2018): 430–434.

[14] Wang, Shang-Rung, Xu Wang and Yaling Zhang. "A secure cloud storage framework with access control based on blockchain." *IEEE Access*, vol. 7 (2019): 112713–112725.

[15] Murthy, C. and M.L. Shri. "A survey on integrating cloud computing with blockchain." *2020 International Conference on Emerging Trends in Information Technology and Engineering (ic-ETITE)* (2020): 1–6.

[16] Blockchain secure cloud: A new generation integrated cloud and blockchain platforms—general concepts and challenges, 2018, https://www.researchgate.net/publication/332704228_Blockchain_Secure_Cloud_a_New_Generation_Integrated_Cloud_and_Blockchain_Platforms_-_General_Concepts_and_Challenges.

[17] Singh, Jatinder and Johan David Michels. "Blockchain as a service (BaaS): Providers and trust." *2018 IEEE European Symposium on Security and Privacy Workshops (EuroS&PW)* (2018): 67–74.

[18] Lu, Y. "The blockchain: State-of-the-art and research challenges." *Journal of Industrial Information Integration*, vol. 15 (2019): 80–90.

[19] Dabbagh, M., Kim-Kwang Raymond Choo, Amin Beheshti, Mohammad Tahir and Nader Sohrabi Safa. "A survey of empirical performance evaluation of permissioned blockchain platforms: Challenges and opportunities." *Computer Security*, vol. 100 (2021): 102078.

Section II

Blockchain Algorithms & Security

5

A Deep Dive into Blockchain Consensus Algorithms

Nupur Kulkarni, Rohini Pise and Sonali Patil

CONTENTS

DOI: 10.1201/9781003203933-7

5.1 Introduction

Blockchain has a great potential to change the way we interact and transact on the Internet. It has features like decentralized systems, security, immutability and transparency. Given that it is a decentralized system and there is no third party involved to verify transactions, security is at risk. Such a system can be highly prone to attacks like double spending and might become vulnerable at times. How is it avoided without having a centralized system? For this system to function at a global scale, a secure algorithm is highly needed. That is where a consensus algorithm comes into play.

5.1.1 Definition of a Consensus Algorithm

Let's understand the definition of consensus algorithm in the simplest manner by considering two different terms, **"consensus"** and **"algorithm"**. Consensus refers to an agreement between two or more stakeholders. An algorithm, in programming terms, can be defined as a set of rules which help to solve a problem. An algorithm can be compared to a roadmap. If we have a look at these two words together, we get a clear understanding of the meaning of a consensus algorithm. A consensus algorithm is the backbone of the Blockchain network. **In technical terms, a consensus algorithm is nothing but a procedure through which all the peers in a Blockchain network agree over the state of a distributed ledger [1].** They come to a consensus depending upon the majority decision and stand by the decision that benefits everyone.

This helps in building trust between the unknown nodes and makes the network more secure. The consensus algorithms ensure safety of the system from malicious attacks in the Blockchain technology.

Example:

To understand this in a better way, let us consider five friends who want to decide the topic of their project. Now, everyone will come up with their own topics, however, the majority of the friends would choose the topic which would be beneficial for them in near future. The ones who didn't select that topic will have to accept this decision, since the majority of them were in favor of the topic. Imagine thousands of people doing the same thing! Doesn't it seem too difficult to handle?

We talked about making a decision on the basis of the majority of votes. But is the majority guaranteed benefit? Not always! Therefore, consensus algorithms not only agree with the majority of votes, but also choose the one that benefits all. Now that we have understood the definition of consensus algorithm, let's look into the different types of consensus algorithms in detail.

5.1.2 Objectives of Consensus Algorithms

The usage of these algorithms is dependent upon the efficiency of the algorithm and they satisfy the following objectives:

1. **Reaching an Agreement**: The consensus mechanism is supposed to ensure that even though the system is decentralized, users should be able to reach an agreement without having the need to trust each other [2].
2. **Participation from everyone**: The consensus mechanism should ensure participation from everyone in the Blockchain network. No one should be missed and everyone's vote should count [2].
3. **Equal value**: Every participant's vote should carry the same value and is equally important [2].
4. **No Double Spending**: Unlike physical currency, cryptocurrency has to deal with the problem of double spending. It simply means copying the transaction details, making it seem legitimate and spending the same cryptocurrency twice. The consensus mechanism should be able to tackle this problem.
5. **Fault Tolerant system**: The consensus mechanism should ensure the reliability of the Blockchain even in case of failure and potential threats.
6. **Equal Activity**: Every participant in the network should be equally active and no one should have more responsibility than the other.

Now that we have looked at the objectives of consensus algorithms, let us learn about each of these consensus algorithms in depth:

5.2 Types of Consensus Algorithms

As of now, more than 30 consensus algorithms exist. Out of those, Proof of Work, Proof of Stake, Delegated Proof of Stake and Practical Byzantine Fault Tolerant are the ones which are widely used in different Blockchain Applications and are most popular in the market [3]. The rest of them are variants of these four algorithms.

5.2.1 Proof of Work

Proof of Work, introduced by Dwork and Moni Naor in 1993, is known to be the oldest consensus algorithm in the Blockchain network [4]. Several blockchain applications use Proof of Work to verify, validate and confirm transactions and create new blocks in the blockchain. Proof of Work is very simple to understand and implement, hence it is the most widely used consensus algorithm. We discussed the "double spending" problem

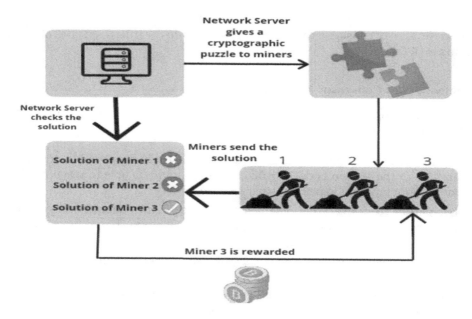

FIGURE 5.1
Implementation of PoW.

earlier. Proof of Work deals with this problem, which can be difficult to solve without a higher authority in the loop. As the name suggests, **Proof of Work is a proof-based consensus algorithm**. This means that it requires a "proof" from a node stating that it has performed the maximum number of computations in order to produce a new block and receive the reward for the same. With Proof of Work, a group of people called miners compete against each other to solve a mathematical puzzle that requires a lot of computational power.

The puzzle can be solved by using a number of mining techniques like CPU mining and GPU mining. The puzzle can only be solved using a trial and error method. On an average, it takes 10 minutes for a puzzle to be solved [4]. Thus, miners use hardware in order to validate the new set of transactions by running algorithms on a software, add the transactions to the public ledger and get rewarded for the same. Refer to Figure 5.1 for understanding it better.

This can only be achieved if miners use expensive computers with enormous computational capabilities and are ready to pay hefty electricity bills. This is certainly a complicated process.

What makes it complicated is that the difficulty of the mathematical or cryptographic puzzle given to the miner keeps on increasing with the number of blocks he is able to add to the blockchain. Sometimes, the difficulty level might even grow exponentially, which makes it a necessity for the miner to increase the number of computations. The more computations he does, the more are his chances to get rewarded for the same [4].

The following flowchart (Figure 5.2) explains the process of proof of work algorithm very clearly.

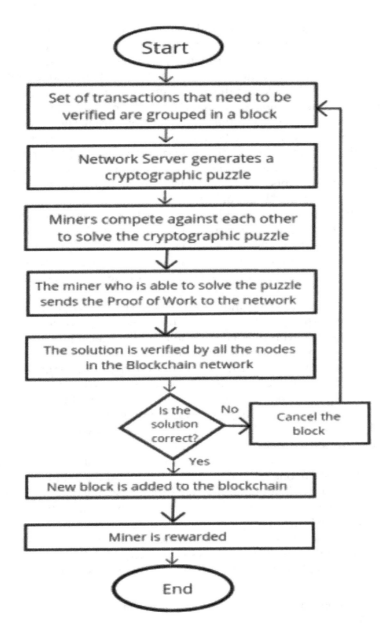

FIGURE 5.2
Flow Chart of Proof of Work.

5.2.1.1 Implementation of "Proof of Work"

Bitcoin was the first cryptocurrency introduced by Satoshi Nakamoto in 2008. Bitcoin, along with many other Cryptocurrencies, uses Proof of Work for validating the transactions and adding them into the block. We'll now discuss the working of Proof of Work in detail. A set of transactions is first announced to a network. The miners include these transactions in a "Candidate Block". A candidate block is nothing but a block which a node, i.e. the miner, tries to mine. Thus, we come to know that, in order to enter the mining competition, a miner needs to create a candidate block. This block is just a temporary block which is validated (if he is successfully able to mine the block, it is added into the block-chain), becomes a confirmed block, and the miner gets rewarded, otherwise it is discarded. But how does a miner mine the block? This remains a valid question. Let's understand that next. The unconfirmed transactions in the candidate block are hashed then and a Merkle Tree is created out of it, which is used to structure all the transactions in the candidate block. Now, you might wonder what a Merkle Tree and a hash is. Let's try to understand the newly introduced terms first. A Merkle Tree is a data structure that can be said to be a way of processing large amounts of data, and hashes are nothing but long strings of numbers that can be accepted as the "Proof of Work".

A Merkle Tree then produces a Merkle hash, which is a single hash that is used to represent all the hashes of transactions in that block [4]. The miner eventually mines the block header, which consists of a Merkle hash, i.e. the root hash, the hash of the previous block and the nonce, which is a number that can be used only once. The output obtained by the miner after mining is called Block Hash. A unique block hash is generated for every block.

The miner then needs to use a trial and error method. He uses a number of nonce values for a large number of hashing functions until a block hash is produced. The valid Block Hash itself proves that the work has been done by the miner. Thus, the algorithm has been named "Proof of Work". Once the valid block hash is obtained, broadcasting of the candidate block takes place, after which all the nodes in the Blockchain network verify if the hash is authentic. If it is verified, the candidate block is considered to be confirmed and added into the existing blockchain. All the nodes which validated the authenticity of the hash update their database. The miner gets rewarded with cryptocurrencies.

Proof of Work is based on the SHA-256 hashing algorithm which generates a unique hash for a variable sized data that you pass through it.

Whatever may be the size of the original data, the hash generated for it will always have the same length. Even if anyone tries to change the original data slightly, the hash function will generate a totally different hash for that input. Also, the data which was given as an input cannot be obtained from the hash that is obtained as an output. Cryptographic hash functions are at the heart of cryptocurrencies, thus maintaining data security. Thus, it becomes possible for the users to detect tampering and the system becomes more secure without the requirement of any intermediaries or a third party.

Till now, we understood how Proof of Work works, so let's summarize the points:

1. Miners require enormous amounts of computational power and electricity to mine a block.
2. Miners who are able to mine the block successfully get rewarded once validated by other nodes.
3. Cryptographic hash functions make the Blockchain network more secure and also ensure data integrity.

5.2.1.2 Applications

Proof of Work is widely used in a lot of cryptocurrencies like Bitcoin, Litecoin, Zcash, Bitcoin SV and Bitcoin cash. Today, Bitcoin, introduced by Satoshi Nakamoto in 2009, is the most widely transacted Cryptocurrency which uses a Proof of Work consensus mechanism [5].

5.2.1.3 Attacks on Proof of Work

1. Proof of Work is prone to 51% attack. What exactly is a 51% attack? A 51% attack or a majority attack occurs when the attacker acquires 51% of the hash rate.

Hash Rate: Hash power or hash rate is the computational power available with a node. We know that Blockchain is a decentralized system which makes it clear that the hash power will be evenly distributed among all the nodes in the network. However, what if this doesn't happen? What if more than 50% of the hashing power is acquired by a node or even an organization? We call one of its possibilities as the 51% attack or majority attack.

When an attacker acquires more than 50% hashing power, he has enough mining power even to change the order of transactions. The attacker can prevent some transactions from being confirmed and broadcasted to the Blockchain network and can even result in a mining monopoly, wherein miners are prevented from mining new blocks. Even though Proof of Work is prone to such attacks, there have been no successful 51% attacks on Bitcoin so far. The primary reason for this is the vastness of the Blockchain network. Since the Bitcoin blockchain is large enough, it's not possible for a node or group of nodes to acquire such a large amount of hashing power, thus making Bitcoin safe. Proof of Work is also prone to Sybil Attacks and Denial of Service (DOS) Attacks, but we can find solutions to prevent them from crashing the Proof of Work Systems.

Hence, we infer that the larger the blockchain, lesser are the chances of it being attacked. However, this isn't the case with smaller cryptocurrencies like Monacoin, Zencash, etc. There have been successful 51% attacks on them previously. We will discuss the Proof of Stake algorithm further, which makes the 51% attack quite unlikely to occur.

2. Proof of Work is also prone to **Selfish Mining attack** [2].

As the name rightly suggests, the miner, after producing a block, doesn't publish it, but keeps it private. He might publish the block gradually over a period of time. Researchers have concluded that this attack is highly beneficial for the selfish miners in the sense of mining power.

3. Apart from 51% attack and Selfish mining attack, Proof of Work is also prone to **eclipse attack.** In this attack, a malicious attacker ensures that a node in the network is completely isolated and is unaware about the incorrect transaction data in its database.

5.2.1.4 Pros and Cons of Proof of Work

The pros and cons of the Proof of Work consensus algorithm are outlined in Table 5.1.

5.2.2 Proof of Stake

After going through Proof of Work in detail, we are going to discuss the most widely used alternative of Proof of Work, which is Proof of Stake. Proof of Stake came into the picture in 2011 and it mainly aimed at achieving consensus in the network. Ethereum previously used Proof of Work, however it has now shifted to Proof of Stake! You might definitely wonder why. The following discussion would help you to find an answer. In Proof of Stake, the nodes which produce blocks aren't usually called miners, but are called validators. Who are validators and what's their job? Let's understand! Validators

TABLE 5.1

Pros and Cons of Proof of Work

Pros	Cons
1. Proof of Work doesn't require some positive balance of cryptocurrency while starting off with mining blocks, unlike Proof of Stake.	1. Proof of Work requires enormous amounts of computational power and costly computers to run algorithms.
2. Proof of Work has been a dominant consensus algorithm for several years now. It has ensured security of the system and preserved its decentralized nature.	2. Proof of Work demands a prior investment from the miner. This is required for costly equipment.
3. Proof of Work is simpler to implement as compared to Proof of Stake	3. A mining pool may be a big threat to the Blockchain network, which might result in centralization of the system.
4. Consensus can be reached very quickly as it is easier to verify the transactions, though it takes much time for a miner to solve the mathematical puzzle.	4. Proof of Work is not much suitable for smaller networks because the probability of gaining a majority in terms of computational power increases with the decreasing number of nodes in a network.

are basically the nodes which have the responsibility of producing new blocks in the blockchain. There lies a criteria upon which the validators are selected. The node's wealth, staking age and several other factors decide if the node will be selected as a validator or not.

5.2.2.1 Implementation of "Proof of Stake"

The Proof of Stake algorithm doesn't expect validators to solve a mathematical puzzle like the Proof of Work algorithm. Rather, it asks the validators to invest some digital assets in the system and put it at stake. The validators need to validate the blocks and carefully place a bet on the one which might have the greater chance of being added to the Blockchain. The blocks added in the blockchain and the bets placed determine the reward received by the validators. Unlike the reward in Proof of Work, Proof of Stake rewards the validators with transaction fees.

As we say in Proof of Work that the blocks are mined, we say in Proof of Stake that blocks are forged. The process of Proof of Stake algorithm is described in detail using the flowchart in Figure 5.3.

The amount of money that users are interested in investing will determine their chances of becoming the validator and forging a block. The higher the invested amount, the higher the chances of being selected as the validator. However, in this process, there is a huge possibility of only the wealthiest nodes being selected as validators. Hence, to ensure fair and random selection of nodes, two methods are used: Coin Age selection and Randomized Block Selection.

As the name suggests, Coin Age Selection clearly means that the selection of nodes is dependent on the time for which their amount has been staked. On the other hand, in Randomized Block Selection, nodes are selected if they have the highest stake and lowest hash value. Once the validator is selected, it has to check if the block containing the transactions is valid, after which it is added to the blockchain. Refer to Figure 5.3 for the flowchart.

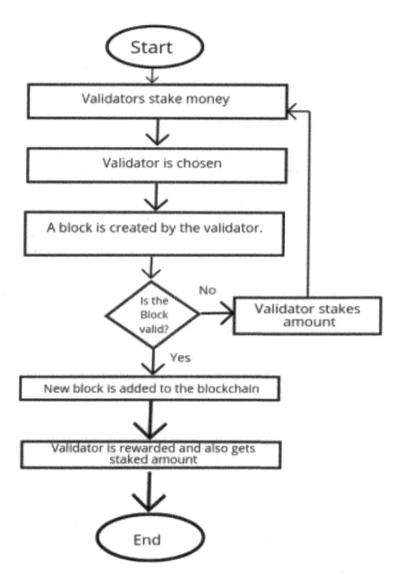

FIGURE 5.3
Flow chart of Proof of Stake.

The concept of stake makes the system more secure as, in this case, the validator cannot encourage fraudulent transactions. The role of the node as a forger might be at risk if it doesn't carefully avoid the fraudulent transactions from happening in the Blockchain network. Proof of Stake doesn't require large computational power and isn't significantly a resource-intensive task. Since the wealthiest nodes don't always get selected, the decentralized nature of the Blockchain network is intact.

Many of the cryptocurrencies use the Proof of Stake algorithms like Peercoin, Shadowcoin, etc. As discussed earlier, Ethereum has also shifted to Proof of Stake.

5.2.2.2 Applications

Many of the cryptocurrencies use the Proof of Stake algorithms like Ethereum, Qora, Peercoin, BlackCoin, Shadowcoin, ShadowCash, etc. As Proof of Stake is said to be energy efficient and has several improvements over Proof of Work, Ethereum has also shifted from Proof of Work to Proof of Stake.

5.2.2.3 Attacks on Proof of Stake

1. **51% attack:** In the case of Proof of Stake, a node or group of nodes need to acquire 51% of the cryptocurrency in order to make this attack possible. Even though the attacker has a 51% stake in a digital asset, he might not want to attack the network, considering the fact that he also has a majority share in it. Hence, attacking a network is not so advantageous for a miner in case of Proof of Stake as compared to Proof of Work. Not only that, but Proof of Work recovers through this attack in a different way than Proof of Stake. In Proof of Work, a rollback takes place and brings the network to a point before the attack took place, in such a way that the attack doesn't count. But still, there are high chances that the attacker might relaunch the attack by purchasing the computer power again.

   On the other hand, Proof of Stake Blockchain blacklists the attacker's address for recovering from the 51% attack, thus deleting the coins. If the attacker wants to relaunch the attack, it might be a big deal since he will have to repurchase the digital asset. Thus, Proof of Stake deals with 51% attack in a much better way than Proof of Work.

2. **Nothing at Stake attack:** In the context of Blockchain, a fork occurs when a blockchain splits into two paths. The miners then need to choose a fork on which they will keep producing blocks. In Nothing at Stake attack, conflicting blocks are generated on all the forks possible in order to get maximum profit even after putting nothing at stake [2].

3. **Grinding attack:** It is important to have an unbiased election process in Proof of Stake and hence, an entropy is introduced among the users to maintain randomization of elected nodes. However, the attacker can manipulate the protocols that bring about entropy. This results in the grinding attack.

5.2.2.4 Pros and Cons of Proof of Stake

The pros and cons of the Proof of Stake consensus algorithm are outlined in Table 5.2.

TABLE 5.2

Pros and Cons of Proof of Stake

Pros	Cons
1. Proof of Stake is comparatively faster than Proof of Work.	1. Proof of Stake is not as sustainable as Proof of Work.
2. Energy-efficient consensus algorithm.	2. The users who have a large amount of coins can greatly impact the Blockchain network.
3. The concept of a decentralized system is highly used because of staking.	3. Proof of work makes it difficult for an average investor to be a part of the blockchain network and earn rewards.

Now, let's summarize proof of Stake using the following points:

1. Proof of Stake is an alternative to Proof of Work and is used to produce blocks and add to the blockchain.
2. Unlike Proof of Work, where miners can voluntarily participate in the mining competition and add blocks to the blockchain, in Proof of Stake, validators are selected on the basis of the digital asset they hold and they can add the blocks to the blockchain.
3. It is a matter of great risk to attack a Proof of Stake system because of the reasons discussed here.

5.2.2.5 Comparison between Proof of Work and Proof of Stake

A comparison between these two consensus algorithms is outlined in Table 5.3.

5.2.3 Delegated Proof of Stake

Introduced by Daniel Larimer in 2014, Delegated Proof of Stake (DPOS), as the name suggests, is a variant of Proof of Stake. It is also an alternative to Proof of Work since it overcomes the resource-intensive nature of Proof of Work. If we talk about the design of DPOS, it's quite eco-friendly. DPOS limits the number of block producers and validators in the blockchain, thereby increasing the scalability [6]. But here is a valid question: How does DPOS ensure that only limited witnesses exist in the network? This is done by vesting the power of voting in the witnesses in the users' hands.

5.2.3.1 Implementation of "Delegated Proof of Stake"

The stakeholders on the network select the block producers, also known as witnesses, who are also responsible for validating the transactions. The users elect nodes who can validate the transactions on the network. The users have the ability to vote directly or give this power to vote on their behalf to other users. Witnesses produce blocks in a round robin manner.

The value of every users' vote depends upon the number of coins a user stakes. The users who have more coins at stake have a greater impact on the process of determining the elected nodes [7].

In a system where all nodes are unknown and everything is based on trust, why would any voter vote for another node? This happens because nodes promise to share block rewards, etc.

TABLE 5.3

Difference between PoW and PoS

Proof of Work	Proof of Stake
1. Large amount of energy and computational power is consumed.	1. No wastage of computational power and not resource intensive.
2. Miners can voluntarily create new blocks in the Blockchain.	2. Validators who create new blocks are selected by an algorithm itself.
3. Cryptocurrency is given as a reward to the miner who is able to solve the cryptographic puzzle first.	3. A transaction fee is given to the one who creates the block.
4. Miners require expensive computers and specialized hardware for creating new blocks in blockchain.	4. The amount at stake determines who will create a new block in the blockchain.

with the users after being elected. If elected, the witnesses validate the transactions on the network on behalf of other voters. It is naturally assumed that they will be honest and won't validate fraudulent transactions. If done so, they will be immediately voted out in the next election and will be replaced by the honest nodes. Thus, if a node remains honest throughout, it stands a higher chance of getting elected and earning block rewards often. This makes the DPOS system quite reputation based, in turn compromising the decentralized nature of Blockchain. Voters also have the ability to vote for delegates who manage the governance of the Blockchain. Delegates have the power to update the codes.

In comparison to Proof of Work and Proof of Stake with regards to performance, DPOS is more scalable and is speedy too.

5.2.3.2 Applications

BitShares, Steem and Steemit, and EOSIO use Delegated Proof of Stake.

5.2.3.3 Attacks on Delegated Proof of Stake

1. **Bribing attack:** In a Bribing attack, as the name suggests, block producers might pay users in order to gain their votes.

This, in turn, changes the results of the election process. The block producers who pay users the most are selected rather than the ones who are best. However, this attack depends on several other features of DPOS, so it is not likely to occur.

2. **Exploit low voter turnout:** This attack occurs especially in a situation where the participation from voters is low. DPOS allows proxy voting in order to resolve this problem.

5.2.3.4 Comparison of DPOS with POW and POS

DPOS is faster in being able to process the number of transactions per second as compared to POS. POS and DPOS are quite similar as both algorithms revolve around stakeholding.

DPOS has a predetermined set of block producers and the number is limited unlike POW, in which a large number of miners can voluntarily compete against each other to produce blocks.

5.2.3.5 Pros and Cons of DPOS

The pros and cons of DPOS are outlined in Table 5.4.

5.3 Other Consensus Algorithms Used in Blockchain Applications

5.3.1 Proof of Importance

Developed by New Economy Movement (NEM), Proof of Importance is a consensus algorithm quite similar to Proof of Stake. However, this algorithm doesn't consider the amount

TABLE 5.4

Pros and Cons of DPOS

Pros	Cons
1. Security is maintained in DPOS systems, as voters can vote out the witnesses who are not honest enough and stop malicious activities immediately.	1. As the power of producing blocks and validating transactions rests in the hands of a small group, 51% attack is easier to make on the network.
2. DPOS blockchain doesn't require more computational power like Proof of Work. It is scalable and can process more transactions per second.	2. Having discussed that only a small group of people is involved in the block creation and validation process, the DPOS blockchain becomes partially centralized gradually, over a period of time.
3. Digital Democracy is offered in DPOS, where voters have the power to choose the block producers.	3. DPOS is not sustainable and dominant as compared to Proof of Work.

of stake unlike Proof of Stake, and also doesn't consider the amount of work, unlike Proof of Work. It considers the entire productivity of the nodes in the network. The rewards earned by the nodes depend on multiple factors like the amount of stake they have, the duration for which they have vested (owned) the stake, net transfers, etc. Unlike other well-known consensus algorithms like Proof of Work and Proof of Stake, Proof of Importance takes into consideration the overall support of the node to the entire network. This helps to overcome the problems faced by Proof of Stake.

5.3.2 Proof of Authority

Introduced by Ethereum co-founder in 2017, Proof of Authority is an efficient consensus algorithm for private Blockchain networks. This makes Proof of Activity a good choice for private companies. In Proof of Authority, users stake their reputation instead of staking coins, hence it is a reputation-based consensus algorithm. There are a limited number of block validators. The candidates willing to become validators have to invest some money and put their reputation at stake. Proof of Authority is very useful for companies who want to leverage blockchain technology and keep their privacy intact. Proof of Authority is also highly useful in giving a solution for supply chains. Microsoft Azure uses Proof of Authority too.

5.3.3 Proof of Elapsed Time

Proof of Elapsed Time has been developed by Intel Corporation in 2016. This is a lottery-based consensus algorithm, which means that it gives every node equal mining rights and an equal opportunity to win among all the participants in the network. This algorithm produces a randomly generated wait time, also known as elapsed time, for every participant in the network. This makes the node sleep for that amount of time. Proof of Elapsed Time is quite similar to Proof of Work, but it consumes relatively less power as it allows the node to sleep for a particular duration. During this time, the miner's machine can complete other tasks, and thus the overall efficiency is increased. The node which wakes up first can add a new block to the Blockchain and can broadcast this information to the entire network.

5.3.4 Proof of Burn

Proof of Burn is an algorithm, invented by Iain Stewart, which solves the problem of energy consumption in Proof of Work. In other words, Proof of Burn acts as an alternative to the Proof of Work consensus algorithm. The problem of double spending is eliminated using Proof of Burn.

This algorithm doesn't burn the electricity or hardware like Proof of Work, but it burns its coins to provide rewards to the nodes in the network. The higher the number of coins sent to burn, the higher the probability of being chosen to mine the block by the algorithm. A reward is received by the node only if it validates transactions successfully and mines a block, otherwise the coins sent to burn are completely wasted. Though the energy consumption is not done in the case of Proof of Burn, resources are still wasted.

5.3.5 Leased Proof of Stake

As the name suggests, Leased Proof of Stake acts as a more effective version of Proof of Stake. In Proof of Stake, the block creators are decided based on the amount of stake that a node holds. However, in the case of Leased Proof of Stake, nodes lease some of their stake to the miners. When mining nodes receive a reward, they share some part of it with the node that leased the stake. A node is not required to mine, but can still earn profit in Leased Proof of Stake, thereby generating passive income. This algorithm is supported by the Waves Platform. The energy consumption in Leased Proof of Stake is low.

5.3.6 Byzantine Fault Tolerance

This algorithm protects against any system failures that might occur [8]. System failures might occur due to the faulty nodes in the network who either don't respond or respond with the wrong information.

Hence, it's important to ensure that the decision making process is not affected and the consensus is reached even in such cases. Thus, the impact of faulty nodes is reduced. The Byzantine Fault Tolerance algorithm is quite energy efficient. However, BFT works efficiently only if the number of nodes in the network is low. BFT is also prone to Sybil attacks and does not scale well.

5.3.7 Proof of Deposit

Proof of Stake in Ethereum is called Proof of Deposit. Proof of Deposit is an improved and modified version of Proof of Stake in which every validator has to pay a certain security deposit in order to be able to produce blocks. In other words, validators freeze a certain amount of coins while the mining takes place. Validators are only allowed to create valid blocks. In case they produce invalid blocks, they are penalized for the same and are not allowed to create further blocks.

5.3.8 Proof of Capacity

Proof of Capacity provides a solution to the resource-intensive nature of Proof of Work. In Proof of Capacity, the users are able to mine cryptocurrencies using the empty space available on their hard disk. The larger the hard drive, the greater the chances of the miner to store the list of solutions and earn a reward. Proof of Capacity is used by cryptocurrencies like Burstcoin, Chia, Storj, etc.

5.3.9 Directed Acyclic Graph (DAG)

DAG is considered to be a rival technology to Blockchain, but at the same time can act as an enabler. In DAG, transactions are recorded to a distributed ledger, just like Blockchain, but in very different ways. In DAG, one transaction is linked to several other transactions. There are no blocks present in DAG. If we consider Blockchain to be a linked list, then DAG is like a tree. DAGs eliminate the need for miners, unlike in Blockchain, and also ensures low consumption of energy. Not only that, but DAGs can scale well and charge less fees to the users. In DAG, validation is provided by individual transactions for one another. The performance of DAG depends upon the volume of transactions. The higher the volume, the faster the process of validation. Hence, if the volume of transactions is reduced, DAG becomes vulnerable to attacks.

5.4 Case Study of Work: Proof of Digitally Owned Content

As the Internet is being widely used today, a lot of digital content is being shared online. But, while the content is being shared, a lot of it is also being stolen. There are several ways of taking the ownership of the digital content, but these ways involve the intervention of third parties like governments, banks, etc. There are other technologies too which secure the digital content, but have their own drawbacks, hence are not so reliable. These technologies include digital rights management, tokenization, etc. But a decentralized way can even be used in order to eliminate the large amount of time required for getting the ownership and securing the content. Blockchain technology can be extremely helpful in achieving this because of its features like Better Transparency, Reduced Costs, Immutability, Time Stamping, etc. [9]

There are different consensus algorithms which can be used for this like Proof of Stake, Byzantine Fault Tolerance, Proof of Work, etc. These are the most widely used consensus algorithms. Algorithms like Proof of Contribution have also been introduced to secure digital content [10]. Ethereum is one the most mature Blockchain platforms, which uses the Proof of Stake Consensus algorithm. Proof of Stake is used because there is less energy consumption. Moreover, Proof of Stake is comparatively faster than Proof of Work and efficient, too. Hence, it is a good alternative for securing digital content in a decentralized manner [11].

Also, Ethereum is backed up by a powerful programming language, i.e. Solidity, which can handle many complex computations, hence making it the best choice for creating an application on ownership of digital content.

References

[1] Sankar, L.S., M. Sindhu and M. Sethumadhavan. "Survey of consensus protocols on blockchain applications." *2017 4th International Conference on Advanced Computing and Communication Systems (ICACCS)* (2017): 1–5, https://doi.org/10.1109/ICACCS.2017.8014672.

[2] Kaur, Sivleen, Sheetal Chaturvedi, Aabha Sharma and Jayaprakash Kar. "A research survey on applications of consensus protocols in blockchain." *Security and Communication Networks*, vol. 2021 (2021): 22, Article ID 6693731, https://doi.org/10.1155/2021/6693731.

[3] Mingxiao, D., M. Xiaofeng, Z. Zhe, W. Xiangwei and C. Qijun. "A review on consensus algorithm of blockchain." *2017 IEEE International Conference on Systems, Man, and Cybernetics (SMC)* (2017): 2567–2572, https://doi.org/10.1109/SMC.2017.8123011.

[4] Yadav, Ashok and Karan Singh. *Comparative Analysis of Consensus Algorithms of Blockchain Technology*, 2020, https://www.researchgate.net/publication/348355281_Comparative_Analysis_of_Consensus_Algorithms_of_Blockchain_Technology.

[5] Nakamoto, Satoshi. *Bitcoin: A Peer-to-Peer Electronic Cash System*, 2009, Cryptography Mailing list, https://metzdowd.com; https://bitcoin.org/bitcoin.pdf.

[6] Yang, Fan, Wei Zhou, Qingqing Wu, Rui Long, Naixue Xiong and Meiqi Zhou. "Delegated proof of stake with downgrade: A secure and efficient blockchain consensus algorithm with downgrade mechanism." *IEEE Access* (2019), https://doi.org/10.1109/access.2019.2935149.

[7] Luo, Y., Y. Chen, Q. Chen and Q. Liang. "A New Election Algorithm for DPos Consensus Mechanism in Blockchain." *2018 7th International Conference on Digital Home (ICDH)* (2018): 116–120, https://doi.org/10.1109/ICDH.2018.00029.

[8] Veronese, G.S., M. Correia, A.N. Bessani, L.C. Lung and P. Verissimo. "Efficient byzantine fault-tolerance." *IEEE Transactions on Computers*, vol. 62, no. 1 (January 2013): 16–30, https://doi.org/10.1109/TC.2011.221.

[9] G. Zyskind, O. Nathan and A. Pentland. "Decentralizing privacy: Using blockchain to protect personal data." *2015 IEEE Security and Privacy Workshops* (2015): 180–184, https://doi.org/10.1109/SPW.2015.27.

[10] Song, Hongyu, Nafei Zhu, Ruixin Xue, Jingsha He, Kun Zhang, Jianyu Wang. "Proof-of-contribution consensus mechanism for blockchain and its application in intellectual property protection." *Information Processing & Management*, vol. 58, no. 3 (2021): 102507, ISSN 0306–4573, https://doi.org/10.1016/j.ipm.2021.102507; www.sciencedirect.com/science/article/pii/S0306457321000170.

[11] Wang, Junyao, Shenling Wang, Junqi Guo, Yanchang Du, Shaochi Cheng and Xiangyang Li. "A summary of research on blockchain in the field of intellectual property." *Procedia Computer Science*, vol. 147 (2019): 191–197, ISSN 1877–0509, https://doi.org/10.1016/j.procs.2019.01.220; www.sciencedirect.com/science/article/pii/S187705091930239X.

6

Blockchain Computing Technology: Challenging Security and Privacy Issues

Sonali Ridhorkar

CONTENTS

6.1 Introduction

The historical overview of Blockchain Technology (BT) has its origin in the 20th century then was widely acknowledged in 2008. In 2011–2013, blockchain technology was used in cryptocurrency most specifically in the transmission of currency and online digital payments. Blockchain technology has developed in numerous function due to its features such as decentralized approach and stability. Figure 6.1 shows the development of BT.

Emerging technology (blockchain) always has security concerns due to security breaches. As many organizations/companies observed that 65% percent of data

DOI: 10.1201/9781003203933-8

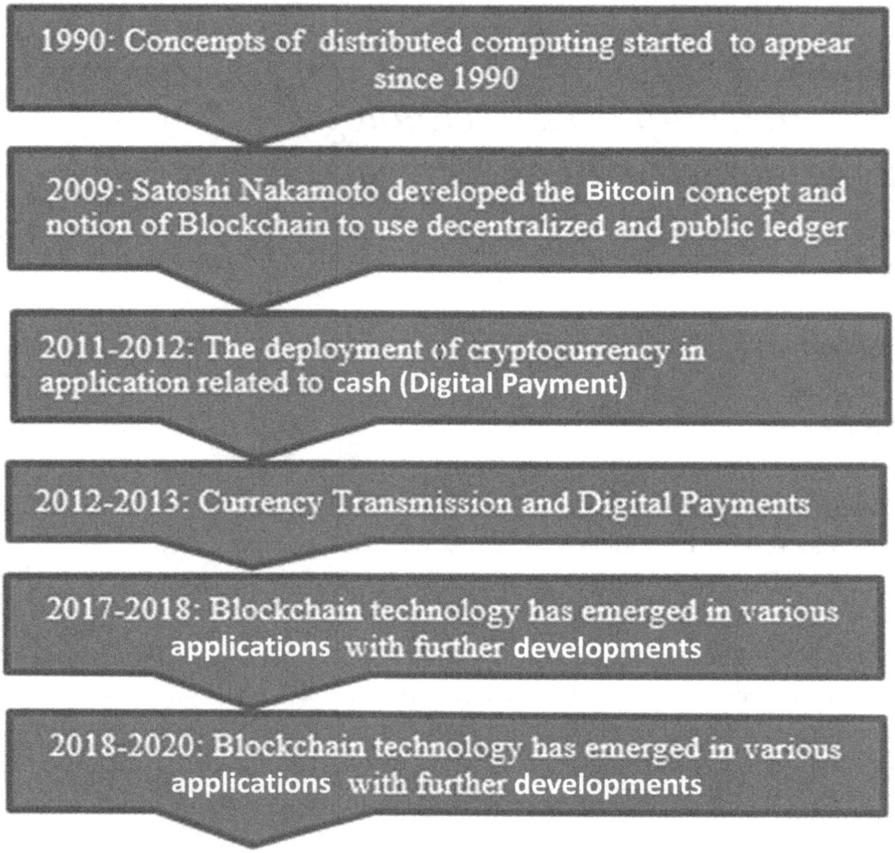

FIGURE 6.1
Development in Blockchain Technology.

infringement happened due to weak passwords and stealing of sensitive information carried out by phishing emails. It is a ground-breaking technology, which was first used by Satoshi Nakamoto with Bitcoin in 2008 [1]. Bitcoin (cryptocurrency) is the notable execution of blockchain, and the most leading practical application of a digital cryptocurrency. Blockchain computing is considered the service and structure of cryptocurrencies to continue records of currency transactions between unauthorized users. Currently, many more application areas depend on BT such as energy transaction, healthcare management, supply chain management, manufacturing process, user identity management, e-government, etc. BT was considered to address the security issues of Bitcoin cryptocurrency as blockchain follows a distributed kind of data structure that is simulated and jointly shared among all entities/users of a network [2, 3, 4]. It was presented with the concepts of cryptocurrency such as Bitcoin [5, 6], which solve the issue of double-spending [7, 8]. Figure 6.2 shows a history of Bitcoin with a timeline of BT development.

The central attraction of BT comes from its attributes which provide security, anonymity, nonrepudiation, and data integrity without the involvement of Kickstarter or third-party risks. A major part of this chapter is focusing on the challenges of BT from a privacy, security, and scalability perspective [9, 10].

A recommended Triad CIA security model consists of three major areas of security services (Confidentiality, Integrity, and Availability) has been referred to evaluate the current state of the maturity level of blockchain technology. BT also enables trustless networks, due to which parties can transact even though they do not have a belief in each other [11, 12].

Blockchain Technology is also known as distributed ledger technology which has been compared with the rapid growth of internet technology comments and arguments that disturb multiple industries, including the healthcare sector, energy public sector, manufacturing unit, and predominantly financial services sector. As the blockchain process is referred to as a distributed ledger, it is worth mentioning that the database is mutually shared between several users in a P2P network environment, deprived the supervision from a central authority.

Major mechanisms involved in blockchain technologies are as follows:

a) **Decentralized Approach:** The elementary feature provided in blockchain that it doesn't provide faith on a centralized node during communication; the data can be recorded, accumulated, and updated in a distributed manner.

b) **Transparency:** The data's record can be carried out by the blockchain system in a transparent way to every node, which means that it transparently keeps data posted, therefore blockchain can be considered as reliable.

c) **Open Source:** Most blockchain systems are open to one and all, the data record can be checked publicly, and participants can also mark the use of blockchain technologies to produce an application as per their requirements.

d) **Autonomy:** In the blockchain system, data can transfer and update securely. The main indication is to create trust from a single person to all the system users.

e) **Immutable:** Some data records (blocks) will be earmarked persistently and can't be altered except somebody can proceed with a mechanism with more than 51% rights of a node at the matching time.

f) **Anonymity:** To address the issue of trust in BTs for each communicating node to node, so that data transfer transaction can be made anonymously, with the specific requirement to recognize the person's blockchain address.

Most transaction systems are typically centralized and controlled by an unbiased observer organization. Blockchain Technology is cast off to generate a distributed computing environment [13, 9, 14]. However, Blockchain Technology is best suited for conducting cryptocurrency transactions and ensure high security of the transaction as well as privacy [15, 16]. So Blockchain Technology is always used for addressing the challenging issues in peer environments such as IoT, and Cloud Computing as BT has evolved with successful usage of cryptocurrency (i.e. Bitcoin)

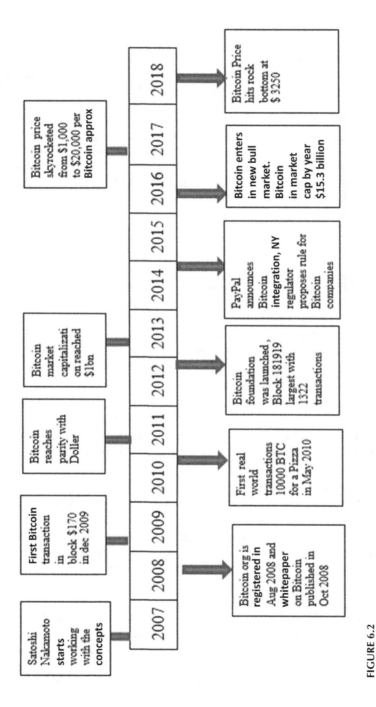

FIGURE 6.2
History of Bitcoin with timeline of Blockchain development.

6.2 Related Works

As blockchain technology is growing day by day and as data records grows, the process of loading and computing will also increase. It takes much time to synchronize the data and, at the same time, data repeatedly increases in size, creating a great problem from server to client when it runs on the system.

6.2.1 Blockchain Technology

The concept of blockchain and Bitcoin was suggested by Satoshi Nakamoto in 2008, who carried out initial research into method of cryptology and an open distributed ledger system that could be combined into a digital currency application. BT represents the chain (public databases) of digital information (block) and is linked using concepts of cryptography. The major advantage of BT is the aforementioned distributed ledger, decentralized approach, information transparency, shielded construction, and susceptibleness. The levels of evolution of blockchain tools and technology fall under three major stages: **Blockchain 1.0**: cryptocurrency and blockchain; **Blockchain 2.0**: smart contract-based ledgers; **Blockchain 3.0**: enterprise and institutional blockchains; and **Blockchain 4.0**: blockchain usable in industry-based infrastructure [17, 18].

Figure 6.3 shows the evolution of blockchain technology and versioning start from v1.0 to v4.0.

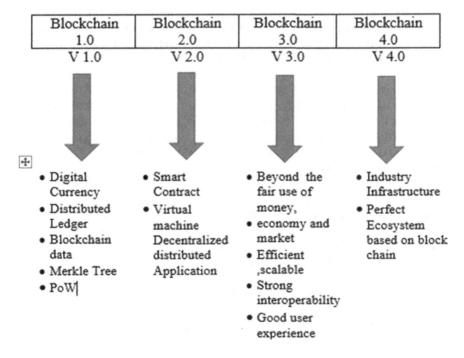

FIGURE 6.3
Evolution of Blockchain Technology.

Blockchain systems can diverge in contribution or participation of users and their accessibility. Network systems are classically characterized as Public Blockchain or Private Blockchain, which is related in terms of who is permissible to contribute based on the permissioned (Open Environment) or permissionless (Close Environment) blockchain, which designates how users/participants gain access to the network. As permissioned (open environment) is suitable for financial applications like cryptocurrency and permissionless (Close Environment) is suitable for business applications like smart contract. However, confidentiality is the major concern to blockchain architecture and is referred to as private blockchain which retains strong security and higher speeds, but does not work in the public domain.

In BT, the block is arranged in the chain (MERKLE TREE) containing main data information like the hash value (code) of the current block, hash code of the previous block, timestamps (Nonces), and other related information [19].

a) **Main data:** Normally dependent upon the types of the services provided by the block, namely bank transaction records, contact records, clearance records, or data records of IoT.

b) **Hash:** After the execution of the transaction, it hashes to code and then broadcasts to other nodes. Blockchain uses the function based on the Merkle Tree to decrease the data communication and computing properties because each node block contains thousands of transaction records, and it records the final hash-to-block header.

c) **Timestamp:** Time duration of block generation.

d) **Other Information**: Mainly block signature, data that user defines, or nonce value are under the categories of other information.

BT has the structured data with security abilities. It is always based on ideologies of cryptography with the approach of decentralization and consensus, which is responsible for ensuring the confidence in communications. Furthermost in blockchains technologies (distributed ledger technologies (DLT)), the data is controlled into blocks and each block contains operation of transactions. Each newly created block links to all the blocks before it if they're available in a cryptographic chain in such a way that it's difficult to tamper with. Altogether, transactions within the blocks are certified and concede through a consensus mechanism, ensuring that each business transaction is correct and accurate.

BT permits the distributed environment approach through the involvement of participants across a distributed network. No single point of failure or individual user can alter or modify the record of transactions, although BTs diverge in more or less critical security characteristics. Blockchain security and privacy has a broad risk management system for managing the blockchain network, which is making use of cybersecurity structures, assurance services, and greatest monitors to diminish hazards contrary to attacks and deception. Figure 6.4 shows the Blockchain connection structure. Each "block" shown in Figure 6.4 contains three major parts of information:

• Information of transaction including date, time, and the aggregate sum of online digital purchase

• Users' individualities (identities/credentials) of all users entangled in the transaction

• Algorithm-based hash code value is associated, which differentiates the block from each other's. Newly formed blocks are added to a blockchain at any moment of time while validating different transaction because it is a unique code that chained all other blocks in the chain.

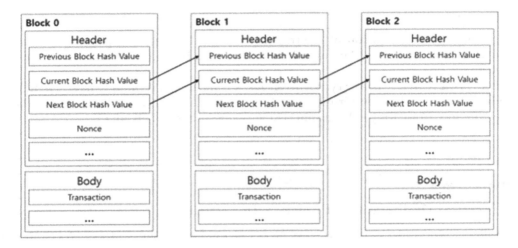

FIGURE 6.4
Blockchain connection structure.

6.2.2 Bitcoin Cryptocurrency

A Bitcoin cryptocurrency (Peer-to-Peer E-cash) system is an electronic system typically based on cryptographic proof rather than trust. In such an environment, transactions are computationally infeasible to reverse. Bitcoin is the key part of blockchain computing Tools. Cryptocurrency like Bitcoin is a completely distributed, peer-to-peer, permission-less technology put forth in 2009 [10, 20, 21, 22].

a) Completely Centralized: No central party for ordering or recording any information.

- Peer-to-Peer Environment: Software that runs on the machine of all stakeholders to or from the system.

b) Permission-less: No need to sign up anywhere to use, no access control; anyone can participate in any role.

Bitcoin is used as a cross-counter untraceable currency that is not under the control of any government agency and hence free from regulation. Current BTC price for 1 BTC = $37,235.50 that is equivalent ₹27,147,43.49 as of the time of writing.

The working of cryptocurrencies has been carried out by the chaining of a 'block' that then gets connected to the preceding chunk (block) to form a 'chain' and gets verified in two different ways: Proof of Work (PoW) and Proof of Stake (PoS) [23, 24].

6.2.2.1 Proof of Work

Code for a Proof of Work (PoW) algorithm is the most time-consuming operation to produce code. While calculating PoW, which is known as miner process, each block is associated with a random value timestamp (Nonce) in the header of block by altering this time Nonce. The PoW algorithm then has to create a value that makes the block header hash value less than the target value, which is the set value in terms of time [25].

6.2.2.2 Proof of Stake

PoW consumes a proportion of electricity power and computing power when compared to a Proof of Stake (PoS) algorithm. It protects from a malicious attack on the network.

Bitcoin is the monarch of all cryptocurrencies. It is the first of its kind to have the highest liquidity value. The best performing cryptocurrencies are Litecoin, Ethereum, Cardano, Tether, Binance Coin, Ripple, Dogecoin, TRON, Dogecoin, and Polkadot.

6.3 Practical Deliberation of Blockchain Security

Blockchain computing technology has been executed as digital money (cyber money), which is expected in today's online transactions. However, many issues arising in blockchain regarding arrangement process (establishment phase), operation, wallet, and software have been reported. The major concern is the security issues raised and the security level of the current blockchain. Effort is required as the consequences can serve as base data for developing future blockchain technology and accompanying security challenges [13, 26, 27].

Blockchain classification is based on the way user participation in blockchain is carried out. It can be categorized as Public Blockchain, Consortium Blockchain, and Private Blockchain. It is further classified as the main and side chain on the relationship of chains. Additionally, several blockchains can be arranged for network and chains of the network that are used for interconnection to generate interchain. BT was established in the online trading of cryptocurrencies such as Ethereum, Bitcoin, etc. Each cryptocurrency operation is assigned a blockchain record that is accessible in the public domain. In addition, all participating users may be required to synchronize these peers with a particular blockchain and receipt of updates as new transactions are added [20–24].

In blockchain, there is 80% business process changes and 20% technology execution. It is an overall modification from conventional ways of carrying out transactions. Even many industries have seen an important conversion transit from digital technologies. BT has the technical challenges like Authentication, Scalability, Privacy, Wasted Resources, Data Malleability, Usability, Bootstrapping, Size and Bandwidth, Throughput, Latency, and Versioning. Blockchain uses security technologies such as public-key cryptography, digital signature, and hashing. Today, blockchain applications go beyond cryptocurrency and bitcoin due to their transparency, fairness approach, and time- and money-saving features for businesses. Blockchain applications also provide opportunities and considerable benefits specifically in terms of efficiency and operations. Technology has an impact on a variety of sectors such as the music industry, education, public services, cybersecurity in healthcare, e-voting systems, secure sharing of medical data, marketplaces for NFTs, tracking systems for music royalties, systems for cross-border payments, real-time IoT-based operating systems, security systems for personal individuality, tracking for anti-money laundering systems, supply chain and logistics monitoring, advertising insights, original content creation, cryptocurrency exchange, and platforms for real estate processing [25, 26].

6.4 Secure Blockchain Solutions in Internet of Things (IoT) and Cloud Computing

A hash value (code) is the tool to prevent mitigation, however nowadays the swiftness of computers completes thousands of hashes per second, and attacks can tamper with the current chunk and then re-estimate the hash code value of another block to mark the block effectively valid. To deal with such issues, Blockchain Technology, using the concept of Proof of Work, decelerates the construction of the new block. In the case of Bitcoin, it takes 10 minutes to compute a Proof of Work algorithm to pair a new block to the chain.

If the number of IoT devices increases, it leads to an increase in chances to determine the security susceptibilities within these devices. These security vulnerabilities result in stealing information and for handling security and privacy challenges in IoT; every user needs to have fully confidential security aspects with the system. Figure 6.5 depicts users/client key agreement on a block operation. Validity is confirmed by distributed nodes of the network, and the block is added further to the growing chain of blocks when the transaction is already complete and payments are finalized [16, 26].

Blockchain technology has the major advantages that are associated with huge scale IoT systems such as tamper-proof data, trustless and peers-to-peer messaging possibility, robustness, great reliability, supplementary to private data records, historical actions, data records of longstanding transactions in smart devices, self-directed functioning, distributed systems for file sharing, exclusion of single control authority, cost-cutting in the development of internet infrastructure, built-in trust, and accelerated transactions [27–29]:

> There are several major concerned challenges identified in IoT in terms of networking, scalability, interoperability, security and privacy, heterogeneity, and big data. Most recommended applications of IoT are home automation, healthcare, smart agriculture, supply chain and logistics, smart city, smart grid, and connected cars.

In a cloud computing environment, user data disclosure or leakage causes monetary and psychological damages. The security aspects such as confidentiality and integrity related to saving and transmitting data in a cloud computing environment is the major concern in such an environment. However, privacy protection and anonymity are not addressed, whereas BT is used to address security and privacy [30–35].

6.4.1 Blockchain Key Solution

There are four persuasive security concerns associated with blockchain technology as suggested in literature and discussed in the following section.

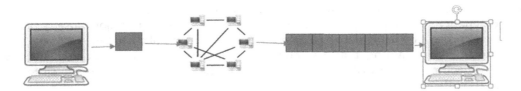

FIGURE 6.5
Overview of Blockchain transaction process.

6.4.1.1 Blockchain Endpoints Vulnerabilities

Although blockchain has worked well in a virtual mode also called 'unhackable', it is required to note that most blockchain transactions have endpoints that have vulnerabilities that grow outside the architecture of blockchain. To illustrate the result of the Bitcoin online investment process, it has an aggregate sum of Bitcoin actually deposited into a 'Public wallet'. These wallet accounts need to be tamper-proof within the structure of blockchain. Some popular illustrations comprise payment processors, smart contracts, and blockchain payment stages. Third-party blockchain vendors have comparatively weedy safety in recommended applications and websites that can be associated with data hacking and access mismanagement [8, 14, 32].

6.4.1.2 Scalability Issues

Blockchains are at the prime of built-in development history of technology, and as acceptance of the technology remains to increase, blockchains are only going to get bigger. The scalability issue has limitations, i.e. response time, block size, and computation cost. Blockchain scalability is always mapped as throughput in terms of the number of concurrent transactions processed in a specified time frame. But most of these large-scale blockchains are unproven. Common concerns center around the issue that, as the blockchain ecosystem grows, it also supports the increased load of transactions and vulnerabilities may be revealed. The technology infrastructure that supports blockchain will become more prone to simple mistakes.

6.4.1.3 Regulation Issues

In BT, the most pressing issue related to security is the lack of perfect regulatory principles. Regulation always has the issue of keeping with advancements in technology. Indeed, cryptocurrency technologies such as the Bitcoin blockchain bypass regulation to tackle inadequacies in intermediate payment networks since many simple standardizations are carried out in blockchain by designers that profit from the errors.

6.4.1.4 Insufficient Testing

The major problem in blockchain is the lack of blockchain testing tools, which has been historically accustomed for cryptocurrency trading since it is being recycled in additional fields. The difficult issue is that the coding accustomed in non-crypto currency solicitations requires a mixed set of testing tools that are unavailable and fail the end-to-end testing.

Blockchain is a significant perception of cryptocurrency (Bitcoin) and essentially has a decentralized database. As the essential technology of Bitcoin, it is a series of data blocks allied with each other using cryptographic mechanisms. The architecture of blockchain is high on energy consumption, which is a scaling problem which is major cause of blockchainen to process by using data based on the copy global /Public Ledger.

Blockchains are adapting, but this underlying technology can be caustic to businesses due to a specific set of security issues. Several blockchain issues related to security were seen as recently as 2019:

6.4.1.4.1 51% Attacks

51% of attacks refer to an attack on the blockchain, mostly on Bitcoin. 51% attacks probably do not destroy Bitcoin but highly damage currency, all transaction made in a cryptocurrency's network, and those that are publicly available to all users. New Bitcoin is approximately generated every 10 minutes. Once the block is mined, it cannot be altered and if it is found, it is rejected by the network's users. The majority of the control is carried out by the network, but attackers can interfere with the process of recording new blocks. Transactions can be upturned and instigate double-spending by the acquisition common mechanism of a blockchain's hash rate by malevolent users. The most prominent cryptocurrencies like ZenCash, Verge, and Ethereum suffered 51% attacks until 2018. Around a great defeat of $20 million was seen due to this blockchain security problem. To prevent a 51% attack, it is required to use a higher hash rate and avoid the use of a consensus mechanism (PoW).

6.4.1.4.2 Exchange Hacks

Cryptocurrency interactions can be affected by various vulnerabilities by malicious entities, but cryptocurrencies are popular amongst technophiles that have huge crypto holdings without sufficient security protection. Several cryptocurrency exchanges platforms became obsolete with the decentralized assistances of blockchains after consolidating the routine. There was a loss of almost $900 million until 2019 due to this blockchain security problem. As digital currency (Bitcoin) transactions are recorded in a digital ledger, hackers can get access to an owner's wallets and still be immune to hacks.

To prevent exchange hacks, it is recommended to accumulate funds via a physical device (paper wallet) which look like USB drives that minimize online endpoints to protect digital money from malicious hackers. Additionally, a decentralized exchange tool to use in systematic transaction directly from a cryptocurrency wallet is encouraged.

6.4.1.4.3 Social Engineering

Social engineering is a mechanism used to get unauthorized access to a phone or device that is linked to multiple accounts. 84% of hackers use social engineering as part of attacks such as phishing, spear phishing, and mining social media. Many forms were available, always trying to acquire private keys, login information, or more directly from cryptocurrency. A phishing attack is one of the most common procedures of social engineering attacks. Malicious performers replicate trust in email IDs, messages exchanges, and social media accounts. Cryptocurrency users are significantly impacted by social engineering scams. There was a loss of $3 million in 2019 due to this blockchain security concern [19].

To preclude social engineering attacks, it is required to never send or share login credentials and private keys, along with not trusting entity as it is always creating the trap.

6.4.1.4.4 Software Flaws

Software used in blockchain technology implementation for cryptocurrency transactions should include code reviews, penetration testing, and use of smart contract audits to test the software and find flaws. There was a loss of almost $24 million in 2019 due to blockchain security issues.

To preclude such software errors, the software needs to be examined for at all errors or gaps by a third party when it is used for blockchain-based software implementation.

6.4.1.4.5 Malware

Cryptojacking is a malicious form of cryptocurrency theft. Mostly, Cryptohackers are involved in Cryptojacking, which causes performance-related issues and increases the usage of electricity and creates an environment for added argumentative code due to the unauthorized and imperceptible work of personal computers. Cryptohackers launch malicious attacks for cryptocurrencies by simply downloading malware to execute scripts to get access to IT infrastructure and cloud services. There are three methods, file-based, browser-based, and cloud-based, that cryptojack cryptocurrency by downloading or transferring of malware such as a virus, worm, keyloggers, klez, Netsky, and spyware towards the execution of crypto mining scripts, hijacking of IT infrastructure, and retrieving cloud services. Due to blockchain security issues, losses of multi-millions have happened.

To prevent such malicious outbreaks, users should have a mechanism for detecting cryptojacking, use anti-crypto mining browser extensions, and not to click unknown links in emails. As malware can be used to infect computers, encrypted files shouldn't be accessed either. Therefore, security software can be used to scan for malware and can help identify malicious scripts.

6.5 Conclusion

Blockchain Technology is the biggest technology development of the last 10 years. The key element of Blockchain Technology is the effective use of the online investing process with security. Security and privacy challenges at the platform, protocols, and application layers of blockchain networks are required to be improved continuously and difficulties have to be tested. Various operative case revisions are available based on security challenges. A hacker tried to acquire rights to use an operator's key warehoused in a device like a computer or a smartphone to crack a cryptocurrency like Bitcoin. Secure token-based trainings are used to safeguard the secret key. Moreover, cybersecurity professionals can utilize technical skills to articulate impending risks to their users/clients. A cybersecurity professional can also recommend tools and practices related to information security, such as the use of fake identities (pseudonyms) in online transactions. Now it is time to comprehend significant challenges of blockchain technology including scalability, hackers and shadow dealing, complexity, privacy, and cost.

References

1. Heilman, E. "One weird trick to stop selfish miners: Fresh bitcoins, a solution for the honest miner (poster abstract)." In: R. Böhme, M. Brenner, T. Moore and M. Smith (eds.), *FC 2014*, *Lecture Notes in Computer Science*. Springer, Heidelberg, 2014, vol. 8438, pp. 161–162, https://doi.org/10.1007/978-3-662-44774-112.
2. Aitzhan, N.Z. and Davor Svetinovic. "Security and privacy in decentralized energy trading through multi-signatures, blockchain and anonymous messaging streams." *IEEE Transactions on Dependable and Secure Computing* (2016): 1545–5971, https://doi.org/10.1109/TDSC.2016.2616861.
3. Gupta, Ashok, Shams Tabrez Siddiqui, Shadab Alam and Mohammed Shuaib. "Cloud computing security using blockchain." *Journal of Emerging Technologies and Innovative Research (JETIR)*, www.jetir.org.JETIR1906X02.
4. Bamert, T., C. Decker, R. Wattenhofer and S. Welten. "BlueWallet: The secure bitcoinwallet." In S. Mauw and C. Jensen (eds.), *Security and Trust Management*, Springer International Publishing, Cham, Switzerland, 2014, pp. 65–80.

5. Herrera-Joancomart, J. "Research and challenges on bitcoin anonymity." In: J. Garcia-Alfaro, J. Herrera Joancomart, E. Lupu, J. Posegga, A. Aldini, F. Martinelli, et al. (eds.), *Data Privacy Management, Autonomous Spontaneous Security, and Security Assurance, vol. 8872 of Lecture Notes in Computer Science.* Springer, Cham, 2015, pp. 3–16. http://doi.org/10.1007/978-3-319-17016-9_1.

6. Anceaume, E., T. Lajoie-Mazenc, R. Ludinard and B. Sericola. *Safety Analysis of Bitcoin Improvement Proposals.* Proceedings of the 2016 IEEE 15th International Symposium on Network Computing and Applications (NCA), Cambridge, MA, 31 October–2 November 2016.

7. Il-Kwon, L., K. Young-Hyuk, L. Jae-Gwang and L. Jae-Pil. "The analysis and countermeasures on security breach of bitcoin." In: *Proceedings of the International Conference on Computational Science and Its Applications*, Guimarães, Portugal, Springer, Cham, Switzerland, 30 June–3 July 2014.

8. Eyal, I. and G.S. Emin. *Majority Is Not Enough: Bitcoin Mining Is Vulnerable.* Proceedings of the International Conference on Financial Cryptography and Data Security, Christ Church, Barbados, Springer, Berlin, Heidelberg, Gemany, 3–7 March 2014.

9. Heilman, E., B. Foteini and G. Sharon. *Blindly Signed Contracts: Anonymous On-Blockchain and Off-Blockchain Bitcoin Transactions.* Proceedings of the International Conference on Financial Cryptography and DataSecurity, Christ Church, Barbados, Springer, Berlin, Heidelberg, Gemany, 22–26 February 2016.

10. Vasek, M., M. Thornton and T. Moore. *Empirical Analysis of Denial-of-Service Attacks in the Bitcoin Ecosystem.* Proceedings of the International Conference on Financial Cryptography and Data Security, Christ Church, Barbados, Springer, Berlin, Heidelberg, Gemany, 3–7 March 2014.

11. Aitzhan, N.Z. and S. Davor. "Security and privacy in decentralized energy trading through multi-signatures, blockchain and anonymous messaging streams." *IEEE Transactions on Dependable and Secure Computing* (2016): 99.

12. Decker, C. and W. Roger. *Information Propagation in the Bitcoin Network.* Proceedings of the 2013 IEEE Thirteenth International Conference on Peer-to-Peer Computing (P2P), Trento, Italy, 9–11 September 2013, Symmetry 2017, 9, 164.

13. Yli-Huumo, Jesse, Deokyoon Ko, Sujin Choi, Sooyong Park and Kari Smolander. "Where is current research on blockchain technology?—A systematic review." *PLoS One* (3 October 2016), https://doi.org/10.1371/journal.pone.0163477.

14. Yuan, Y. and F.-Y. Wang. *Towards Blockchain-Based Intelligent Transportation Systems.* Proceedings of the 2016 IEEE 19th International Conference on Intelligent Transportation Systems (ITSC), Rio de Janeiro, Brazil, 1–4 November 2016.

15. Christidis, K. and D. Michael. "Blockchains and smart contracts for the internet of things." *IEEE Access*, vol. 4 (2016): 2292–2303.

16. Kogias, E.K., P. Jovanovic, N. Gailly, I. Khoffi, L. Gasser and B. Ford. *École Polytechnique Fédérale de Lausanne (EPFL): Enhancing Bitcoin Security and Performance with Strong Consistency via Collective Signing.* Proceedings of the 25th USENIX Security Symposium (USENIX Security 16), Austin, TX, 10–12 August 2016.

17. Lin, Iuon-Chang and Tzu-Chun Liao. "A survey of blockchain security issues and challenges." *International Journal of Network Security*, vol. 19, no. 5 (September 2017): 653–659, https://doi.org/10.6633/IJNS.201709.19(5).01.

18. Eyal, I., A.E. Gencer, E.G. Sirer and R. van Renesse. *Bitcoin-ng: A Scalable Blockchain Protocol.* Proceedings of the 13th USENIX Symposium on Networked Systems Design and Implementation (NSDI 16), Santa Clara, CA, 2 February 2016.

19. Yli-huumo, J., D. Ko, S. Choi, S. Park and K. Smolander. "Where is current research on blockchain technology?—a systematic review." *PLoS One* (2016): 15–27.

20. Bonneau, J., A. Miller, J. Clark, A. Narayanan, J.A. Kroll and E.W. Felten. *Sok: Research Perspectives and Challenges for Bitcoin and Cryptocurrencies.* Proceedings of the 2015 IEEE Symposium on Security and Privacy (SP), San Jose, CA, 17–21 May 2015.

21. Bozic, Nikola, Guy Pujolle and Stefano Secci. "A tutorial on blockchain and applications to secure network control-planes." *Smart Cloud Networks & Systems (SCNS)* (2016), https://doi.org/978-1-5090-4476-4/16IEEE.

22. Paul, G., P. Sarkar and S. Mukherjee. *Towards a More Democratic Mining in Bitcoins.* Proceedings of the International Conference on Information Systems Security, Hyderabad, Springer International Publishing, Cham, 16–20 December 2014.
23. Natoli, C. and V. Gramoli. *The Blockchain Anomaly.* Proceedings of the 2016 IEEE 15th International Symposium on Network Computing and Applications (NCA), Cambridge, MA, 31 October–2 November 2016.
24. Nakamoto, S. *Bitcoin: A Peer-to-Peer Electronic Cash System.* https://bitcoin.org/en/bitcoin-paper (accessed 29 June 2017).
25. Huang, H., X. Chen, Q. Wu, X. Huang and J. Shen. "Bitcoin-based fair payments for outsourcing computations of fog devices." *Future Generation Computer Systems,* vol. 78 (2016).
26. Huh, S., C. Sangrae and K. Soohyung. *Managing IoT Devices Using Blockchain Platform.* Proceedings of the 2017 19th International Conference on Advanced Communication Technology (ICACT), Bongpyeong, Korea, 19–22 February 2017.
27. Zhang, J., X. Nian and H. Xin. "A secure system for pervasive social network-based healthcare." *IEEE Access,* vol. 4 (2016): 9239–9250.
28. Vasek, M. and T. Moore. *There's No Free Lunch, Even Using Bitcoin: Tracking the Popularity and Profits of Virtual Currency Scams.* Proceedings of the International Conference on Financial Cryptography and Data Security, San Juan, Puerto Rico, Springer, Berlin, Heidelberg, Gemany, 26–30 January 2015.
29. Kaskaloglu, K. *Near Zero Bitcoin Transaction Fees Cannot Last Forever.* Proceedings of the International Conference on Digital Security and Forensics (DigitalSec2014), The Society of Digital Information and Wireless Communication, Ostrava, Czech Republic, 24–26 June 2014.
30. Ziegeldorf, J.H., R. Matzutt, M. Henze, F. Grossmann and K. Wehrle. "Secure and anonymous decentralized bitcoin mixing." *Future Generation Computer Systems,* vol. 80 (2016).
31. Tschorsch, F. and B. Scheuermann. "Bitcoin and beyond: A technical survey on decentralized digital currencies." *IEEE Communications Surveys and Tutorials,* vol. 18 (2015): 2084–2123.
32. Park, Jin Ho and Jong Hyuk Park. "Blockchain security in cloud computing: Use cases, challenges, and solutions." *Symmetry,* vol. 9 (2017): 164, https://doi.org/10.3390/sym9080164; www.mdpi.com/journal/symmetry.
33. Armknecht, F., G. Karame, A. Mandal, F. Youssef and E. Zenner. "Ripple: Overview and outlook." In: M. Conti, M. Schunter and I. Askoxylakis (eds.), *Trust and Trustworthy Computing,* Springer, Cham, Switzerland, 2015, pp. 163–180.
34. Singh, S., Y.-S. Jeong and J.H. Park. "A survey on cloud computing security: Issues, threats, and solutions." *Journal of Network and Computer Applications,* vol. 75 (2016): 200–222.
35. Swan, M. *Blockchain: Blueprint for a New Economy.* O'Reilly Media, Inc., Sebastopol, CA, 2015.

7

Decentralization in Blockchain and its Impact on Identity

*Shailaja Nitin Lohar and Sachin Babar

CONTENTS

7.1 Introduction: Introduction to Blockchain Technology

Technology has advanced in every aspect with respect to faster data manipulation and extended security mechanisms. The security in digital systems has gained prime importance in recent years, along with the need to protect data from illicit tampering and the demand for faster data processing. Mapping all the real-world entities into digital counterparts has become the foundation of many technologies over the last decade. One such example was the digital currency, Bitcoin. It was introduced in 2009 and was the first

DOI: 10.1201/9781003203933-9

digital currency which uses peer-to-peer technology without any trusted third party [1]. Bitcoin, along with providing immutable security, now stands as the most popular cryptocurrency because users are able to transfer money from one digital wallet to another without any third party or use of a public ledger to record transactions. The underlying technology which made this happen is Blockchain.

This chapter will aim at analyzing the impact of decentralization in Blockchain with respect to identity management systems. Integration of Blockchain technology with other technologies is also discussed with respect to the challenges which may affect the efficient working of both technologies. Blockchain has emerged as a strong contender for decentralizing [2] certain applications and securing data and transactions. Blockchain is a secure, shared, distributed ledger through which each user has the copy of records that can be updated only if all the users in the network consent to it. It is a distributed database which contains records of all transactions that have been executed by the participating users. Once the information is entered in the database, it cannot be deleted. Since the concept of a centralized authority or controller is eliminated in Blockchain, there needs to be some control over the network when deciding priorities of certain transactions and participation of the nodes. This is achieved by agreements between the nodes in the network conducted by consensus algorithms [3]. As per the application, the power of the network processors and number scalability of the nodes dictates the appropriate consensus algorithm that is decided and implemented.

7.1.1 Decentralization in Blockchain

The technological advancements have reached a peak with the invention of newer and efficient technologies. The huge amount of data processed per second through the internet is proof of the digitization of maximum applications. The interconnectivity is growing day by day with the advent of new applications bringing the world closer. This increasing connectivity is also raising concerns with respect to security, integrity and threats to digital assets. These concerns are addressed by advanced security mechanisms but if we closely think over it, if the technology like Blockchain is itself tamper-proof, the problem of threats will be solved more easily. It does not use any centralized authority to control, modify or

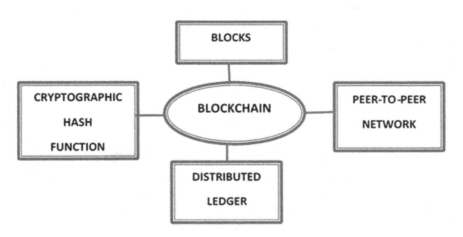

FIGURE 7.1
Important aspects of Blockchain [4].

authenticate the data (see Figure 7.1). Instead, all the participant nodes of a Blockchain network can append their data to this ledger with the help of some agreement. Any modifications to the ledger are done with consent of all the nodes. The data is tamper-proof because the ledger hashes to previous blocks in the chain, which reflect even minor changes. Any identity management system focuses on three main activities regarding digital identity, authentication, identification and authorization. The real-world claims made by a user and the proofs to authenticate his identity are applicable for his digital identity too. This authentication and verification process is implemented using Blockchain to avail the benefit of decentralization for identity management. The following sections give a brief of decentralization, its importance and a comparison to the previous identity management systems.

7.1.2 Decentralization and Identity Management

To build an application with minimum trust concerns, the technology must rely on distributing the processes, authority among the participants, rather than relying on a centralized authority. To achieve this, decentralization is a core concept from Blockchain which addresses the major concerns and drawbacks of centralized systems. Identity management systems [5] is one such area which is of prime importance in every domain and which has evolved over the years. The identity is an integral part on any virtual entity. It proves the authenticity of that entity with a unique identity. In the initial years of the computer and internet world, this identity was always centralized, which can be termed as a centralized identity management system. The next type of management for identities were the federated identities, which we are currently using. For example, many of our login accounts to various applications are done through Google Mail or a Facebook login. This may not be a centralized approach, but it is still giving control of our identities to specific domains. Both these approaches face the issue of centralized or controlled identity management. To overcome these shortcomings, Blockchain is emerging as a new identity provider with the help of its decentralized approach. Table 7.1 gives us the advantages and disadvantages of each approach.

TABLE 7.1

Types of Identity Management Systems

Identity Management System	Advantages	Disadvantages	Examples
Centralized	User needs to sign in at only one workspace for accessing all the tools and applications needed.	More dependency on the centralized authority. Data loss can have more severe effects.	OpenId [1]
Federated	User need not create multiple logins for multiple applications; specified domains will handle all the identity management of the user.	Authority is given to the specified domains only. Denial of service from these domains at any point will delete the user's identity related to those specific accounts from all applications.	Using Google sign-in.
Decentralized	User's digital identity is not managed or owned by any centralized authority; instead it is decentralized and retained in any case.	Majority of domains do not use a decentralized approach to keep reviving their customers.	uPort [6], Civic [6]

The table shows the reasons to consider decentralized identity models for user authentication and verification.

The traditional identity management models do not give the user authority to control their own identities, which can be done using the decentralized identity management system.

7.2 Blockchain Aspects Supporting an Identity Management Solution

With the expansion of Blockchain from being a cryptocurrency-related technology, other domains like healthcare, supply chain and banking are using various aspects of Blockchain to transform the business. In each of these domains, too, identity management is an integral part and is built on top of the following blockchain concepts.

7.2.1 Distributed Ledger Technology (DLT)

In simple terms, distributed ledger [7] is a distributed database where all the transactions are recorded simultaneously. It does not use any central storage and control, rather it is managed by multiple nodes. The blockchain's feature of securing the digital transactions is implemented in DLT by applying cryptography for each transaction update and verification [8].

DLT provides peer-to-peer connection between all the distributed ledgers along with keeping them tamper-proof [9]. This has helped in considering it for identity management solutions.

The three main aspects of digital identification (identity claim, identity issuer and identity verifier) are at the core of digital identity systems. Verification of issuer and verifier is done using DLT instead of relying on a third party [7]. This has leveraged the user by owning their identities. The concept which supports the new dimension for "User owns Identity" is the self-sovereign identity (SSI) [10], based on Christopher Allen's ten principles of SSI [10]. The two main concepts relate to SSI are the DID (Decentralized Identifier) and VC (Verifiable Credentials) [7]. DID are the unique identifiers which have their own format (see Figure 7.3). They are pointers to the DID document (DDOs) which include methods and functions to manipulate the DIDs. The DID document can describe a verification method to assess a proof. The Verifiable Credentials are digital proofs for verification of the credential holder which is created by issuer. Figure 7.2 shows the workings of the decentralized approach of self-sovereign identity.

The figure explains the working of SSI; there can be multiple verifiable credentials associated with a single entity and only the related identity is presented to the verifiers in the application context only. The verifiable credential is the DID owner's authentication.

For example, if a user is at a shopping mall, he can do the transactions on his DID, which will not reveal his entire identity, but only the necessary part and he does not need to subscribe to the shopkeeper's website to receive any discounts. The claim he makes can be verified by the shopkeeper. The user can carry multiple verifiable credentials to use in various contexts and application. He does not need to provide the complete identity information each time, but rather only the necessary details as is required.

This ensures the users control their identity and makes use of Blockchain benefits for identity management.

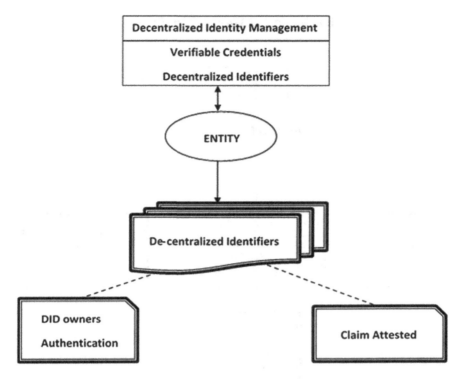

FIGURE 7.2
Self-Sovereign identity concepts.

7.2.1.1 Key Aspects of DID

- They are not dependent on any centralized issuing authority or any identity provider.
- DIDs have the capacity to manage all the keys at their end.

The World Wide Web Consortium Credentials Community Group (W3C-CCG) [11] is working for the standardization of these decentralized identifiers and verifiable credentials [12]. Sovrin and uPort are some of the frameworks using the SSI approach for decentralization of identity management systems based on SSI principles.

7.2.2 Smart Contracts

The authentication on a distributed ledger is done by smart contracts [11]. The third-party verifier in any type of transaction is responsible for the mutual agreement between identity verifier and issuer. A smart contract is the verifier which will execute only if the transaction is authenticated by the verifier. Smart contracts allow transactions which are trusted through the agreements and used for verification between different entities on the blockchain network. It eliminates the use of a central authority and surpasses the paperwork of agreements in a more secure and trusted way. Before execution of a smart contract on a Blockchain, a transaction fee is incurred, which is in the form of cryptocurrency Ether or Gas. This fee is necessary in order to execute the smart contract.

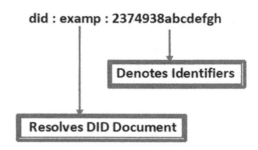

FIGURE 7.3
DID Syntax [8]

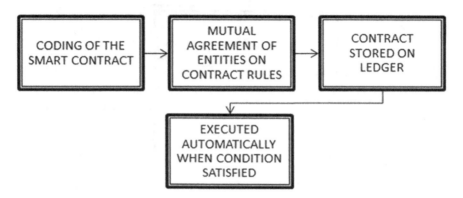

FIGURE 7.4
Flow of smart contract execution [1].

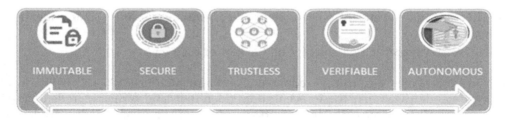

FIGURE 7.5
Benefits of smart contracts.

Figure 7.4 shows the flow of execution of a smart contract [13]. Both the entities can mutually agree on the virtual contract, and that can be coded into the smart contract code. The execution of this contract will be triggered once the specified condition is satisfied. The decentralized approach towards verification and authentication through smart contracts also highlights its benefits, which are shown in Figure 7.5.

Smart contracts can be written and executed on any Blockchain, but its most popular use is on Ethereum Blockchain because it has its own cryptocurrency called Ether, which can be used to pay for transactions virtually on the Ethereum chain. It enables the developers and smart contract users to create and deploy the contracts on the decentralized ledger, supporting maximum applications. Many smart contract platforms like Ethereum work on public networks where participants can join randomly; the contracts cannot be modified due its immutable nature [4].

7.3 Case Study—Home Temperature Monitoring System (DID-Based)

Smart systems based on the Internet of Things (IoT) have gained a wide popularity in recent years. One such application is the automated temperature monitoring and controlling system at home. With the use of wireless technologies like Zigbee, Wifi, Bluetooth and the temperature sensors, this system can be implemented as a part of home automation. The popularity of these systems has also paved the way for attackers and intruders who have tampered with such projects maliciously. To avoid this, this system can be made DID-based, so that only the trusted user can modify or control this system.

In this case, the identity of the IoT device used will be shared only with the legitimate user [14]. If the user is away from home and needs to maintain the temperature at his home, he will access the system and provide his DID necessary to access it and then only the system can be controlled remotely. Here, the user needs to provide his mutual identity with the device and then access is granted. To establish a mutual identity, the device and the user agree through a smart contract, which is deployed on a decentralized Blockchain and triggered when the user needs to access the system. The use of decentralization will give the following benefits in this case study:

- Intruders cannot access the system in any malicious way.
- The mutual identity established will ensure that no third party will be able to intercept the communication between the system and the user.
- Safety and security can be ensured by the user because of immutable functionality added to the system with the help of a smart contract and DID.

This system can be extended to other functionalities of the smart home project, like giving visitors access to WiFi, identifying recognized visitors and managing automated notifications for grocery shopping by providing personal DID. In every scenario, the respective DID will be provided by a user instead of giving every personal detail for each functionality.

7.4 Identity Management Applications

7.4.1 Healthcare

There are several use cases like electronic medical records, remote monitoring of patients and the pharmaceutical supply chain related to blockchain uses in healthcare [15]. The distributed ledger of Blockchain can store the expanding data of patients along with recording and accessing authorized data of patients by creating a trusted healthcare record. There are companies like Burstiq and Factom which are using blockchains to manage the huge amount of patient data, storing it in digital form on the distributed ledgers. Remote patient monitoring can be done with the combination of mobile devices, sensors and IoT devices [15].

7.4.2 Digital Voting

The important requirements of e-voting or digital voting are privacy, eligibility, convenience and verifiability. Initially, Direct Recording Electronic (DRE) [16] voting systems were used for digital polling and prior to this, Estonia was the first country to implement online voting. The important part of this system is the national ID card given to Estonian citizens. These cards contain files which identify the owner and allow the owner to carry out a number of online and electronic activities, including online banking services, digitally signing documents, access their information on government databases and electronic voting. There were flaws observed, like monitoring of client machine through malware and modification of the votes cast. All such drawbacks are overcome with Blockchain technology. With the use of a distributed ledger, end-to-end verifiability and immutable data modifications, voters can securely cast their votes. There are a number of systems proposed for this, which have proofed the efficiency of Blockchain in e-voting.

7.4.3 Document Verification

The authentication and verification of official, educational documents is one of the processes which require centralized authorities and is also time consuming. Use of Blockchains in these use cases is proving beneficial due to the elimination of a centralized authority, direct verification between issuers and claimers of the proof. The decentralized nature of blockchain allows the data to be accessed freely from the ledger, at the same time providing added benefits of claim revocation in certain cases. The time stamping property of blockchain can be very useful because it will indicate the change in the latest document verification, any revoked documents, modifications and malicious contenders. This will help banks, educational institutes and the healthcare industry verify documents in less time securely and more efficiently.

7.4.4 Identity Management System Using Blockchain

The chronology of identity management systems ranges from centralized, user centric, federated and towards a self-sovereign identity. The virtual identities are authorized, stored using either centralized systems or federated systems like Google giving its users email verification for multiple applications. But the risk in these systems is the central point of failures and the dominance of federated systems. The solution is a self-sovereign identity (SSI) [17], the concept in which users have complete control over their own identities. SSI is implemented using blockchain for user authentication and verification. Iroha, Hyperledger, Civic [1], uPort [1] and Cryptid are some of the examples of SSI implementations. Some applications like, Trinsic (which use the hyperledger Blockchain), allow users to create their own digital wallets which can be used for verification and authorization of claims anytime [19] with any organization.

7.5 Challenges of Blockchain

The range of applications shows the popularity and wide use of Blockchain technology, but there are some aspects of this technology which still need improvement or re-assessment.

Blockchain's integration with other technologies is noteworthy, but there are some critical challenges which are listed in the following section.

7.5.1 Scalability

A Blockchain network processes thousands of transactions per second, but applications with limited resources need a scaling solution [18] to accommodate this network of blockchain. Since the validation process increases with a greater number of participant nodes in the network, scaling the system for a larger number of blocks becomes difficult. When scaling the network, the power consumptions must also be taken into consideration because the consensus algorithm might need more power for execution of a transaction on the scaled network. Every participant must be coordinated accordingly even after the addition of multiple new modes.

7.5.2 Interoperability

Most existing Blockchains work independently and do not interoperate with other peer networks. Since different Blockchain networks use different consensus algorithms and types of Blockchains, the compatibility between multiple Blockchain networks [19] is also a challenge.

7.5.3 Computational Power

The consensus mechanisms used in Blockchain networks consume a lot of computational power [20] to solve mathematical puzzles. Also, replicating all the nodes with the same copy of the ledger across the network is a tedious and time-consuming process. Increasing the number of nodes gradually increases this computational complexity. Observing Bitcoin, the chain is always growing at a rate of 1MB per block every 10 minutes [21], proportionally increasing computational power and storage. Adapting Blockchains in an IoT environment thus is a major challenge with the constrained nature of devices in IoT [22, 23].

7.5.4 Legal Issues

Although there are applications of Blockchain in finance, the lack of a centralized authority poses security issues with respect to financial transactions. Regulating all the transactions according to a legal framework will require coordination between governments and stakeholders. All the applications of Blockchain will require legal protection in case of fraudulent mishaps which might affect the use of Blockchain for a particular application. But this again regresses the decentralized nature of a Blockchain by binding it to a legal authority.

7.6 Conclusion and Discussion

Blockchain being a beneficial technology for a range of applications, it is a promising approach towards security embedded in technology. The features of Blockchain support the data integrity, immutability and the decentralized approach for financial as well as non-financial applications. The comparative approach of identity management systems with the decentralization of identity verification and authorization is sure to solve the drawbacks of federated and user-centric systems. The various aspects of a decentralized identity management system discussed in this chapter show a promising approach for a variety of applications where identity management can be effectively implemented in a secure, immutable, shared and distributed manner.

Also, the high computational complexity being one of the challenges is a reason why applying Blockchain to some applications will be difficult. The removal of a centralized authority and giving right to every participant node in networks comes with a trade-off of consensus algorithms, which are computationally intensive and may be a hindrance in implementing identity solutions for IoT systems because of their constrained nature. Considering all the challenges and limitations, Blockchain still is a promising technology for many applications like identity management systems, where a centralized authority could be eliminated and the authentication of users will be safeguarded with the help of a decentralized approach.

References

[1] Lewis, Antony. "Blockchain Technology Explained." *Blockchain Technologies* (2015): 1–27, www.blockchaintechnologies.com/blockchain-definition.

[2] Bartolomeu, Paulo C., Emanuel Vieira, Seyed M. Hosseini and Joaquim Ferreira. "Self-sovereign identity: Use-cases, technologies, and challenges for industrial IoT." *IEEE International Conference on Emerging Technologies and Factory Automation, ETFA* (September 2019): 1173–1180, https://doi.org/10.1109/ETFA.2019.8869262.

[3] Bruyn, A. Shanti. *Blockchain*, 2017, https://doksi.net/en/get.php?order=DisplayPreview&lid=26583.

[4] Zheng, Zibin, Shaoan Xie, Hongning Dai, Xiangping Chen and Huaimin Wang. "An overview of blockchain technology: Architecture, consensus, and future trends." *Proceedings—2017 IEEE 6th International Congress on Big Data, BigData Congress 2017* (2017): 557–564, https://doi.org/10.1109/BigDataCongress.2017.85.

[5] Witkovski, Adriano, Altair Santin, Vilmar Abreu and Joao Marynowski. "An IdM and key-based authentication method for providing single sign-on in IoT." *2015 IEEE Global Communications Conference, GLOBECOM 2015* (December 2015), https://doi.org/10.1109/GLOCOM.2014.7417597.

[6] Dunphy, Paul and Fabien A.P. Petitcolas. *A First Look at Identity Management Schemes*, 2018, https://arxiv.org/abs/1801.03294.

[7] Zhu, Xiaoyang and Youakim Badr. "Identity management systems for the internet of things: A survey towards blockchain solutions." *Sensors (Basel, Switzerland)*, vol. 18, no. 12 (2018): 1–18, https://doi.org/10.3390/s18124215; W3C VCWG.

[8] Yaga, Dylan, Peter Mell, Nik Roby and Karen Scarfone. "Blockchain technology overview." *NIST Blockchain Technology Overview* (2019), https://doi.org/10.6028/NIST.IR.8202.

[9] Grüner, Andreas, Alexander Mühle and Christoph Meinel. *On the Relevance of Blockchain in Identity Management*, 2018, 1–7, https://www.researchgate.net/publication/326570310_On_the_Relevance_of_Blockchain_in_Identity_Management.

[10] Allen, C. *The Path to self-Sovereign Identity*, 2016, www.lifewithalacrity.com/2016/04/the-path-to-self-soverereign-identity.html (accessed 10 September 2019).

[11] Verifiable Claims Working Group, https://w3c.github.io/webpayments-ig/VCTF/charter/faq.html (Accessed 8 October 2018).

[12] Lux, Zoltan Andras, Dirk Thatmann, Sebastian Zickau and Felix Beierle. "Distributed-ledger-based authentication with decentralized identifiers and verifiable credentials." *2020 2nd Conference on Blockchain Research and Applications for Innovative Networks and Services, BRAINS* (2020): 71–78, https://doi.org/10.1109/BRAINS49436.2020.9223292.

[13] Wang, Shuai, Yong Yuan, Xiao Wang, Juanjuan Li, Rui Qin and Fei Yue Wang. 2018. "An overview of smart contract: Architecture, applications, and future trends." *IEEE Intelligent Vehicles Symposium, Proceedings,* vol. IV (June 2018): 108–113, https://doi.org/10.1109/IVS.2018.8500488.

[14] Monti, Matteo and Steen Rasmussen. "RAIN: A bio-inspired communication and data storage infrastructure." *Artificial Life,* vol. 23, no. 4 (2017): 552–557, https://doi.org/10.1162/ARTL_a_00247.

[15] Fekih, Rim Ben and Mariam Lahami. 2020. *Application of Blockchain Technology in Healthcare: A Comprehensive Study.* Lecture Notes in Computer Science (Including Subseries Lecture Notes in Artificial Intelligence and Lecture Notes in Bioinformatics), vol. 12157 LNCS, Springer International Publishing, Cham, https://doi.org/10.1007/978-3-030-51517-1_23.

[16] Mehboob, Kashif, Junaid Arshad and Muhammad Khan. "Secure digital voting system based on blockchain technology." *International Journal of Electronic Government Research,* vol. 14 (2018): 53–62, https://doi.org/10.4018/IJEGR.2018010103.

[17] Machine Identity—DIDs & Verifiable Credentials for Trust & Interoperability in IoT—Mrinal Wadhwa, https://ssimeetup.org/machine-identity-dids-verifiable-credentials-trust-interoperability-iot-mrinal-wadhwa/.

[18] Reyna, Ana, Cristian Martín, Jaime Chen, Enrique Soler and Manuel Díaz. 2018. "On blockchain and its integration with IoT: Challenges and opportunities." *Future Generation Computer Systems,* vol. 88 (May): 173–190, https://doi.org/10.1016/j.future.2018.05.046.

[19] Deng, Qing. "Application analysis on blockchain technology in cross-border payment." *Proceedings of the International Conference on Financial Innovation and Economic Development (ICFIED),* vol. 126 (2020): 287–295, https://doi.org/10.2991/aebmr.k.200306.050.

[20] Makridakis, Spyros and Klitos Christodoulou. "Blockchain: Current challenges and future prospects/applications." *Future Internet,* vol. 11, no. 12 (2019), https://doi.org/10.3390/FI11120258.

[21] Dash, Chinmaya and Prakash Chandra Behera. "Blockchain technology: A revolutionary bitcoin technology." *International Journal of Information Science and Computing,* vol. 4, no. 1 (2017): 27, https://doi.org/10.5958/2454-9533.2017.00004.7.

[22] Sneha, K., M.R. Manu, B. Balamurugan and S. Sreeji. "Blockchain identity management." *Essential Enterprise Blockchain Concepts and Applications* (December 2021): 123–142, https://doi.org/10.1201/9781003097990-7.

[23] Tasatanattakool, Pinyaphat and Chian Techapanupreeda. 2018. "Blockchain: Challenges and applications." *International Conference on Information Networking* (January–July 2018): 473–475, https://doi.org/10.1109/ICOIN.2018.8343163.

[24] Der, Uwe, Stefan Jähnichen and Jan Sürmeli. "Self-sovereign identity—opportunities and challenges for the digital revolution." *ArXiv,* 2017, https://www.semanticscholar.org/paper/Self-sovereign-Identity-Opportunities-and-for-the-Der-J%C3%A4hnichen/54f4c4fa0db5b94f2f146af1ea051a3218f1ce32.

8

Threat to the Current Blockchain Cryptosystems Due to the Advancement of Quantum Computers

Maulik Hiten Pandya

CONTENTS

8.1 Introduction

Blockchain has proved to be useful in many diverse fields due to its features like immutability, transparency, accountability, etc. All of these advantages we enjoy are provided through hashes and public-key cryptography. It is because conventional (classical) computers do not have enough computational power to decrypt and reverse a public-key and a hash, respectively. The security of these cryptography and hashing algorithms are based on mathematical problems which are tough to solve by the current most powerful supercomputers. This is why algorithms like DSA, RSA- 256, RSA-3072, ECDSA, ECDH, Diffie-Hellman, etc. (hashing algorithms, like SHA-256, are quantum resistant.), were considered to be safe until the development of quantum computers. The recent developments in the quantum computing field have changed the perspective of the world who considered these algorithms to be safe forever.

Quantum computers use algorithms like Shor's algorithm and Grover's algorithm for prime factorization and linear search, respectively. Most of the used cryptographic functions are based on the prime factorization of two large integers which can easily be broken by a few thousand qubits of the quantum computer. There are still many primitive

DOI: 10.1201/9781003203933-10

symmetric cryptographic systems, like AES-256 and SNOW 3G, which are quantum-resistant, i.e., they are not very prone to quantum attacks. There is another field where new cryptographic systems are being developed to overcome these current complications and are termed as "Post-Quantum Cryptography".

8.2 Cryptography in Blockchain

As already mentioned, hash functions are quantum-resistant, so mostly it is only digital signature schemes that are vulnerable to quantum attacks.

The generation of a public key is done by applying a cryptographic system to a private key. This is an irreversible operation because, if the outcome (which is the public key) and generator point are given, then it is nearly impossible to find the input (which is the private key). Now, this public key is hashed twice to generate the address which is then used throughout the nodes for transactions [1]. Furthermore, we'll know how this cryptography and the mathematics related to it works.

8.3 Cryptography in Bitcoin

Bitcoin uses the Elliptic Curve Digital Signature Algorithm (ECDSA)[2] as the algorithm to generate its pair of private and public keys. The private key is selected at random or by the user and then it uses ECDSA to generate its public key, which is then hashed with SHA-256 to create the addresses.

As ECDSA is a Trapdoor function: the only way to guess its private key is by brute force, which can take several years to solve by any supercomputer. Hence, we can use this private key to sign any transaction or document digitally. Since the signature will always comprise of the message (the message will always be different) and the private key, the signature will always be unique. Therefore, there is no way to find or guess the private key unless it is shared. Now, let us understand the real mathematics for the generation of the keys.

8.4 Mathematics of ECDSA

Bitcoin uses Secp256k1[3] to generate its private and public keys, and is defined by the equation $y3 = x2 + 7$, and the general equation of ECDSA is shown in Figure 8.1

A private key is generated at random which is multiplied by the generation points, a constant value, to get the public key. The multiplication is not that simple and is not the traditional multiplication; instead, we use (a) Addition and (b) Point Doubling [4].

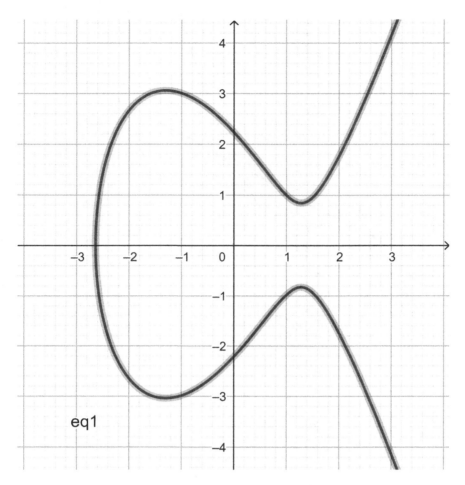

FIGURE 8.1
y3 = x2 + ax + b

A) **ADDITION:** To add points on an elliptic curve, we take the slope of the generator points and find the intersect on the curve. Since the curve is symmetric around the x-axis, we take the reflected image of the intersect point. In the example that follows and illustrated in Figure 8.2, we find the slope of points A and B and find the intersected point (C) which is reflected on the x-axis to get the final addition D = A+B.

B) **POINT DOUBLING:** Instead of taking two points, we start with the only point. Here we take the tangent of the point and find the intersection made by the tangent on the curve. Then the point of intersection is reflected on the x-axis to get the doubled point. In the following example depicted in Figure 8.3, the tangent of point A is used to find the intersection. Its image is reflected along the x-axis to get the double of point A.

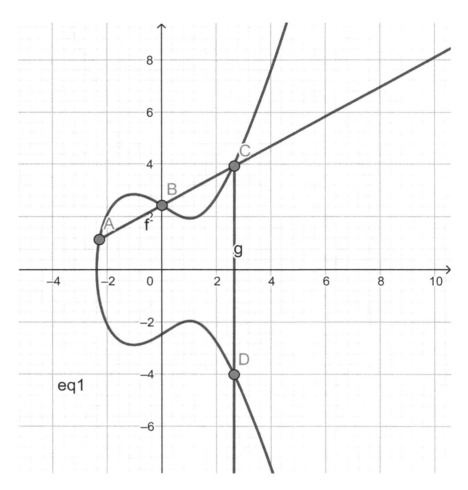

FIGURE 8.2
Elliptic curve addition.

8.5 Quantum Computing

Unlike conventional computers, quantum computers are built upon completely different fundamentals. They are built using the properties and laws of quantum mechanics such as quantum superposition, quantum entanglement, quantum interference, etc.

A bit in a conventional computer is either 1 or 0. But, in quantum computers, the quantum bit or the qubit is 0 and 1 at the same time; this happens because of quantum superposition which allows a qubit to be in both states at the same time until it is measured. By measuring, we collapse the superposition state and a single state is then observed. The outcome of these qubits is probabilistic.

Being in both states allows it to work in parallel for many different outcomes. In a simple language, 1 qubit can do a work of 2 bits (conventional bits), 2 qubits can do work of 4 bits, 3 qubits can do a work of 8 qubits, and so on. This number increases exponentially, and hence we gain quantum supremacy. If there are 'n' qubits, then it can perform

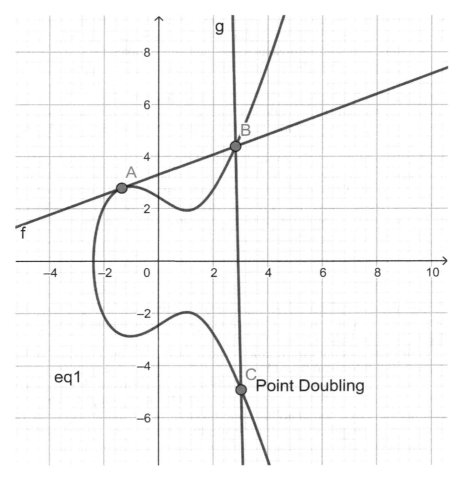

FIGURE 8.3
Elliptic curve point doubling.

computations equal to 2^n bits of a classical computer. This is the reason quantum comput-ers are immensely fast than classical computers. Since the outcomes of quantum bits are probabilistic, we can develop algorithms that can give us the desired outcome with high probability [4].

Using quantum algorithms, we can speed up the entire process and can find the solu-tions for problems which weren't possible to be solved by classical computers. The two most famous quantum algorithms are Grover's Search algorithm and Shor's algorithm. Further, in the note, we'll see how these two algorithms can cause real problems to the blockchain cryptosystem.

8.5.1 Grover's Algorithm

It is a searching algorithm for unstructured data. Classical computers have a time com-plexity of $O(N)$ to find an element from unstructured data, but using Grover's algorithm in quantum computers, this time complexity comes down to $O(\sqrt{N})$ [5]. This is not a great increase in speed, but is still much better than the classical search algorithm. For example, if a search is to be performed in unstructured data, and it takes 1,000 steps to be solved by the classical computer, then the quantum computer can do it in approximately 32 steps ($\sqrt{1000} = 31.622$).

It uses amplitude amplification to find the desired element, which is the reason for the increase in speed. As I already mentioned, outcomes of quantum computers are probabilistic, hence amplitude amplification is a great idea to increase the probability of the required element.

Since it is faster to find items, it is theorized that this algorithm can be used to find the collision of hashes which was not possible by the classical machines. It is theorized that the collision hash of SHA-128, AES-128 can be found using this algorithm but that can be resolved just by increasing the size of key length to 256-bits [6, 7]. We can look at it as, if the 128-bit key length is difficult for classical computers, then the 256-bit key length will be difficult for quantum computers.

8.5.2 Shor's Algorithm

Blockchain mainly uses ECDSA because it is based on the logarithmic problem that cannot be solved by classical computers. But this can be possible by quantum computers in the coming future with the help of Shor's algorithm.

Shor's algorithm solves the logarithmic problem of ECDSA by a method called period finding. We can call this a real threat because it can solve this complexity in polynomial time [8, 9]. This is a great increase in speed when compared to classic computers, which have complexity in exponential time (see Figure 8.4). Quantum computers use fundamentals like quantum interference, quantum superposition, and Quantum Fourier Transform (QFT) to maximize the required probabilistic output. In the coming section, we'll see which are some different cryptosystems that may not be prone to quantum attacks.

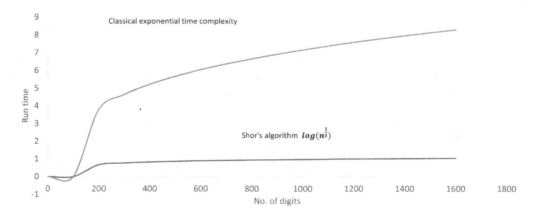

FIGURE 8.4
Shor's algorithm vs classical algorithm.

8.6 Post-Quantum Cryptography

To overcome the threats, we need to develop cryptosystems for blockchain that might not be vulnerable to any kind of quantum attacks. Massive researches are being conducted to find alternatives to the presently used traditional cryptosystems that will be quantum-resistant. If Shor's algorithm in quantum computers can break the present most prominent cryptosystems like RSA, ECDSA, then we will need a new type of cryptosystem to protect our data. The different types of new cryptosystems are as follows:

1. LATTICE-BASED CRYPTOSYSTEM: It is one of the most appealing cryptosystems as it uses multi-dimensional lattices for security. The traditional cryptosystems have an algebraic approach, but this has a geometrical approach. In theory, the easy problems are also difficult to solve by classical computers and even by quantum computers. This is because there is still no quantum algorithm that can solve lattice-based questions like SVP (Shortest Vector Problem) [10–12]; hence we can probably say that this cryptosystem could be quantum-resistant, looking at the difficulty of the problem. Consider a 2D plane having multiple points on the plane that forms a lattice with a period structure. Now, if we choose a point on the lattice and are asked to find the shortest non-zero vector, we can easily find it, but when we increase the dimensions to 100 or let's say 1,000, then it becomes difficult to answer the same question because it is difficult to even imagine 100 dimensions. The lattice-based cryptosystem uses this difficulty to increase security, probably making it quantum-safe.

There are several ways to implement this lattice-based cryptosystem, one of them is the LWE (Learning With Errors) problem. It is implemented using matrices. It can be used to create public keys that can be shared. Any random matrix A is selected, which is known publicly. But, with it we also have a secret 's' matrix and an error 'e' matrix; 's' and 'e' are private. Therefore, to calculate matrix B, we multiply A by 's' and then add 'e' [13, 14].

A					s		e		B
4	1	11	10		6		0		4
5	5	9	5				-1		7
3	9	0	10		9		1		2
1	3	3	2	✖		➕	1	=	11
12	7	3	4		11		1		5
6	5	11	4				0		12
3	3	5	0		11		-1		8

The values of A and B can be shared as public keys and 's' can be kept as a secret key.

We can also implement this by Ring-LWE; the processes are the same as the LWE, but here we use polynomials. Like LWE we use the same method but with the same procedure: we use coefficients of polynomials.

A random value of 'A', 'q' (which is the modulus), and 'n' (the highest coefficient power) is made known publicly. We find 'b' by multiplying 'A' by a secret 's' and then add it to an error 'e'. 's' and 'e' are not made public, so only the person knows it. Consider an example: Alice and Bob want to communicate, but they first will have to create a shared key to encrypt and decrypt a message. They first share the values of 'A', 'q', and 'n'. Then they individually create new values of 's' and 'e'[15]. After this, they calculate their values of 'b' and exchange them with each other. To understand this, let's look at the following equations:

Alice will create bA from 's' and 'e' and the same will be done by Bob to create bB:

$$bA = A \times sA + eA \quad bB = A \times sB + eB$$

Now, Alice and Bob will share this bA and bB with each other. Both will now multiply it by their s and then divide it by $(x^n + 1)$:

$$sharedA = (bB \times sa)/(xn+1) \quad sharedB = (bA \times sb)/(xn+1)$$

Thus, both Alice and Bob have the same key so now they can securely communicate.

Lattice-based cryptosystems also have other encryption schemes like GGH encryption scheme and NTRUEncrypt.

2. HASH-BASED CRYPTOSYSTEM: As we have seen, the quantum algorithm (like Shor's algorithm) can solve some of the mathematical problems of signature schemes in polynomial time, making the current schemes futile.

Hash-based cryptosystems have been studied for years and can prove to be quantum-resistant.

This can be done by using LMS and XMSS. These are the Merkle Tree-based signature schemes with One Time Signature (OTS)[16]. OTS is used to sign a message with a private key. The problem with this is that, using OTS, only one message can be signed at a time using a private key. To solve this, we combine OTS with the Merkle Tree. Leaves are OTS public keys and the nodes of the tree are the hashes of the two children, which in continuation forms the root of the tree. This root is the public key of the Merkle Tree formed.

If any of the nodes have been tampered with, then the final public key of the Merkle Tree changes, which makes it difficult to tamper. The verifier tries to compute the OTS public key and then it authenticates it by going through the tree path. If the final root hash matches, then it can be said that the OTS public key was valid and no data has been tampered with.

This is called the Hash-Based Signature Scheme (HBS), where we use OTS to sign the messages which are equivalent to the public key of a leaf.

This seems quite useful, but it also gets non-efficient with the increase in the size of the tree. Consider if the height of a tree is H, then the tree can sign a 2^H number of messages. So, if H is greater than 40, then it becomes very difficult to compute the signatures for every message [17].

To tackle this, we make use of a multi-level HBS Tree (see Figure 8.5). Here, the entire Merkle Tree is divided into more sub-level trees. Each root of a tree is signed by the OTS of the tree just above it.

This makes the height of each subtree a reasonable height, which consequently reduces the signing time. If H1 + H2 + H3 + ... + Hn is the heights of the tree, then the maximum number of signed messages would be $(2^{H1 + H2 + \ldots + Hn})$ and the key generation time would be $O(2^{H1} + 2^{H2} + 2^{H3} + \ldots + 2^{Hn})$. Further, in the note, we'll talk about LMS and XMSS.

a. *LMS:* It is a stateful scheme that includes 4 bytes of index that represents the state when the message is signed. This helps in preventing multi-collision attacks as now it can only be used one time. LMS uses Winternitz One-Time Signature (WOTS) as its OTS [17]. LMS is restricted to SHA-256 as it doesn't allow the other versions of the hashing algorithm.

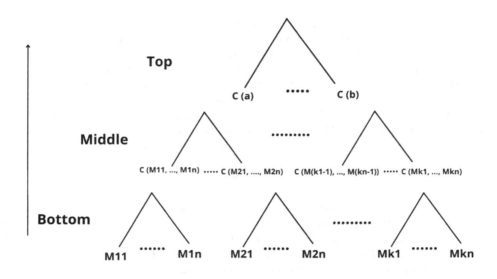

M = Message   C = Combination

FIGURE 8.5
Multi-level HBS.

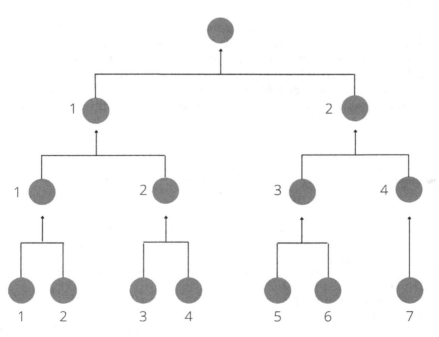

FIGURE 8.6
L-tree signature scheme.

The other disadvantage of LMS is the size of the keys. The entire PQ-Cryptosystem has the same problem of large size keys, and sometimes it makes it impractical to generate the keys.

As anyone could have noticed, in the HBS there is a lot with the hashing. Both the person who signs and the person who verifies has to compute a lot of hashing to send or receive the correct message. In an experiment done by Panos Kampanakis and Scott Fluhrer in their "LMS vs XMSS: Comparison of two Hash-Based Signature Standards" paper, they demonstrated the time required by the LMS and XMSS for the compression of hashes during an OTS computation [16]. In their conclusion, they found that XMSS has smaller signature sizes compared to LMS with equivalent parameter sets.

b. XMSS (eXtended Merkle Signature Scheme):

It is similar to LMS, but the difference is that XMSS uses a binary L-tree (see Figure 8.6). It is generated from the numbers of the WOTS + public key numbers. Here, the number cannot be an exponent of 2, i.e., it can happen that a node on the right side of the L-tree may not have a pair, so the right-side leaf that does not have a pair is raised upwards until it gets a pair, and it is then merged with them in the tree.

The larger the tree's size, the more difficult it becomes for the generation of the tree. A tree a with the height of more than 20 will take more than 10 minutes to generate. If the height is 10, then the XMSS can sign 1,024 transactions, and so on.

Unlike LMS, XMSS supports SHA-512 and it can also be extended as the time comes.

8.7 Conclusion

In conclusion, we can say that the development of advanced quantum computers is still far away but is not impossible. With the advent of quantum computers, the security of major DLTs will be at stake, and perhaps we'll also develop quantum-resistant cryptosystems until then. As we saw, two of the four post-quantum algorithms are still in their development phases and will fully be developed in the coming future. As blockchain is all based on its tough security that allows the transaction between two untrusted entities, it cannot be compromised.

8.8 References

[1] Sharma, Toshendra Kumar. "Can blockchain be under quantum attacks?" *Blockchain Council*, www.blockchain-council.org/blockchain/can-blockchain-be-under-quantum-attacks/ (accessed 19 May 2021).

[2] Anhao, Noah. *Bitcoin Post-Quantum*, https://bitcoinpq.org/download/bitcoinpq-whitepaper-english.pdf.

[3] Secp256k1. *Wikipedia*, https://en.bitcoin.it/wiki/Secp256k1.

[4] Samtani, Neeraj J. 2018. *How Would Quantum Computing Impact the Security of Bitcoin by Enhancing Our Ability to Solve the Elliptic Curve Discrete Logarithm Problem?* https://papers.ssrn.com/sol3/papers.cfm?abstract_id=3232101.

[5] Grover's algorithm. *IBM, Qiskit,* https://qiskit.org/textbook/ch-algorithms/grover.html (accessed 19 May 2021).

[6] Li, Maggie. *Grover's Search Algorithm Using IBM's Qiskit,* 2020, https://medium.com/@ziyu.lili.maggie/grovers-search-algorithm-3233592820d3.

[7] Real Security. *State of Symmetric & Hash Algorithms After Quantum Computing,* 2019, www.real-sec.com/2019/08/state-of-symmetric-hash-algorithms-after-quantum-computing/.

[8] Shor's Algorithm. *IBM, Qiskit,* https://qiskit.org/textbook/ch-algorithms/shor.html.

[9] Shor's Algorithm. *IBM Quantum Composer,* https://quantumcomputing.ibm.com/composer/docs/iqx/guide/shors-algorithm.

[10] Campagna, Matthew, Lidong Chen, et al. *Quantum Safe Cryptography and Security,* June 2015, www.etsi.org/images/files/ETSIWhitePapers/QuantumSafeWhitepaper.pdf.

[11] Micciancio, Daniele and Oded Regev. *Lattice-Based Cryptography,* 22 July 2008, https://cims.nyu.edu/~regev/papers/pqc.pdf.

[12] Fernández-Caramès, T.M. and P. Fraga-Lamas. "Towards post-quantum blockchain: A review on blockchain cryptography resistant to quantum computing attacks." *IEEE Access,* vol. 8 (2020): 21091–21116, https://doi.org/10.1109/ACCESS.2020.2968985; https://ieeexplore.ieee.org/abstract/document/8967098.

[13] Prof Bill Buchanan OBE. *Python and Crypto: Learning With Errors (LWE) and Ring LWE.* The Cyber Academy, https://asecuritysite.com/public/lwe_ring.pdf (accessed 18 May 2021).

[14] Buchanan OBE, Bill. 2018. *Learning with Errors and Ring Learning with Errors,* https://medium.com/asecuritysite-when-bob-met-alice/learning-with-errors-and-ring-learning-with-errors-23516a502406 (accessed 18 May 2021).

[15] Buchanan OBE, Bill. 2019. *Ring Learning with Errors for Key Exchange (RLWE-KEX),* https://medium.com/asecuritysite-when-bob-met-alice/ring-learning-with-errors-for-key-exchange-rlwe-kex-5dc0ce37e207 (accessed 20 May 2021).

[16] Kampanakis, Panos and Scott Fluhrer. *LMS vs XMSS: Comparison of Two Hash-Based Signature Standards,* 2017, https://eprint.iacr.org/2017/349.pdf.

[17] Kampanakis, Panos, Peter Panburana, Michael Curcio and Chirag Shroff. *Post-Quantum Hash-Based Signatures for Secure Boot,* 2020, https://eprint.iacr.org/2020/1584.pdf.

Section III

Applications of Blockchain

9

Digital India Digital Economy Using Blockchain Technology

K.S. Thakre*, Gargi Kulkarni and Prajwal Sameer Deshmukh

CONTENTS

DOI: 10.1201/9781003203933-12

9.1 Introduction

Today, money is not safe in the form of cash and banks. Consider this scenario: Rs 10 lakh invested in a fixed bank for 2 years. Interest for every quarter of the seven areas was received or accepted, but a few months before the deposit matures, the bank, due to an increase in financial problems (which eventually lead to the bank's regulator placing more controls), doesn't pay hard work on maturity. In many such cases, investors have lost their hard-earned money to banks due to financial mismanagement—as a result, the Reserve Bank of India (RBI) has taken Prompt Corrective Action (PCA) against them. Currently, Central Bank of India, UCO Bank, Maharashtra Co-operative (PMC) Bank, United Bank of India, Indian Overseas Bank, Punjab, to name a few, are under RBI's PCA. The record-breaking history of cooperative banks is daunting. According to RBI data, there were 1,926 bank cooperatives (UCBs) in 2004; and 16 years ago, the RBI was forced to merge 129 weak alliances with strong banks. About 246 UCBs have fallen in the last 16 years. Day by day, the risk of automatic failure is swiftly increasing; potential risks are well-organized and things can get out of hand quickly if timely measures are not taken. The latter, namely the 21st edition of the Financial Stability Report (FSR) released by the RBI, identifies a number of negative risks, although India's financial system remains stable. All major indicators of risk, global risk, financial market risk, and expected macroeconomic risk remain in the 'high' to 'high' range. The RBI has warned all stakeholders of the potential increase in the sector's Gross Non-Performing Assets (GNPAs) in the future. As natural calamities, pandemics and man-made disasters continue to affect health and livelihoods, the impact on debt growth, the quality of banking assets, and banking adequacy is severe.

The redistribution of corporate balance sheets that made steady progress in the pre-pandemic era had a significant impact on the economy of countries. Macro's credit risk assessment shows that the GNPA rating for all SCBs could rise from 8.5% in March 2020 to 12.5% in March 2021 in the first round. If the macroeconomic situation worsens, the rate could rise to 14.7% under greater pressure, according to RBI's Financial Stability Report. According to the FSR, approximately 67% of public bank customers (PSBs) and 49% of the private sector customers received a suspension from April 30, 2020. About 1/3 of the private sector bank loan and 2/3 of the PSBs were under suspension. This is an ominous situation. In many cases, the government has made sure that the bank depositors are safe, but such guarantees cannot be entirely trusted. Given that the NPAs of many banks are increasing, customers' hard-earned money is not 100% secure in banks. Financial pressures on the Indian banking system (and the credit market) are very constructive, and this rise in the level of the system could explode the investors' money without error.

The government introduced the Financial Dispute Resolution and Financial Insurance (FRDI) Bill in Parliament in August 2017, but withdrew it in August 2018. Bail-in is contrary to bail release. When a government rescues a bank, it primarily uses taxpayers' money to save the business. Conversely, the bail-permit clause allows the use of the investors' money to reduce bank debt. But with so much media opposition, the government has had to back down from the proposal. Just before the COVID-19 pandemic hit the country in March, the government was considering introducing a modified version of the FRDI and re-introducing it as the Bill Sector Development and Regulation (FSDR) Bill. And now that the banking and financial sector is under a lot of pressure in the midst of COVID-19, negotiations to establish a solution under the legal framework of the new FSDR system have begun to form. Non-Banking Companies (NBFCs), payment banks, insurance companies, major market players, cooperatives, and local banks will be under the proposed settlement authority. A systematic approach to formal funding to deal with depressed assets is required, according to former RBI Governor Shaktikanta Das.

_____

9.2 Literature Review

India is currently the seventh largest economy in the world. It currently has an estimated population of about 1.34 billion people, or about 18% of the world's population, according to the World Economic Forum. Despite its GDP dropping by roughly 5.7% in the quarter that ended June of 2017. India remains the fastest growing large economy in the world after China. If estimates are anything to go by, India will have overtaken China as the world's most populous country by 2024, which would help solidify its position as the nation with the world's largest youth population. The World Economic Forum also projects that India's economy will be the second largest economy in the world by 2050, with China occupying the first position. Poor as the policy might have been for average Indians, though, there were bright spots for proponents of a cashless economy.

The World Economic Forum reported that the number of digital transactions in India increased following the demonetization policy, which was a plus for the government, who would now have increased its ability to track the flow of money within the economy. The growth in digital transactions in India is, in turn, a big plus for Blockchain and cryptocurrency. Just about 0.5% of the people in India are into Bitcoin, the cryptocurrency that popularized Blockchain technology. By inference, if such few people in India know about Bitcoin, it's safe to say that only about 0.55 of India's population is familiar with Blockchain technology. However, on the national level, a lot of work is going on to

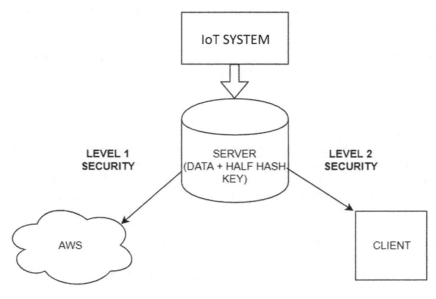

FIGURE 9.1
RFID-based digital payment system.

integrate Blockchain technology into various sectors of the economy including the financial and health sectors. In 2016, the Indian bank, ICIC Bank, announced that it had completed a cross-border transaction executed on Blockchain. In September 2017, the Institute for Development and Research in Banking Technology, or IDRBT, founded by the Reserve Bank of India, announced plans to launch a new Blockchain platform. The Reserve Bank of India is India's central bank. The announcement followed a report published by the IDRBT in January 2017 that India could use Blockchain to digitize its national currency, the rupee. Given the positives of increased tax payments, for instance that the demonetization policy in India has yielded through increased digital transactions [1], it's plausible that the Indian government will double down on its drive to grow a cashless economy. There are some challenges, but it seems promising. If, as in any place in the world, the Indian government wants to boost its cashless economy, it needs to find lasting solutions to the challenges confronting the propagation of a cashless economy. Some of those challenges include financial inclusion, high setup and transaction costs, and transaction times.

The practice of money laundering and the realization of everyday life began in the 1990s, when electronic banking was on the rise, with digital payment methods becoming more widespread in 2010. In 2016, only about 2% of the value generated in Sweden was cash, and only about 20% of commercial transactions were in cash. Less than half of the country's banking branches conduct cash transactions [2]. Examples include mediators such as PayPal, digital wallet systems such as Apple Pay, telecommunications and NFC payments via electronic or smartphone card, and electronic bills and banking, all broad uses. [3] At this point money was no longer desirable in other types of transactions that would historically be the norm to pay by tangible tender, and large sums of money in some cases were treated with suspicion, due to its flexibility and ease of use in money laundering and terrorist financing [4]. In addition, payments in large amounts have been strictly prohibited by some suppliers and retailers, [3, 5] to the point of coining the term 'money war'. [6] The 2016 U.S. Consumer User Survey states that 75% of respondents have chosen a credit or bank card as their payment method while only 11% of respondents prefer cash. [7] Since the establishment of the two companies in 2009, digital payments can now be made through mechanisms such as Venmo and Square. Venmo allows people to pay directly to other people without earning money.

Existing online payment systems are vulnerable to cyberattacks and are undemocratic [8]. Cyberattacks like ransomware attacks are especially prominent in existing online payment systems. The dependency on a single central authority for payments is a major cause of these attacks.[9]

S. Kumari et al 'Blockchain based Data Security for Financial Transaction System', [10] focuses on providing security to a Blockchain system using various mechanisms. The proposed model consists of the financial transaction-based system which works on RFID technology. The data obtained from the system can only be accessed by clients who are authorized, hence providing the first level of security by providing authentication to the valid client using M2M authentication. Once the user is authenticated, the proposed system is a financial transaction-oriented system that uses RFID technology. The data from the RFID passive tag is captured and collected from the RFID reader and is placed in the server (local system). The data that is stored in the server is stored using a Blockchain mechanism (see Figure 9.1).

The hash is divided, and one part is stored in the cloud which is Amazon s3. This mechanism incorporates the first level of security. The second level of security is achieved by authenticating the client with M2M authentication. The user who wants to access the data present in the Blockchain needs to get authenticated first; the process of authentication is provided by the RSA algorithm. The keys are generated using the RSA (Rivest-Shamir-Adleman) mechanism. The purpose of the key is to enable mutual authentication between a user and the IoT system. The key size ranges from 1,024 to 4,096 bit are typical. The keys are private and public, which are employed by RSA. Here, the public key is kept at the server and a private key is given to the client. The process of encryption and decryption takes place, that is an OTP is generated using the random class method where the OTP is encrypted using the public key of the server and sent to the user. If the client is a valid user, then the client will be able to decrypt using his private key and tell the OTP to the server. For this process to take place, the keys are exchanged in the form of the certificate. The OTP, certificate, and private and public keys are kept in the database and filled by the server and the client when it's time to fill their fields.

Technologies and Algorithms used: IoT Environment RFID for data communication, Amazon S3 for data storage, RSA Algorithm for process of authentication, and SHA-1 Algorithm to generate hash for the blocks.

Following the advent of digital payment systems, several efforts have been made to leverage the advantages of Blockchain technology to better digital payments.

One such study, E-commerce payment model using Blockchain by Shee-Ihn Kim1 et al., [11] attempts to do away with the payment gateways associated with the digital payment system. This paper proposed that a Blockchain e-commerce payment system comprises the merchant, customer's smartphone application, and blockchain system.

The payment processing procedure is as follows:

1) After selling its products and services, the merchant requests that the customer makes payment using a blockchain cryptocurrency; the merchant makes the payment request through a QR code displayed on the customer's web browser where QR code contains the information of M_Address, Amount, Time Stamp, M_TX_ID, and Merchant's Digital Signature as a QR code.

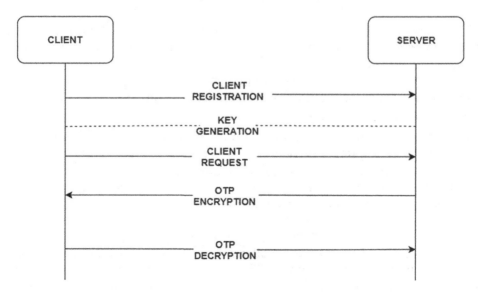

FIGURE.9.2
Client server interaction

2) To confirm whether the customer has made the payment, the merchant requests confirmation from the Blockchain system.

3) After purchasing products and services from the merchant, the customer scans the QR code to pay the price to the merchant. The payment is not transmitted directly to the merchant. A request is made to the Blockchain system, which contains the transaction ledger.

4) The Blockchain system deducts the payment amount from the customer's account and raises the amount in the merchant's account. After executing this transfer between the accounts, the Blockchain system transmits the results to the merchant. The merchant confirms the payment and begins to provide the purchased service to the customer. The blockchain system also transmits the payment result information to the customer's smartphone application (See Figure 9.2).

As a result, they have successfully implemented the e-commerce payment system for both merchant and customer. So first, when the customer selects a product on the merchant's online shopping mall, the payment screen generates. The customer scans the QR code to execute the payment procedure. The Blockchain subsystem transmits the payment result to the merchant and the customer. Tests were run sequentially on the merchant, customer, and Blockchain subsystems. The verification process confirmed whether the digital signature for the merchant's message, as well as that for the customer's message, was accurately created.

Another such system was proposed in R. Gupta et. al [12], 'Acceptance Towards Digital Payments and Improvements in Cashless Payment Ecosystem', 2020 International Conference for Emerging Technology (INCET), 2020.

This proposal leverages the use of the relatively new smart contract payment system using Ethereum: a reliable, secure, and contemporary working model for a Digital Payment Wallet where a shared e-wallet is used primarily to support transactions made by minors under the supervision of their parents. Therefore, a rather secure and contemporary transaction technology. Here, the following steps have been followed:

1) Create an account to deploy Smart Contract on Ropsten Test Network.

2) From Ropsten Test Faucet, transfer 1 ether to the user account created by mentioning the account address.

3) Transfer funds from one wallet to another by providing the primary account address and the amount of transaction to *'transferTo'* function.

4) Primary 1 receives the notification for confirming the transfer of funds.

5) When the transaction is confirmed, funds are successfully transferred, and the wallet balance is updated suitably.

6) For adding a new participant (primary or minor digital user), Primary 1 can add another primary account, Primary 2, by calling the function *'add_owner'* in the backend, using the address of the Primary 2. This will send a request to add 'Primary 2' to the other primary users of the shared wallet. If accepted, Primary 2 is successfully the added owner of the shared wallet.

7) We can also check the current wallet balance by executing the *'wallet_balance'* function in the backend of Remix IDE.

8) If a minor account makes a transaction of amount greater than spending limit, the primary account receives an alert to grant or decline permission.

TABLE 9.1

Summary of Improvements Required in Online Payment Systems Using Blockchain Technology

S.No.	Features of Digital Payment Systems	Existing Features of System	Proposed Features	System Improvement Expected
I.	Development of distributed ledger to create and store blockchain	Remix ide (deployed on ethereum network)	Netbeans ide	Increased system flexibility
II.	Currency	Ether	Indian rupee	Prevents need to buy separate currency
III.	User application security	Password	Email-based, one-time password	Improved resistance to cyber attacks
IV.	Programming language used	Solidity	Java	Java is comparatively more robust, secure, and universally supported

While this proposed system does a commendable job of using the Ethereum ecosystem, there is still the need to ease Indian economy trusting and accepting cryptocurrencies as a norm. While research is ongoing on such topics, it is important to keep in mind that not every layman possesses the knowledge or the resources to carry out payments by making use of cryptocurrencies. Summary of Improvements Required in Online Payment Systems Using Blockchain Technology is given in Table 9.1.

9.3 Digital Wallets Using Blockchain Technology

One way to overcome the problems associated with existing online payment systems is the use of Blockchain technology to create a decentralized system that uses distributed databases. Such systems have been previously conceptualized, which suggest an architecture to seamlessly integrate e-wallets of different banks and participating institutions using blockchains that shall act as a foundation of Digital Ledger Technology (DLT) for the financial sector in India. A swarm-based peer-to-peer network is designed for the proposed e-wallet system. The proposed solution shall minimize the load on the Core Banking Solution of the banks, thus reducing the load on the servers at the data centers.[9] While such systems provide a better level of protection against cyber-crimes, there is still some scope for levelling up the security of transactions, especially at the user's end. There is scope for improvement.

A Blockchain is an electronic ledger of transactions. It is a distributed database with no central server, and it offers transparency and trust without the need for a governing agency. Blockchains are decentralized by design. This means there's no one person or organization that can control it, and that changes can only be approved by consensus. Blockchains make securing transactions convenient for users. They eliminate the need for trusted central authorities and allow users to audit their transactions.

A lot of Indian contenders have tested the usage of Blockchain in the areas of trade finance, cross-border payments, bill discounting, supply chain financing, and loyalty and digital identity areas. Some of the Indian banks, business conglomerates, and one stock exchange are among the pioneers of exploring Blockchain in India.[13]

Though all these early adopters wanted to experiment with Blockchain to identify a futuristic solution, the road that led to these experiments was full of challenges. The major reasons for this were lack of awareness, evolving nature of Blockchain platforms, and application integration challenges.

9.4 Survey and Trend Analysis

From survey and analysis, we observe in Figure 9.3 that the most prominently used mobile payment apps are Paytm (85.9%), Google Pay (68.1%), BHIM UPI (42.3%), and PhonePe (41.7%), while other apps being serviced include Freecharge, PayPal, Mobikwik, etc. [12]

The Reserve Bank conducted a pilot survey on retail payment habits of individuals in six cities between December 2018 and January 2019, with a focus on the awareness and usage of digital payments. The survey results indicated a widespread awareness of digital payments among respondents, with a point in favor of digital payment being its convenience. The awareness was similar across men and women (See Figures 9.3–9.8). The awareness was positively associated with ownership of bank accounts, levels of literacy, and income of the users. However, there were concerns about a low level of awareness among respondents of the basic safety norms to be followed for digital payments (See Figures 9.3–9.8).[13]

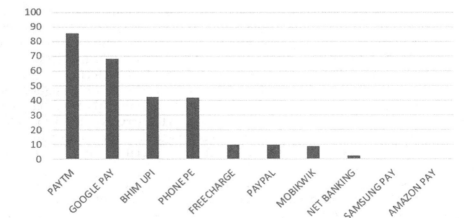

FIGURE 9.3
Percentage of users of various digital payment applications.

OCCUPATION-WISE AWARENESS OF DIGITAL PAYMENTS

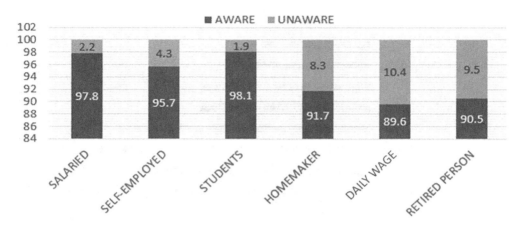

FIGURE 9.4
Occupation-wise awareness of digital payment methods (in percentage) [13].

ANNUAL INCOME-WISE AWARENESS OF DIGITAL PAYMENTS

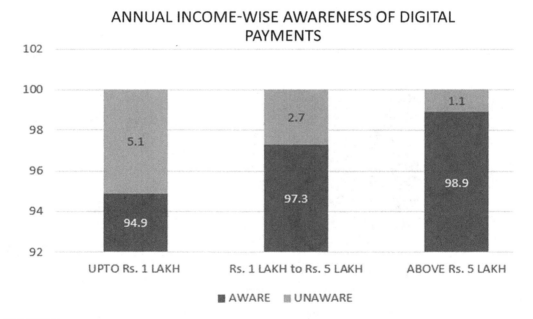

FIGURE 9.5
Annual income-wise awareness of digital payment methods (in percentage) [13].

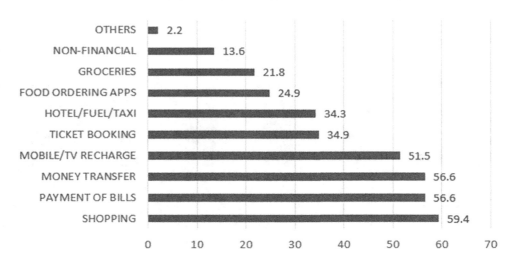

FIGURE 9.6
CHART 13: Purpose of digital transactions (in percentage) [13].

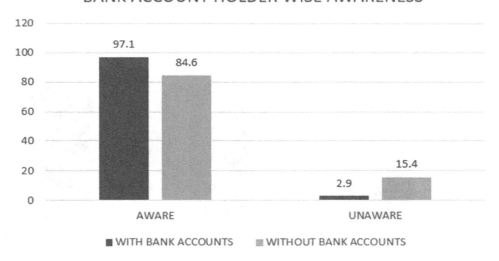

FIGURE 9.7
CHART 14: Bank account holder-wise awareness of digital payment methods (in percentage) [13].

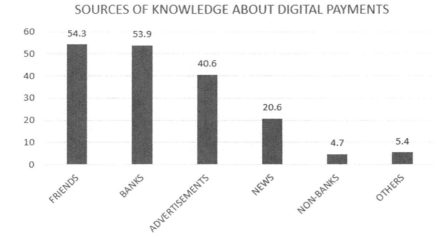

FIGURE 9.8
CHART 15: Sources of knowledge of digital payment methods (in percentage) [10].

9.5 Proposed System

In this study, we have developed a novel decentralized application framework that implements a new form of security for digital wallets that implements enhanced security using distributed ledger architecture. Following is the proposed system architecture:

The system in Figure 9.9 is a combination of two separate entities, i.e., an Android application on the user's end to initiate the transactions. The users added to a bank's database are managed by the trusted authority using a web interface, created using JSP servlets. Each time a new user (customer) creates an account in a bank, her data is stored in an encrypted database. The data is encrypted using the Advanced Encryption Standard (AES). When the user successfully initiates a transaction, the details of the transaction are stored securely in the form of an encrypted block. Each block is 'connected' to the previous block by creating a chain of sorts by using hash values. These hash values are generated each time using the details of the current transaction and the hash value of the previous block.

The Secure Hash Algorithm (SHA-256) is used to generate unique hash values for each block. As shown in the diagram, the important components of the diagram are an AES encryption block, an AES decryption block, a Transaction Block, Blockchain, and databases. So, whenever a user registers to a system with the information, it will first be encrypted and then stored to the DB1 and DB2 simultaneously, whenever a user wants to log the information from the database, it will first be decrypted, i.e. regained into original format and feed for the login. When bank logs in, the bank can add a user, can add money to a user account, which will be also stored simultaneously in both the databases. Whenever a user logs into the system, they can add a beneficiary and transfer the amount or make a transaction, after which a block will be generated and added to the Blockchain.

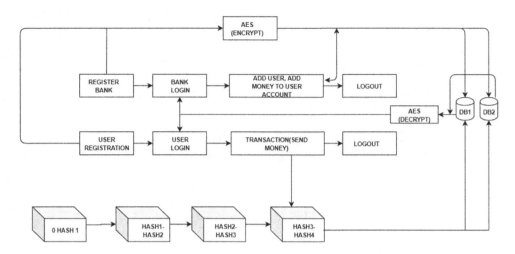

FIGURE 9.9
Proposed system architecture.

Whenever a transaction takes place in the system, a record of that transaction is kept in the form of a hash value in the block. Each subsequent block will be attached to the previous block and in this way a series of visible blocks will occur. The current block hash value is determined using current block data and the previous block hash. This way, if any block is invalid, then all hash blocks should be changed.

Many such copies are stored on separate servers, which will ensure data security and confidentiality and will provide immunity to the users' data against cyberattacks, such as a distributed denial of service.

Whenever a transaction takes place in the system, a record of that transaction is kept in the form of a hash value in the block. Each subsequent block will be attached to the previous block, and in this way a series of visible blocks will occur. The current block hash value is determined using current block data and the previous block hash. This way if any block is low, then all hash blocks should be changed. Many such copies are stored on separate servers, which will ensure data security and confidentiality. Since this system uses distributed trust, it will maintain the visibility of the transaction.

9.6 Algorithms

1. Advanced Encryption Standard (AES):

The encryption process uses a set of especially derived keys called round keys. These are applied, along with other operations, to an array of data that holds exactly one block of data, the data to be encrypted. This array we call the state array.

Following are the AES steps of encryption for a 128-bit block:

1. Derive the set of round keys from the cipher key.
2. Initialize the state array with the block data (plaintext).
3. Add the initial round key to the starting state array.
4. Perform nine rounds of state manipulation.
5. Perform the tenth and final round of state manipulation.
6. Copy the final state array out as the encrypted data (ciphertext) (see Figure 9.10).

The reason that the rounds have been listed as 'nine followed by a final tenth round' is because the tenth round involves a slightly different manipulation from the others. The block to be encrypted is just a sequence of 128 bits. AES works with byte quantities so we first convert the 128 bits into 16 bytes. We say 'convert', but, in reality, it is almost certainly stored this way already. Operations in RSN/AES are performed on a two-dimensional byte array of four rows and four columns. At the start of the encryption, the 16 bytes of data, numbered from D0 to D15, are loaded into the array.

Each round of the encryption process requires a series of steps to alter the state array. These steps involve four types of operations called Sub Bytes and Shift Rows.

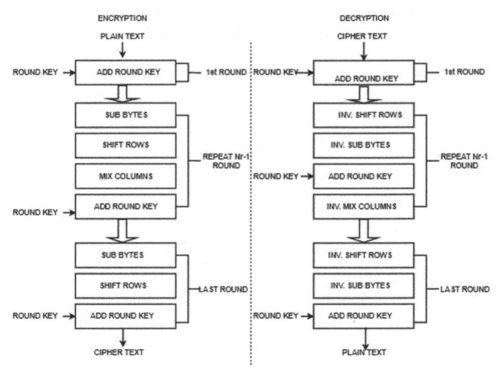

FIGURE 9.10
Advanced encryption standard (AES).

2. Secure Hash Algorithm 256 (SHA 256)

SHA-256 (secure hash algorithm FIPS 182–2) was created as a cryptographic hash function with a digest length of 256 bits. It's a keyless hash function; i.e., an MDC (Manipulation Detection Code). A message is processed by blocks of 512 = 16 × 32 bits, each block requiring 64 rounds.

A cryptographic hash (sometimes called 'digest') is a sort of 'signature' for a text or data file. SHA-256 generates an almost unique 256-bit (32-byte) signature for a text. A hash isn't 'encryption'—it cannot be decrypted back to the original text (it's a 'one-way' cryptographic function, a fixed size for any size of source text). This makes it suitable to match 'hashed' versions of texts, instead decrypting the text to get the initial version of the text (see Figure 9.11).

The methodical procedure adopted for the development of a fully functional decentralized app for digital wallet services using Blockchain is defined as follows:

1. Problem statement designed.

    All necessary logic requirements, edge cases, and consistency conditions were defined.

2. Development of the distributed database and securing it on MySQL server and NetBeans IDE.

    Two structured databases with identical attributes are created using MySQL. They are updated simultaneously after each valid transaction.

3. Implementation of the Blockchain technology using a web application.

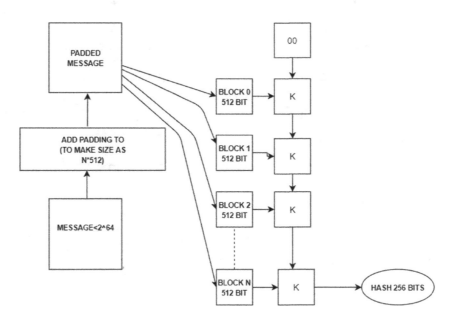

FIGURE 9.11
Secure hash algorithm (basic working).

The generic logic constituted of several functions such as 'processTransaction', 'addBlock', and 'getBalance' to make transactions, encrypting a transaction before storing it in a MySQL database and adding blocks to the Blockchain, to then check the balance from the user's wallet, etc. These were developed using Java language on NetBeans IDE and deployed using the ApacheTomcat Server. Constraints like available balance, validity of account, transaction amount, etc. were also integrated.

4. Creating an Android application for users

An Android application is developed for users to login to and send and receive money. It has features that allow users to check their account balance and transaction history.

Once the web application was deployed on the web, to initiate and support the transactions, the application was made capable of supporting trial transactions; an Admin account was created to add dummy users with available balances to the system and carry out transactions.

The various cases and outcomes of the activity of the developed blockchain application are discussed in the following section.

Before users can actually start using the Android app to send money, they have to be added to the cashless payment ecosystem for them to carry out transactions. This is done by the Admin of the system, using the web application.

1. Logging into the web application:

   After logging in as the Admin, new users and banks can be added to the system. Once customers have been added to the database, they are sent their login credentials for the Android application to the email address they used to register.

2. Users can log into the Android application as an Admin or customer. On logging in as an Admin, they can add new users to the ecosystem. A user needs to enter credentials, i.e. email address, password, and the IP address of the network, to carry out transactions. At each step, users' credentials are verified with the encrypted database, allowing for the avoidance of any malicious transactions.

3. Once the user has successfully logged in, the home screen allows a user to select various functions such as viewing balance, viewing transaction history, starting a new transaction, and viewing existing beneficiaries.

4. To add a new beneficiary, the Admin adds a new beneficiary by entering a username, email address, and beneficiary address.

   Step 1: Add the account type, i.e. savings or current.

   Step 2: Add the beneficiary's account number.

   Step 3: Add IFSC of bank account.

   Step 4: Add personal details of the beneficiary, such as name, email address, and residential address.

5. Viewing transaction history

   User can check the valid transactions that have already been completed by the user. Any account can access the transaction history of its account by simply clicking on transaction.

6. Transfer money

   After adding a new beneficiary, the user can send money to any of the added beneficiaries.

   Step 1: Select beneficiary from the existing beneficiaries list.

   Step 2: Enter amount to be transferred. Before typing in the amount to be sent, a user can easily see the current available balance displayed on the screen.

   Step 3: Click on the 'TRANSFER MONEY' button to send money.

   If the available balance amount is sufficient, the transaction is initiated.

   This is a crucial step because, after a transaction is initiated, control is transferred to the web app, where the Blockchain is validated and a new block is added, representing the latest transaction.

   This is done by assigning the block a new hash value, which is calculated using the hash of the previous block and the transaction details of the current block. Each new block points to its preceding block, keeping in mind the architecture of a Blockchain system.

7. Checking wallet balance

   The app allows a user to check the latest account balance before initiating new transactions, and afterward the successful transfer of money to a beneficiary.

9.7 Assumptions and Dependencies

This document will provide a general description of the project, including user requirements, product perspective, and overview of requirements and general constraints. In addition, it will also provide the specific requirements and functionality needed for this project such as interface, functional requirements, and performance requirements.

9.8 External Interface Requirements

9.8.1 User Interfaces

The user interface or UI for the web application should be compatible with any standard browser such as IE, Mozilla, or Google Chrome. Using this UI, the user can have access to the system. The proposed system will make use of Google Chrome and the Apache Tomcat server. The web application is developed on NetBeans version 8.2. For the customers, the Android application should be compatible with Android 8 and subsequent releases and is developed on Android Studio 4.1.3.

9.8.2 Hardware Interfaces

A hardware interface is needed to run the software. Java (JDK) and NetBeans compatible hardware is required, which is the minimal requirement.

9.8.3 Software Interfaces

Java has been used as the front-end programming tool on NetBeans 8.2. MySQL has been used as back-end application tool for constructing and storing data in a distributed database. The latest version of Java higher than 7.0 can be used.

9.8.4 Non-Functional Requirements

9.8.4.1 Performance Requirements

1. System can work optimally or faster on 8 GB or more of RAM.
2. The system is targeted to be available all time. Once there is a fatal error or system down, the system will provide understandable feedback to the user.

9.8.4.2 Software Quality Attributes

1. Usability: This relates to how easily people can use the app or website. A measure of usability could be the time it takes for end users to become familiar with the app or website functions without training or help.
2. Performance: This is essentially how fast the app or website works. A performance requirement for the app or website could be to start in less than 20 seconds.
3. Security: Say that the app or website saves all the previous code and lets you reuse a saved code.

9.9 System Requirements

1. Database Requirements
   MySQL Database

MySQL is on open-source database, which is mainly a RDBMS, i.e. a relational database management system. As a database server, the primary function of this software is to store and retrieve data as requested by others from end software applications like Java, which may or may not run either on the same computer or on different computer. This can be across the network either in internet or intranet.

2. Software Requirements
   2.1 Operating System: Microsoft Windows 7 and above.
   2.2 Programming Language: Java.
   2.3 IDE: NetBeans, Android Studio.
3. Hardware Requirements
   3.1 Processor: Intel Core I3 or Higher.
   3.2 RAM: 4 GB or Higher.
   3.3 Hard Disk: 100 GB (min.).

9.10 Project Scope

1. To develop a prototype model for cashless India using MySQL database for the distributed database and NetBeans IDE 8.2 and Android Studio 4.2.1 to develop the Android application. This model will be run at local host using Apache Tomcat server.
2. Blockchain features such as decentralization, cryptography, and hash codes will be implemented using Java language.
3. Java has been selected for implementation instead of other object-oriented languages due to its robustness, security, and wide acceptance.

9.11 Data Flow Diagrams

A data flow diagram (DFD) is a graphical representation of the 'flow' of data through an information system, modeling its process aspects.

1. In this project, the cashless system comprises of two secure, remote databases and a website for the trust authority to maintain it. The customer interacts with the system through an android application.
2. In order to be able to use the BCT transaction system, the user first gets registered in the database by providing details such as an email address, name, and account balance to the trust authority.
3. Once registered, in order to login, the customer provides login details. The cashless system verifies these credentials from the data stored in the online database.
4. After successfully logging in, the application gives the user access to their account information such as viewing past transactions and beneficiaries. The user can also add new beneficiaries after logging in.
5. To carry out a transaction, i.e. send money, the user selects a beneficiary and adds the amount to be sent.
6. Again, the application takes data from the user's database and verifies whether the required amount is present to carry out the transaction. Data Flow diagram of Casless India project level 0 and level 1 are given in Figures 9.12 and 9.13.

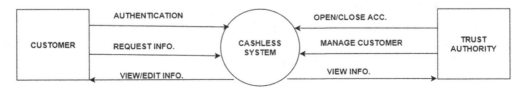

FIGURE 9.12
Data flow diagram: Level 0.

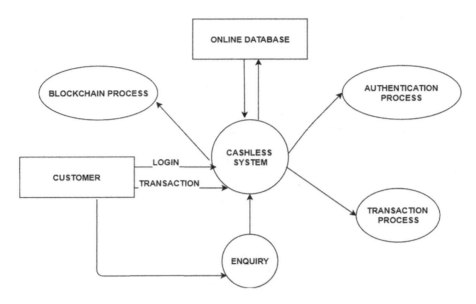

FIGURE 9.13
Data flow diagram: Level 1.

7. If funds are available, the transaction is carried out and the user's balance is updated in the database. The details are then added to the Blockchain in the form of a new block. Data is given by the BCT system to the blockchain process.

9.12 Uml Diagrams

9.12.1 Use Case Diagram

Dynamic behavior is most important aspect to capture the model of any system.

A Use Case Diagram represents the interaction of the users with a system on a very basic level. In this system, the following main scenarios are represented in the use case diagram:

USE CASE ID	01
USE CASE NAME	LOGIN
USE CASE DESCRIPTION	After successfully opening an account in the bank, user is given unique login credentials. To log into the system, they must enter these credentials correctly, after which they're allowed to interact with the system. Extends: If incorrect details are entered, the session is rendered INVALID.
ACTORS	User
PRE-CONDITIONS	User must have a valid account in the system.
NON-FUNCTIONAL REQUIREMENTS	User must have and enter correct credentials.

USE CASE ID	02
USE CASE NAME	Add Beneficiary
USE CASE DESCRIPTION	User can add a new beneficiary to whom money is to be sent. For this, the user needs to login first and add beneficiary details, i.e. their account number and name.
ACTORS	User
PRE-CONDITIONS	User must be logged into the system.
NON-FUNCTIONAL REQUIREMENTS	Beneficiary details must be correct.
USE CASE ID	03
USE CASE NAME	TRANSACTION
USE CASE DESCRIPTION	User 'A' can send money to user 'B'. This includes: I) Checking if A has sufficient funds.
	If funds are present, A sends money to B and extended use cases are: I) Adding a new block of transaction to Blockchain (if transaction is successful).
	ii) Updating sender's account balance (if transaction is successful).
ACTORS	User, Trust Authority.
PRE-CONDITIONS	Sender and receiver must have correct credentials and be logged in.
NON-FUNCTIONAL REQUIREMENTS	Sender must have sufficient funds.

USE CASE ID	04
USE CASE NAME	Update account
USE CASE DESCRIPTION	After a user makes a successful transaction, the bank updates their account balance by adding or subtracting the appropriate amount that was received or sent, using the correct credentials of the user who has received/sent the amount.
ACTORS	Trust Authority
PRE-CONDITIONS	Transaction must be successful.
NON-FUNCTIONAL REQUIREMENTS	Sender and receiver must have correct credentials.

9.12.2 Activity Diagram

An activity diagram is a flowchart that represents the flow from one activity to another.

The system has a flow as follows:

i) Admin logs in, adds bank.

ii) Bank logs in, adds new user.

iii) User logs in and adds money (cash) to his account.

iv) Bank converts user's money to digital format.

v) User adds beneficiary or views existing beneficiaries.

vi) After selecting a beneficiary, user initiates a transaction.

vii) New block representing the latest (valid) transaction is created.

viii) Transaction is processed and the user's balance amount is updated.

ix) User logs out. Use case diagram of system can be seen in Figure 9.14 and Figure 9.15.

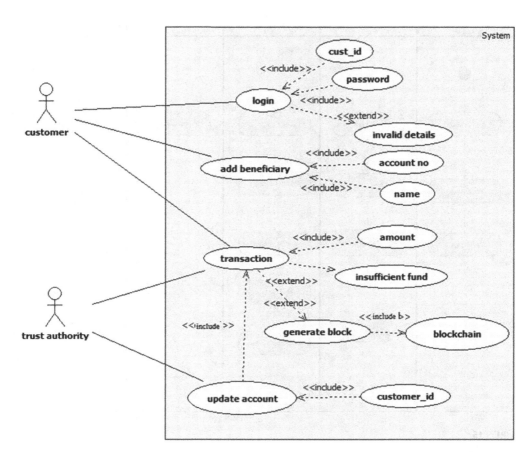

FIGURE 9.14
Use case diagram.

9.12.3 Sequence Diagram

Sequence diagrams can be used to provide a graphical representation of object interactions or object coordination over time.

In the following diagram (See Figure 9.16), the sequence of actions and object interactions are shown:

i) update_account_details (): The trust authority creates a new account for a user and adds balance. Object is passed to Customer.

ii) view_transactions (): The trust authority views all transactions made by users from the Transaction entity.

iii) login(): The customer logs into the system. Object stays with Customer.

iv) add_beneficiary (): Customer adds new beneficiary.

v) update_account_details (): Balance is updated after money is sent/received.

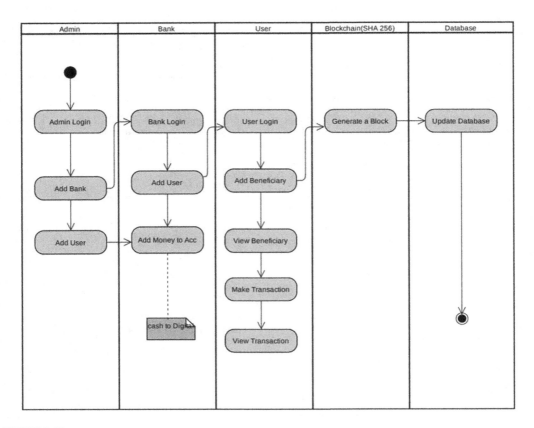

FIGURE 9.15
Activity diagram.

vi) Send/receive amount (): The customer may send or receive money and gives the information such as their and receiver's/sender's details, amount to be sent, and date and time of transaction.

vii) validate_transaction (): Transaction entity checks information received and validates the transaction.

viii) update_status (): If the transaction is invalid due to wrong credentials or insufficient balance, the status is updated as 'INVALID'.

    1. generate_block (): If the transaction is successful, a new block to represent that transaction is created, and the information is sent to the Blockchain.

    2. Validate_block (): The newly added block is validated.

    3. Add_block_to_blockchain (): The new block, if valid, is added to the Blockchain.

    4. Update_status (): The transaction status is updated and is conveyed to Transaction.

        Update_transaction_status (): Once the new block is successfully added to the Blockchain, the customer can now see its status as 'VALID'.

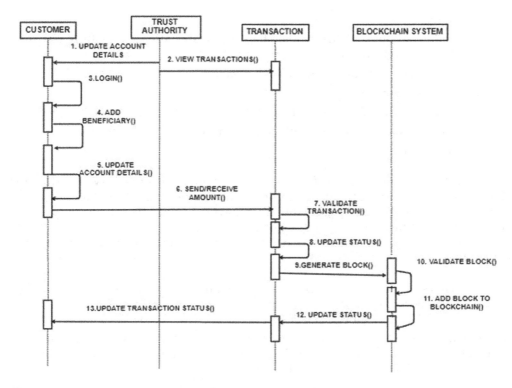

FIGURE 9.16
Sequence diagram.

9.12.4 Collaboration Diagram

These diagrams can be used to portray the dynamic behavior of a particular use case and define the role of each object (See Figure 9.17).

In this system, the entities are identified as:

1. Customer:
    i) Log into the system
    ii) Add beneficiary: Add new beneficiary to whom money is to be sent.
    iii) Update account details: Add new email address, user name, change password.
    iv) Send/receive amount: Send money to one of the beneficiaries or receive money.
2. Trust Authority:
    i) Validate_transaction: Verify if new transaction particulars such as sender/ user details are correct and check if money has been sent.
    ii) Update status: Update status of transaction as valid or invalid.
    iii) Generate block: Generate new block for the transaction if it is valid.

3. Transaction:

    i) Update account details: Update balance of user after successfully transferring/receiving money.

    ii) View account details: View user's account details.

4. Blockchain system:

    i) Validate block: Validate the Blockchain every time a new block is added.

    ii) Add block to Blockchain: If block is valid, add it to the Blockchain.

5. Entity Relationship Diagram:

An entity relationship diagram (ERD) shows the relationships of entity sets stored in a database. An entity in this context is an object, a component of data. An entity set is a collection of similar entities. These entities can have attributes that define its properties. By defining the entities, their attributes, and showing the relationships between them, an ERD illustrates the logical structure of databases. In the proposed system, there are four main entities:

    i) User: This stores the users' details such as email address, name, address, account balance, and user ID. User ID is the primary key. This entity has a 1:1 relation to the Virtual Account entity, i.e. one user has one virtual account.

    ii) Virtual account: Each user has a virtual account that has a foreign key User ID to identify the User entity in the database. Other information such as transaction ID and available balance is stored in this table.

    iii) Bank: This is the trust authority. It can access user information in the Virtual Account entity and has information such as name of the bank, branch where user holds account, name of manager, and User ID as primary attribute.

    iv) Transaction: This entity holds the information of all transactions that have been carried out. The primary key here is the User ID, and other attributes are the amount transferred, date of transaction, receiver's email address, sender's email address, and name of the manager (See Figure 9.18).

6. Class Diagram

1. Customer: The data members of this class are: customer ID (cust_id), password, account number, balance amount, beneficiary details, mobile number, and email address. The methods included are:

    i) add_beneficiary ()—to add new beneficiaries to transactions.

    ii) view_beneficiary ()—to view existing beneficiaries.

    iii) transaction ()—to make a new transaction.

    iv) view_transaction ()—to view old transactions.

    v) update_account_details ()—to update balance after successful transaction. Interacts with the class Transaction through this function.

2. Transaction: The data members of this class are: Transaction ID (trans_id), amount, Sender ID, Receiver ID, date of transaction, and status of transaction. The methods include:

    i) fetch_account_details ()—to verify user and check for sufficient balance for transactions.

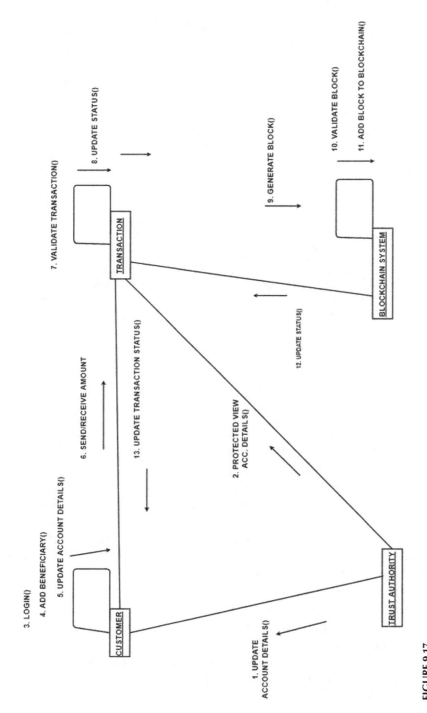

FIGURE 9.17
Collaboration diagram.

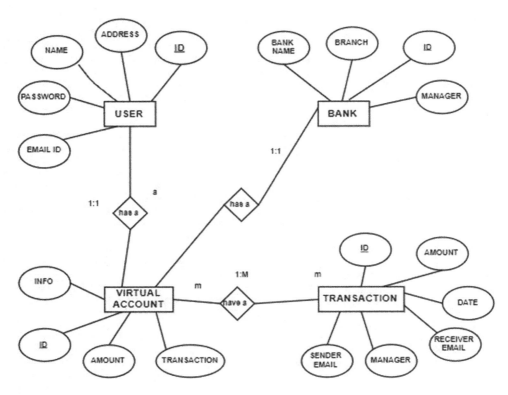

FIGURE 9.18
Entity relationship diagram (ERD).

    ii) update_account_balance ()—to update user's account balance if the transaction is successful, i.e. if money is sent or received.

    iii) change_status ()—to update transaction status: either successful or failed.

    iv) generate_block ()—to add block representing a (successful) transaction to the blockchain.

3. Block: The data members of this class are: Block ID (block_id), data (amount sent in transaction), hash of current block, hash of previous block (prev_hash), and date and time of transaction (timestamp), The methods include:

    i) generate_hash ()—to generate a new hash value for current transaction.

    ii) validate_block ()—to validate the Blockchain.

    iii) add_block_to_chain ()—to add block representing a (successful) transaction to the Blockchain.

4. Trust_Authority: The data members of this class are: Customer ID (cust_id), amount sent in transaction (amount), date of transaction (date), and account number (account_no). The methods include:

    i) view_account_details ()—to view user's account details.

    ii) view_transaction_details ()—to view transaction details.

iii) update_account_details ()—to update balance after successful transaction. Interacts with the class Transaction through this function

9.13 Result

As a result, a digital wallet system has been created to support the online transfer of money using a local area network.

The system makes use of the existing banking architecture for the convenience of users. Each user must have an existing bank account. The money in customers' account details is encrypted using Advanced Encryption Standard (AES). An Admin then logs into the web application and adds the desired banks where the customer has their account.

Once user is registered in the system, they receive their login credentials to their registered email address. The user can now log into the Android application using these credentials and perform the transactions. This transfer of money takes place over a Local Area Network (LAN). Each transaction is stored in form of a 'block'. One block is constituted of the transaction information such as sender's and receiver's email address, amount, and time of transaction using the Secure Hash Algorithm 256 (SHA 256).

These transactions are stored in form of a Blockchain. Each time a new transaction takes place, it is validated along with the entire Blockchain. This protects the payment ecosystem from potential threats such as ransomware attacks, social engineering attacks, or a distributed denial of service (DDoS).

1. Logging into the web application:

   After logging in as Admin, new users and banks can be added to the system. Once customers have been added to the database, they are sent their login credentials for the Android application on the email address with which they have been registered.

2. Users can log into the Android application as an Admin or customer. On logging in as an Admin, they can add new users to the ecosystem. A user needs to enter credentials, i.e. email address, password, and the IP address of the network to carry out the transactions. At each step, users' credentials are verified with the encrypted database and this step allows for the avoidance of any malicious transactions.

3. Once the user has successfully logged in, the home screen allows a user to select various functions such as viewing balance, viewing transaction history, starting a new transaction, and viewing existing beneficiaries.

4. To add a new beneficiary, Admin adds a new beneficiary by entering a user name, email address, and beneficiary address.

   Step 1: Add the account type, i.e., savings or current.

   Step 2: Add the beneficiary's account number.

   Step 3: Add IFSC of bank account.

   Step 4: Add personal details of the beneficiary, such as name, email address, and residential address. A Detailed class diagram is given in Figure 9.19.

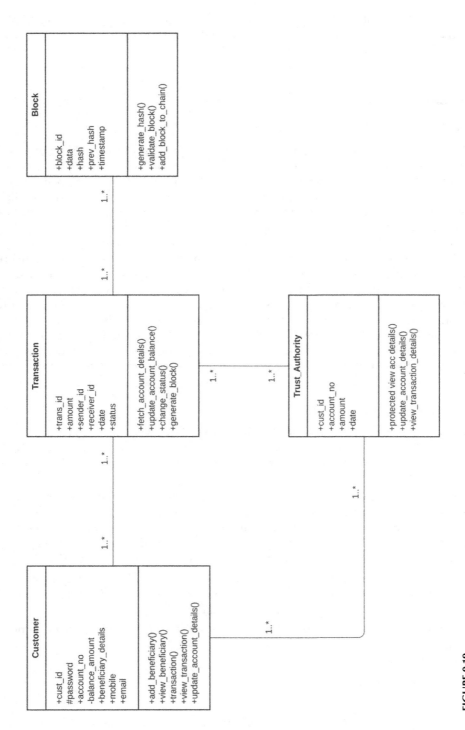

FIGURE 9.19
Class diagram.

5. Viewing transaction history

User can check the valid transactions that have already been completed by the user. Any account can access the transaction history of its account by simply clicking on transaction.

6. Transfer money

After adding new beneficiary, user can send money to any of the added beneficiaries.

Step 1: Select beneficiary from the existing beneficiaries list.

Step 2: Enter amount to be transferred. Before typing in the amount to be sent, a user can easily see the current available balance displayed on the screen.

Step 3: Click on the 'TRANSFER MONEY' button to send money.

If the available balance amount is sufficient, the transaction is initiated.

This is a crucial step, because after a transaction is initiated, control is transferred to the web app, where the blockchain is validated and a new block is added to the Blockchain, representing the latest transaction.

This is done by assigning the block a new hash value, which is calculated using the hash of the previous block and the transaction details of the current block. Each new block points to its preceding block, keeping in mind the architecture of a Blockchain system.

7. Checking wallet balance

The app allows a user to check the latest account balance before initiating new transactions, and after the successful transfer of money to a beneficiary.

9.14 Conclusion

Indeed, the road towards complete digitization is very long. The Indian government is undertaking stern measures to promote digital payment services, for instance, the Data Protection Bill 2019. A recent initiative as of 2019 is FASTag, a digital service that mandates tolls to be paid digitally. However, while pacing up with everyday advancements, one often neglects parallel factors that slow India's digital growth by a significant rate. The fundamental objective of this study was to determine possible, yet inexplicable factors slowing down complete digitization and to discover feasible solutions that can generate improvements in a potential cashless ecosystem. Apart from noncryptic facts, like poor network and connectivity, and ineffective security and support, we find that a significant population of minors (users below 18 years of age) transact digitally, although they may not be legally allowed to do so. We see that KYC authentication is not yet mandatory at all digital platforms, and at platforms where it is mandatory, the procedure for KYC completion is not entirely digital. Also, additional fees for making wallet-to-bank transactions, partial acceptance of digital payments by merchants, unreliable processes, and the complex nature of navigation and transaction protocols, etc. cause a reduction in the digital customer base. As an outcome of these findings, an improvement scope has been discussed wherein two main advantageous suggestions have been made, including an encrypted, distributed ledger as opposed to a central database, and most importantly the consumer doesn't have to bother with the intricacies and details associated with using cryptocurrency. This proposed system allows a user to keep using online payment applications as they are used to, with the added advantage of allowing the transactions and database to be secured. With a concerned focus on securing millions of users' bank accounts and ease of making transactions online as regular digital users, we propose an online payment service based on Blockchain technology that implements usability, enhanced security, and a decentralized network of transacting nodes. Implicit consistency and effective security are maintained in the projected model.

9.15 Future Scope

Although the technology of Blockchain is relatively simple, effective, and highly secure, its implementation without the use of cryptocurrency is trickier. Blockchain technology will boost India's initiative to make the Indian financial system free of corruption and robust to cyber threats that are prevalent in today's day and age. Here, we recommend a capable model for advancements in the existing digital payment system. Nonetheless, a vast scope lies beyond this study: exploitation of confidential transaction information, applicability of short-term loans, improvements in the use of biometrics or reliable authentication, and necessary user-oriented policy changes essential for India's growing economy. In future, we will try to get sponsorship from the government after which we can use commercial servers and host with large amount of space where we can implement a Blockchain on a large scale, where the communication medium will be WAN (Wide Area Network), i.e. internet and communication between the servers will take place worldwide. To make the system more inclusive for people from all walks of life, options for using the system in native languages of the country may be included.

References

[1] Cashless-Society.org. *Cashless-Society.org*. Archived from the original, 14 December 2017, https://en.wikipedia.org/wiki/Cashless_society (accessed 27 January 2017).

[2] Sheffield, Hazel. "The UK is getting closer to becoming a completely cashless society." *The Independent*, 21 May 2015.

[3] Wikipedia Article, *Cashless Society*, https://en.wikipedia.org/wiki/Cashless_society.

[4] Dowd, K. "The war on cash is about much more than cash." *Economic Affairs*, vol. 39 (2019): 391–399, https://doi.org/10.1111/ecaf.12377.

[5] Tompor, Susan. "A cashless society? Some retailers turn noses up at currency." *USA Today*, 4 September 2016 (accessed 3 July 2020).

[6] 2016 U.S Consumer Payment Study, www.tsys.com/Assets/TSYS/downloads/rs_2016-us-consumer-payment-study.pdf.

[7] Neroy, Rounaq, "Are you assuming money in bank deposits as safe? Watch out!." *Personal FN*, www.personalfn.com/dwl/are-you-assumingmoney-in-bank-deposits-as-safe-watch-out.

[8] Albesher, Abdulaziz and Kareem Kamal A. Ghany. *Avoid Shortcomings of Cashless Transaction System using Blockchain*, 2019, https://ieeexplore.ieee.org/document/8930799, 978-1-7281-1232-9/19/$31.00c2019IEEE.

[9] Singh, Karan, Nikita Singh, Dharmender Singh Kushwaha. "An interoperable and secure e-wallet architecture based on digital ledger technology using blockchain." *International Conference on Computing, Power and Communication Technologies (GUCON)* (2018): 165–169, https://doi.org/10.1109/GUCON.2018.8674919.

[10] Deloitte-ASSOCHAM. *India-Blockchain Technology in India—Challenges and Opportunities*, https://www2.deloitte.com/content/dam/Deloitte/in/Documents/strategy/in-strategy-innovation-blockchain- technology-india-opportunities-challenges-noexp.pdf.

[11] Shee-Ihn, Kim and Seung-Hee Kim. *E-Commerce Payment Model Using Blockchain.* © Springer-Verlag GmbH Germany, part of Springer Nature, Cham, 2020 (received 6 March 2019, accepted 4 September 2020).

[12] Gupta, R., C. Kapoor and J. Yadav. "Acceptance towards digital payments and improvements in cashless payment ecosystem." *2020 International Conference for Emerging Technology (INCET)* (2020): 1–9, https://doi.org/10.1109/INCET49848.2020.9154024.

[13] RBI Retail Payment Habits in India—Evidence from a Pilot Survey, www.rbi.org.in/Scripts/BS_ViewBulletin.aspx?Id=20205.

10

Blockchain-Based Secure Evidence-Management Police Assistance System

Sonali Patil and Rohini Pise

CONTENTS

10.1 Introduction

Blockchain is the buzzword in today's technological world. Security is the prime objective of Blockchain. Along with security, many other aspects as immutability, confidentiality, distributed and decentralized nature makes Blockchain more popular. Blockchain technology has the scope in not only cryptocurrencies, but also in many applications such

DOI: 10.1201/9781003203933-13

as the education sector, Internet of Things, healthcare, agriculture, supply chain, digital identity, digital asset exchange, government services, crowdfunding, finance, intellectual property, entertainment and many more.

Before deciding to implement any Blockchain application for any use case, we have to first understand whether the traditional database is sufficient to handle the data and provide the security to that use case. If this is not the case, we have to provide more security to the application using Blockchain. When there is enormous data, and privacy and security are the concern, Blockchain can be used.

There are also certain challenges while implementing Blockchain such as initial cost, energy consumption, certain Blockchain security and privacy issues, and integration with legacy systems. So, to identify any use case, anyone should check the urge of security, feasibility, network availability, etc.

10.1.1 What is a Police Complaint?

The police complaint is an accusation made by a complainant or informant to the police department about an offense that has been committed. The details about the event, its place or situation are mentioned in the complaint so that the police department can take the necessary legal action to rectify the situation.

A criminal case begins from the filing of a First Information Report (FIR). Whenever any complainant lodges a complaint, the police department is bound to resolve it within a specific time. But sometimes many genuine complaints do not get resolved within time. The reasons like lack of alertness, vigilance of police officers, malpractice happening in the department or lack of transparency cause such delay.

10.1.2 FIR

Any type of crime is recorded with an FIR. It initiates the actions against criminals. If anyone reports a crime and wishes to initiate criminal proceedings by the police, the initial thing is to file an FIR. The FIR should contain details about facts to which the informant is a witness. It should not be based on vague or hearsay communication which the informant may have received.

Figure 10.1 shows the format of a police complaint and gives an idea of what is actually needed to log a complaint. The details about incidence, date and time, and contact details are included. This format is standard as it will not create confusion if the case is handed over to a different police department.

10.2 Related Work

A survey on Blockchain technology-related applications specifically to tracking the complaints and reports is performed.

The first application of Blockchain was Bitcoin, a cryptocurrency which was introduced by Satoshi Nakamoto [1]. The transactions were recorded in distributed ledger.

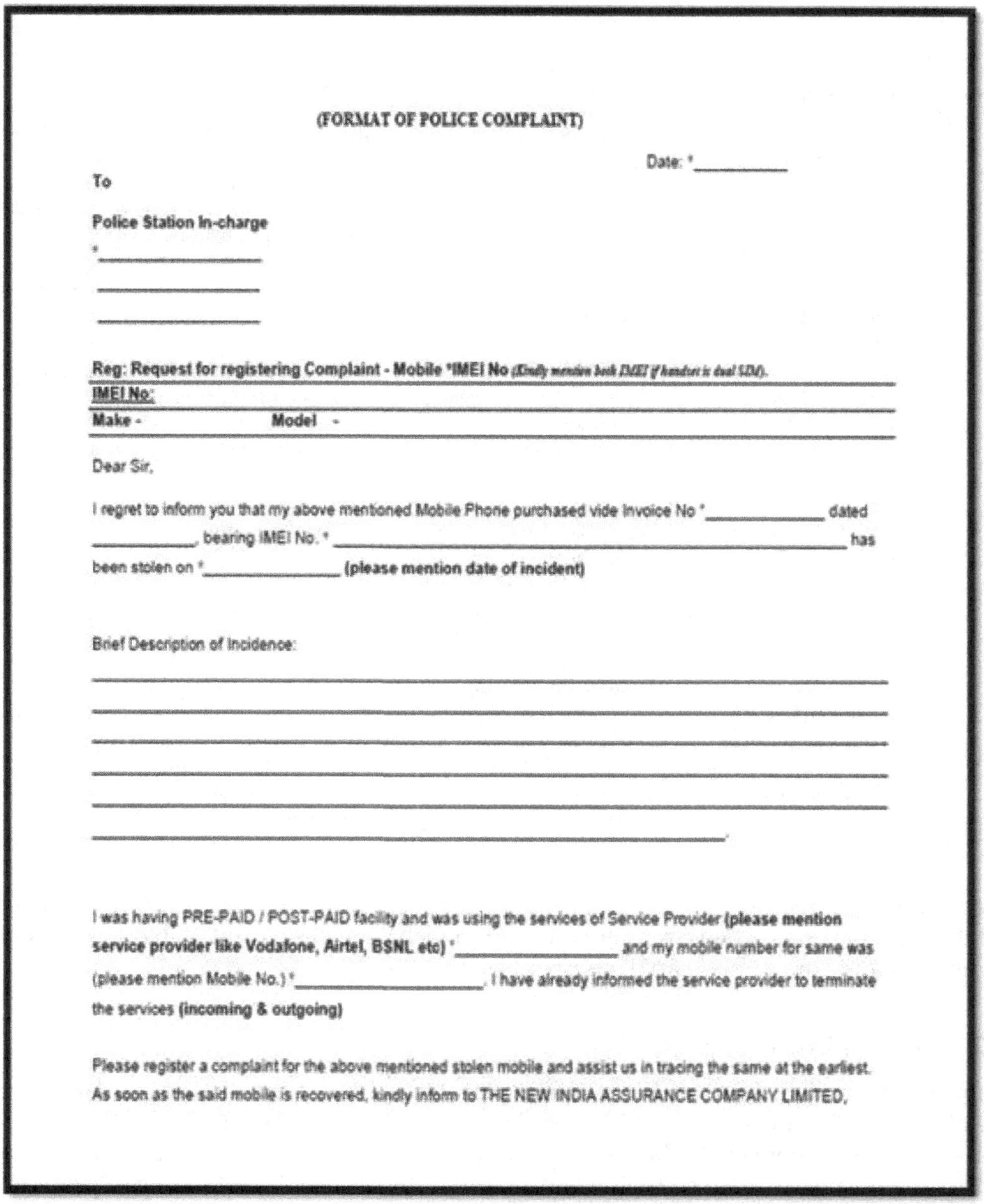

(FORMAT OF POLICE COMPLAINT)

Date: *__________

To

Police Station In-charge

*________________

____

____

Reg: Request for registering Complaint - Mobile *IMEI No *(Kindly mention both IMEI if handset is dual SIM).*

IMEI No:

Make - **Model -**

Dear Sir,

I regret to inform you that my above mentioned Mobile Phone purchased vide Invoice No *__________ dated __________, bearing IMEI No. *______________________________ has been stolen on *__________ **(please mention date of incident)**

Brief Description of Incidence:

____

____

____

____

____

________________________________.

I was having PRE-PAID / POST-PAID facility and was using the services of Service Provider **(please mention service provider like Vodafone, Airtel, BSNL etc)** *__________ and my mobile number for same was (please mention Mobile No.) *__________. I have already informed the service provider to terminate the services **(incoming & outgoing)**

Please register a complaint for the above mentioned stolen mobile and assist us in tracing the same at the earliest. As soon as the said mobile is recovered, kindly inform to THE NEW INDIA ASSURANCE COMPANY LIMITED,

FIGURE 10.1
Format of police complaint.

Blockchain Architecture [2], different consensus algorithm like Proof of Stake, Proof of Work, etc. are described along with their features, advantages and limitations.

Proof of Work is one of best and most suitable algorithms in complex problems and is explained in paper [3]. A systematic process and methods of dealing with FIR system is explained in paper [4].

TABLE 10.1

Comparative Analysis

Sr. No	Title of the Paper	Author	Contribution
1	Bitcoin: A peer-to-peer electronic cash system (White Paper)	Nakamoto, S. 2008	In this paper the need of online payments, the direct transactions between two parties without the intervention of financial institutes, can be performed. It includes a peer-to-peer version of electronic cash.
2	A Survey about Consensus Algorithms Used in Blockchain	Giang-Truong Nguyen, Kyungbaek Kim, 2018	Presents different consensus algorithms like Proof of Work and Proof-of-Stake
3	A systematic literature review of blockchain-based applications: Current status, classification and open issue.	Fran Casinoa, Thomas K. Dasaklis, Constantinos Patsakis 2018	Presents Blockchain-based applications across multiple domains and investigates the current state of Blockchain technology and its applications.
4	A Method to Secure FIR System using Blockchain	Antra Gupta, Deepa. V. Jose 2019	FIR system is discussed.
5	Forensic identification reporting using automatic speaker recognition systems.	J. Gonzalez-Rodriguez, J. Fierrez-Aguilar and J. Ortega-Garcia 003 IEEE International Conference, 2003	Describes how to deal with the issue of forensic reports.
6	A Survey of Blockchain from the Perspectives of Applications, Challenges and Opportunities	Ahmed Afif Monrat, Olov Schel´en, Karl Andersson2008	Explains the architecture and taxonomy of Blockchain. Presents a comparative study of the trade-offs of Blockchain. Different consensus mechanisms are explained.

Paper [5] explains the issue of forensic Scientists regarding reporting to the judge/jury and their conclusions when Speaker recognition techniques are used. Table 10.1 provides a summary and comparative analysis of studied papers.

10.2.1 Gaps in Existing System

A police department handles various complaints registered by victims, and the main thread between them is trust. Police complaints are handled with the help of online systems [6]. Online systems help the department register the complaint, store all evidence and records regarding any case so that, when required, the police department can produce it. But the very important part missing is the security of the system. Though data is available easily with these systems, there are high chances of a security breach and no assurance of data integrity. As per a survey, it is found that many cases are not resolved even after many years due to tampering of data or evidence. Because of these malpractices, the system is no more trustworthy for the complainer and, ultimately, society. To build the trust of a common man on the system, this system should be transparent, secure and reliable. The motivation behind proposing our new system or application is to have a transparent police complaint tracking system to track the complaint registered by the victim and so that he can see the progress or details of it anytime.

Another aspect of online data is in the prosecution of cybercrime as it is used to associate people with criminal activity. Therefore, maintaining the credibility, reliability and auditability of digital evidence is of extreme importance as it travels through various stages in cybercrime investigation. The potential of Blockchain technology to allow a detailed log of transactions [7] from its origination gives the forensic community tremendous hope. In the case of cybercrimes, digital evidence plays an important role in forensic analysis since there are higher chances of tampering with the evidence. So security of forensic reports and transparency regarding this aspect is the need of time. Lack of trust, integrity, improved provenance, availability and resilience scalability demands a more secure solution. In this chapter we suggest a Blockchain application that can be leveraged for tracking police complaints and providing security to forensic reports, particularly bringing transparency, security, faster processing, traceability and process integrity.

We have proposed a system to improve the security and transparency in tracking police complaints with the help of Blockchain technology. The main focus is to process the FIR securely by avoiding malpractices while processing the registered complaints. To achieve this, a system is proposed, which it will make the tracking and processing of a complaint easy. This system would also help to get ongoing details and alert investigating officers to solve the complaints within a stipulated time. The important features like transparency and integrity of Blockchain technology will be helpful in this application as the user can track the complaint at any time. Immutability is another feature which will make our system tamper-proof and safe. Smart contracts can be written to avoid the delay. Thus, all these features of Blockchain technology create a trustworthy system.

10.3 Proposed System

As there is need for a transparent, secure, traceable and trustworthy Blockchain application that can be leveraged for tracking police complaints and providing security to forensic reports, here in this section the proposed solution is explained.

10.3.1 How Blockchain Is Used in Police Complaints

Blockchain [8] is a transparent, distributed and decentralized ledger in which transactions are stored. Blockchain is chain of blocks created after the transactions are executed. These blocks are connected to each other with the hash values. Each block in a Blockchain has the data such as transaction ID, block number, Merkle root, nonce, hash of previous block, hash of current block and other fields [9]. Thus, hash value helps to make Blockchain immutable. Further it also provides security to forensic reports generated from a pathology lab and then forwarded to a police department. As discussed earlier, the transparency feature of Blockchain technology helps the user to track the complaint at any time. The data can be tamperproof as any change in data can be easily identified. Smart contracts are another feature provided by Blockchain. Smart contracts can be written to avoid delay in solving the case. Thus, the goal of transparency, security, reliability and immutability in the police department can be achieved.

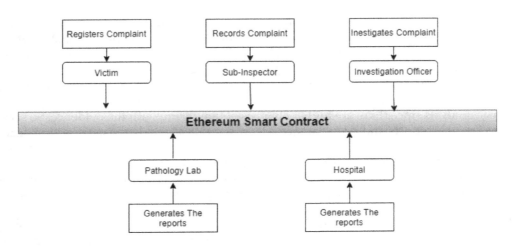

FIGURE 10.2
Schematic view of proposed system.

The objectives of this application would be:

- Alteration and tampering of data should be identified and avoided in case of police complaints.
- Avoid the problem of tampering with the forensic report.
- Achieving transparency in every process to resolve the complaint.
- Decentralizing the whole process to avoid corruption.

Figure 10.2 shows the five modules involved in the application.

10.3.2 Complainer/Victim

The victim registers a new complaint. Instead of the regular process of registering the complaint manually, a digital approach is implemented. Viewing the progress of a complaint will be easy for the victim.

10.3.3 Sub-Inspector

Whenever a new complainant is approaching to register a complaint, it is registered through a sub-inspector. A soon as a new complaint is registered, a new block is created in the Blockchain. After that, the same is communicated to the corresponding victim and inspector or investigating officer for further enquiries.

10.3.4 Investigating Officer

After a complaint is registered, it will be forwarded to an inspector or investigating officer. During the investigation process, when the officer is getting new information, he can add blocks to the chain about data related to the case.

10.3.5 Pathology Lab

The report of a crime or report of a victim is generated in the laboratory and confidentially forwarded to the hospital or doctor. In the proposed system, we upload a document into the Blockchain network, which is an immutable and distributed network. Blockchain is a highly secure network which can never be hacked or tampered with.

10.3.6 Hospital

The hospital receives the files from the pathology lab. The hospital verifies the document and sends to the police department for further investigation. This report or document cannot be altered or modified as the Blockchain generates hash code of this document, which is static; if the content of the document changes, then the hash code change. Then we can easily trace and track the document modification process. The hospital ledger contains its own file in its own node.

10.3.7 Technologies Used

- Solidity programming as a medium to write a smart contract
- Ethereum Virtual machine to deploy the smart contract on public Blockchain platform
- ReactJS and Material UI for creating user interaction for different modules
- IPFS for storing data, thereby ensuring security
- Web3.js to interact with local or remote Ethereum nodes
- Truffle as an environment to develop decentralized healthcare application
- Ganache for testing purposes
- Metamask Software

10.4 Architecture Diagram

1. All the data and details like victim details, user details and complaint details are stored in the distributed database.
2. Business logic consists of different algorithms like the hashing algorithm SHA-256, block mining algorithms, cryptographic algorithms, etc.
3. After login of inspector or sub-inspector, the details will get added to a database of users.
4. Whenever a new complaint gets added, a new block will be created that has its own hash values and other details like a timestamp.
5. At the same time, a new account of the victim will be created that will them to see what has been added or what is the progress of the complaint.
6. Whenever there is an update, the block will get added to the chain and the chain will grow. Architecture diagram of proposed system is given in Figure 10.3.

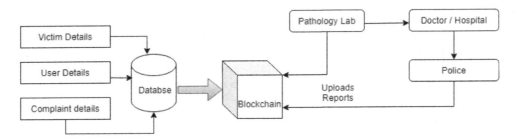

FIGURE 10.3
Architecture diagram for proposed system [9].

7. In the pathology lab, the report of the victim is generated and forwarded to a doctor for further action.

8. Hospital receives the files from the pathology lab. Hospital verifies the document and sends to the police department handling the police inquiry. If there is a change to the content of the document, then the hash code will change. Then we can easily trace and track the document modification process. Hospital ledger contains its own file in its own node.

9. Police department will get input from the doctor. Using Blockchain, we can provide ledger reports to the police department for investigation.

11. At the final stage, the report is generated and uploaded on a network that should be verified. The hash code of the generated report at the pathology lab and uploaded report on the network is checked. If both are the same in all nodes, the report is tamper-proof. If the reports are modified, then we can track and trace them using the Blockchain network.

12. No one will be able to make changes to the report because, in every block, its hash of the previous block and its current hash will get stored; the hash is computed with the help of all the details of the current blocks using SHA-256 algorithm.

10.4.1 Deployment Diagram

Figure 10.4 describes the process of deployment of the application. The transactions are stored in blocks of Blockchain. The smart contracts are executed on EVM [10]. An Ethereum distributed app is deployed on the web server; the user will access the DApp through a web browser.

10.5 Results and Discussions

The proposed system gives better performance while creating the blocks. The transaction time and the number of transactions executed per second also improved.

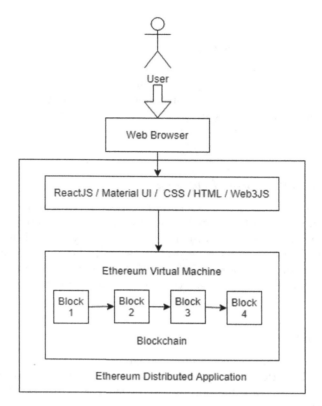

FIGURE 10.4
Deployment of proposed application.

10.5.1 Results

1. Latency: The transaction latency is the sum of the block inclusion latency and consensus latency [11]

   L (tx) = LB (tx) + LC (b), where LB (tx) is block inclusion latency,

   Moreover, LB (tx) is calculated as: LB (tx) = time (block (tx)) + T −time(tx)

2. Throughput: It is the number of transactions in unit time [11].

   Throughput (tps) = Total committed transactions/Total time for committed nodes.

3. CPU and memory utilization [11]: The time for which CPU and memory are busy performing the operations is calculated.

4. Gas: Number of transactions and size of blocks determine the consumption of Gas [12].

5. Computational Cost [12]: Cost involved in computation of transactions.

6. Security analysis [12]: As Blockchain comes with confidentiality, integrity and immutability, it provides the most security to this application.

10.5.2 Discussions

- *Transparency in Tracking Complaints*

In the system, transparency is achieved when a victim is able to view the FIR (uploaded by sub-inspector) and all the investigation reports uploaded by the inspector. When a victim logs into the system, he will have an option to view the investigation reports. The victim will be provided with a web page, where he would enter his username and password. If the username and password entered by the victim matches the one that is in database, then he would get option to view it.

- *Immutability for Prevention from Tampering*

In the system, we use the concepts of Blockchain, especially that of hashing. In this, whenever a sub-inspector or inspector upload a file, it will be stored in block, and whenever a new report is uploaded it is stored in the next block. Newly created blocks will have the hash of the previous block. Whoever tries to tamper with the uploaded content will cause the hash to change and it will not match the hashes of the further Blockchain. This check of hashes is done when a block is mined or created. For hashing, SHA-256 algorithm [13, 14] is used.

- *Decentralization in System*

As the system uses blockchain concepts for storage of a database, the database is not centralized. The system includes different nodes, and every node contains the complete database. Thus every node can track happenings in the system, building a kind of trust in the peers that use the system.

10.6 Conclusion and Future Scope

The proposed system is a transparent and light-weight Blockchain system. The security in tracking of a police complaint and generating forensic reports is achieved. The system is evaluated based on parameters as throughput, latency and storage. An immutable, transparent and decentralized system can be designed and implemented to improve the trust on a police department. As future enhancement, we suggest the security provided to the documents in the law of court.

References

1. Nakamoto, S. *Bitcoin: A Peer-to-Peer Electronic Cash System*, 2008, p. 9, www.Bitcoin.org.
2. Nguyen, Giang-Truong and Kyungbaek Kim. "A survey about consensus algorithms used in blockchain." *Journal of Information Processing Systems*, vol. 14, no. 1 (February 2018): 101–128, ISSN 1976-913X (Print), https://doi.org/10.3745/JIPS.01.0024.

3. Porat, Amitai, Avneesh Pratap, Parth Shah and Vinit Adkar. *Blockchain Consensus: An Analysis of Proof-of-Work and Its Applications*, 2017, www.scs.stanford.edu.

4. Gupta, Antra, Deepa V. Jose. *A Method to Secure FIR System Using Blockchain*, Blue Eyes Intelligence Engineering & Sciences Publication, 2019, https://www.semanticscholar.org/paper/A-Method-to-Secure-FIR-System-using-Blockchain-Gupta-Jose/12836d07a98cb536b238 37b1e14914a75e1c94ea.

5. Gonzalez-Rodriguez, J., J. Fierrez-Aguilar and J. Ortega-Garcia. "Forensic identification reporting using automatic speaker recognition systems." *IEEE International Conference on Acoustics, Speech, and Signal Processing*, vol. 2 (2003).

6. Giova, G. "Improving chain of custody in forensic investigation of electronic digital systems." *International Journal of Computer Science and Network Security*, vol. 11, no. 1 (2011): 1–9.

7. Saraf, Chinmay and Siddharth Sabadra. *Blockchain Platforms: A Compendium*. IEEE International Conference on Innovative Research and Development (ICIRD), 2018, https://ieeexplore.ieee.org/document/8376323.

8. Pourmajidi, William and Andriy Miranskyy. *Logchain: Blockchain-Assisted Log Storage*. IEEE 11th International Conference on Cloud Computing (CLOUD), 2018, https://ieeexplore.ieee.org/document/8457918

9. Hamid Lone, Auqib and Roohie NaazMir. "Forensic-chain: Ethereum blockchain based digital forensics chain of custody." *Scientific and Practical Cyber Security Journal (SPCSJ)*, vol. 1, no. 2 (2017).

10. Androulaki, Elli, Christian Cachin and Christopher Ferris. "Hyperledger fabric: A distributed operating system for permissioned blockchains." (April 2018), https://www.coinresear.ch/snapshots/Androulaki2018, arXiv:1801.10228v1.

11. Zohar, A. "Bitcoin: Underthehood." *Communications of the ACM*, vol. 58, no. 9 (2015): 104–113.

12. Casinoa, Fran, Thomas K. Dasaklis and Constantinos Patsakis. "A systematic literature review of blockchain—based applications: Current status, classification and open issue." *Telematics and Informatics*, vol. 36 (2018).

13. Monrat, Ahmed Afif, Olov Schel'en and Karl Andersson. "A survey of blockchain from the perspectives of applications, challenges and opportunities." *IEEE Access* (2019), https://doi.org/10.1109/ACCESS.2019.2936094.

14. Zheng, Zibin, Shaoan Xie, Hongning Dai, Xiangping Chen and Huaimin Wang. "An overview of blockchain technology: Architecture, consensus, and future trends." *IEEE International Congress on Big Data (BigData Congress)* (2017): 557–564.

11

Blockchain for Healthcare Systems

Shreeya Patil

CONTENTS

11.1 Introduction

Traditional information management systems are centralized, i.e. a single authority manages all data and transactions resulting in various interoperability, security, privacy, integrity, accessibility, and ease of use concerns. Centralized systems are lacking in terms of interoperability, accessibility, and availability and result in negative consequences such as loss and fragmentation of data and ransomware attacks, which have become urgent problems. [1] The most important benefit of blockchain that resolves these issues and has made it such a crucial technology in all sectors is that it is a purely distributed application, thus removing the need for any central authority and eliminating problems concerning a single point of failure. Beyond the dominance of blockchain in cryptocurrency, various key features of blockchain such as privacy, security, transparency, immutability, decentralization, data provenance, distributed ledger, anonymity, and smart contracts have broadened the scope of blockchain applications in other domains. Decentralized Applications (DApps) are a major application of decentralization using blockchain technology. [2] Blockchain is being implemented in several industries such as finance, insurance, supply chain management, copyright protection, etc.

One such revolutionary application of blockchain is in the healthcare industry. Blockchain solutions in healthcare are currently being explored to securely store health records, secure patient and healthcare provider identities, maintain a single source of truth, manage pharmaceutical supply chains, medical fraud detection, and data sharing among medical researchers. Using blockchain, sensitive and confidential patients' medical

DOI: 10.1201/9781003203933-14

health records can be protected. The integrity of historical medical records can be pre-served to accurately diagnose and treat patients using the property of immutability of blockchain. Access control and auditing of data can be effortlessly handled due to the application of blockchain in healthcare. [3, 4] Building a patient-centric healthcare system instead of the traditional centralized medical systems currently in use is important, and blockchain helps accomplish this.

The subsequent sections in this chapter are organized as follows. Firstly, the issues and challenges with traditional healthcare systems are identified. Next, the workflow of a blockchain-based healthcare system consisting of medical data, blockchain technology, healthcare applications, and stakeholders is explained. Furthermore, the architecture of a blockchain-based application which consists of the creation of medical records, its storage via databases, blockchain and cloud storage, and the retrieval of these records is presented. The following section explores the use cases of blockchain in healthcare such as EHR, supply chain management, remote patient monitoring, supply chain, insurance claims management, and health data analytics. Next, some challenges in the implementa-tion of this system such as scalability, navigating regulations, interoperability, transaction speeds, integration of blockchain with existing healthcare systems, the accuracy of health-care data and progress of cultural adoption of blockchain technology, and availability of blockchain developers and experts are discussed. Further, a case study highlighting the implementation of a DApp using blockchain and IPFS for secure storing and sharing of medical records is explained. And finally, a summary of the conclusion and future scope of blockchain technology in the healthcare space is covered.

11.2 Issues and Challenges of Traditional Healthcare Systems

The healthcare industry continues to face a lot of challenges concerning interoperability, privacy, and security despite the advent of technological applications. For example, certain legal compliance requirements such as the U.S. Healthcare Law (HIPAA) requires that healthcare practices must comply with certain privacy and security regulations to ensure that the patients' security and confidentiality are protected as they generate sensitive, pri-vate health information. [1, 5, 6]

Following is a brief description of the various challenges that pre-existing healthcare systems are currently facing:

- Ensuring interoperability between organizations for secure and effective infor-mation transfer of EHRs to provide efficient functionality to patients and data handlers involved, beyond any geographical limits. [5, 7, 8]

- The current healthcare systems that are centralized and contain highly sensitive patient data are vulnerable to various cyberattacks (such as DDoS and ransom-ware attacks) that might cause data breaches and leak important patient informa-tion, thus violating the rules and regulations of health organizations and posing serious threats to the patients and the organization involved. [9, 10]

- In today's healthcare systems, organizations have permanent and complete control over medical data provided by patients. Instead, a patient-centric model must be established where the patients can control to whom their medical data is shared, to what extent, and for how long. [5]

- The data generated by IoT smart healthcare devices to collect and store health and wellness related data should be easily integrated with high-fidelity health records recorded by healthcare practitioners. This system must follow certified medical equipment standards and licenses to establish interoperability and trust between all parties. [11–13]

- Today's healthcare systems require that patients maintain hard copies and electronic copies of all the medical data over one's lifetime and have to share these medical records with doctors. This ineffective data sharing system is insecure, slow, and lacks trust and interoperability. Secure data sharing for collaborative treatment and accuracy of diagnosis through the efficient opinion-seeking of various doctors to prevent errors in treatments and medications is extremely important. [5, 8, 10, 14]

- All medical data in massive amounts and various formats should be available securely via a single platform to all the stakeholders such as patients, pharmacies, doctors, and lab test centers for easy retrieval, storing, and sharing for an optimized user experience. [5]

- The healthcare sector is transitioning from a volume-based (more payment leading to better treatment) to a value-based (patient-centric treatment with high quality) system. Thus, patients should be well informed and involved in the decision-making process. In a value-based model, data is collected digitally and gives easy access, preventing data inaccuracy and data fragmentation. [15]

- Healthcare systems must maintain a mutual trust relationship between parties via mutually agreed-upon rules and regulations before any communication and exchange of data takes place to maintain a security standard. [15]

- Presently, the cost of healthcare is a major concern due to the absence of proper drug supply chain tracking infrastructures. Patients are victims of exploitation by having to purchase medication and other medical commodities at higher prices. Drug supply chain monitoring can help prevent this exploitation. [16]

- The existing patient billing management systems are vulnerable to manipulation. Recently, excessive billing and false billing of patients for services not performed has resulted in 50% of healthcare billings being fraudulent. [17]

- Clinical trials are a vital part of the healthcare industry and help perform human testing to study the status and intensity of diseases. But unfortunately, 50% of these clinical trials are estimated to go unreported and thus create pressing safety concerns for the patients involved and may result in a serious threat to their lives. [5]

The subsequent section describes the workflow of a blockchain-based healthcare system consisting of medical data, blockchain technology, the healthcare applications to be incorporated with blockchain, and the stakeholders using this system.

11.3 Workflow of Blockchain-Based Healthcare Systems

Blockchain technology is redefining the way data is modeled and governed in healthcare systems. The workflow of a blockchain-based healthcare system can be divided into four primary layers comprising the sources of data, blockchain technology, the healthcare system, and the end-users/stakeholders. Firstly, all medical data from labs, smart wearable devices, etc. are consolidated as raw material that eventually grows into the scale of big data. This is the most important element in this system and creates the first layer. The second layer is the phase of the core blockchain platform used in this healthcare system. Blockchain platforms help users perform data transactions in this healthcare system. Hyperledger Fabric and Ethereum are some examples of blockchain platforms currently in use. [18, 19] The primary components of blockchain are smart contracts, digital assets, membership, wallets, events, and signatures. An array of protocols (for instance P2P, decentralized, distributed, and centralized) can be used for communicating with other programs and frameworks across various networks. The blockchain for the particular healthcare systems can be chosen to be public or private as is required. E.g. a private blockchain network can be confined to a specific healthcare provider and a public blockchain network can be used for the implementation of a drug supply chain management blockchain application. This blockchain platform will have to be integrated with the rest of the components of the healthcare system. The third layer consists of core healthcare applications such as data management applications, supply chain management (SCM) applications such as pharmaceuticals and clinical trials, and the Internet of Medical Things (IoMT) applications including healthcare IoT, medical devices, data security, and artificial intelligence (AI). The fourth and final layer comprises the end-users/stakeholders such as doctors, patients, pharmacies, test labs, and researchers who use this blockchain-based healthcare system. Users at this layer should be able to efficiently share and manage data without any security and privacy risks. [20]

The following section provides a description of the architecture of a healthcare system implementing blockchain comprising of the creation of the medical records, the storage of these documents using blockchain, database, and cloud storage, and the accessibility of these records.

11.4 Architecture of Blockchain-Based Healthcare Systems

With the recent progress in electronic healthcare-related technology, cloud data storage for healthcare, and regulations for patient data protection and privacy, new arenas have opened for healthcare data management and the ease of use, accessibility, and sharing of patients' data at their convenience. [21] Blockchain technology in healthcare has the potential to resolve critical issues concerning the storage, security, transactions, and management of health data in an effective way. Figure 11.1 shows the basic architecture of a blockchain-based healthcare data management system. This application performs data sharing, data storage, data management, and EHR in a healthcare system. [20]

Following are the steps of this healthcare data management system using blockchain:

1) Primary data such as medical history, diagnosis, and other physiological information is generated from the patient-doctor interaction.

2) An EHR is created using primary data and other medical information such as details of the particular health organization, lab test reports such as MRIs, X-rays, and drug history.

3) The ownership and customized access control are given exclusively to the specific individual patient who is the owner of this entity. Any party who wants access to

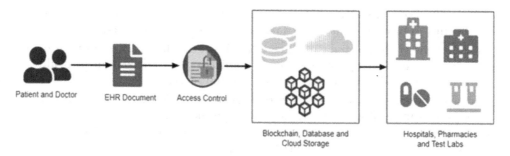

FIGURE 11.1
Data management using blockchain in healthcare [20].

this valuable information in the future must request access permission, which is then forwarded to the owner of the EHR and only the owner can decide to whom this access can be granted.

4) This is the core step of the process which includes the database, blockchain, and cloud storage. The blockchain provides privacy and security, and the database and cloud storage facilitate the storage of the EHRs in a distributed manner. The patient's data stored on the blockchain is encrypted using the patient's private key. This data can be decrypted by the doctor or researcher by using the patient's public key, provided by the patient.

5) The end-users comprising of healthcare providers such as hospitals, private clinics, labs, pharmacies, and public hospitals request access to the medical data safely and transparently to the authorized owner. Irrespective of geographical location, these health records are accessible and available via the web on mobiles and devices, and will be validated via the blockchain public ledger, which will continue to have medical records added to it over time. [20, 22]

In the next section, some use cases of blockchain in healthcare are described such as EHR, supply chain management, remote patient monitoring, supply chain, insurance claims management, and health data analytics.

11.5 Use Cases of Blockchain In Healthcare

Understanding the practical applications of blockchain-based healthcare systems directs us to understand the optimal implementation of this technology along with the challenges and limitations present.

- EHR applications such as the MedRec blockchain technology application by MIT Digital Media Lab handles sensitive health record data appropriately. [4]
- Many advanced prototypes are developed based on IBM Hyperledger for drug supply chain application in order to maintain the sanctity and quality control of pharmaceutical supply chains. [23]

- Ethereum-based blockchain platforms are developed as prototypes to demonstrate clinical trials and maintain data sanctity in the process. [24]
- Remote Patient Monitoring can be facilitated through IoT devices, Ethereum, and Hyperledger to develop patient-centric applications of blockchain in healthcare for health record data creation, analysis, and maintenance. [5]
- Various Ethereum-based prototypes have been implemented for insurance claims applications in healthcare. Some examples are the MIStore—a biomedical insurance system—and Poditok—an organization partnered with Intel for advanced implementations of blockchain technology. [5]
- An advanced application of blockchain technology is health data analytics wherein blockchain is incorporated with business intelligence, analytics, and cognitive capabilities for superior processing of data. An example of this is Moamosihna, which is a blockchain framework to help harness the benefits of artificial intelligence, machine learning, and natural language processing. [5, 25]

The various challenges encountered when implementing a blockchain-based healthcare system are explained in the next section.

11.6 Challenges for Blockchain Applications in Healthcare

The implementation of blockchain in healthcare does come with its own set of unique challenges described as follows:

- Scalability is a major issue due to the transaction speed of the processing nodes in a blockchain network. [26]
- The regulations and compliances, for example HIPAA, on blockchain vastly varies from country to country and across organizations. [26]
- Interoperability is a major challenge due to different transaction mechanisms, consensus models, and smart contract functionalities. [26]
- Integrating blockchain with the pre-existing healthcare systems for an end-to-end healthcare system is a difficult challenge to surmount due to the amount of time, detailed planning, and human resources and expertise required to incorporate blockchain technology into healthcare. [5, 26]
- Blockchain cannot assure the authenticity, i.e. accuracy of the stored data, and this is a sensitive issue when it comes to healthcare data that affects patients' lives. [26]
- Also, quantum computing can pose a major security threat to public-key cryptography-based blockchain systems. Blockchain technology should be robust in working with other technologies such as IoT and analytics. [26]
- Involvement and interaction with all stakeholders, for example the elderly and children, should be as simplistic and intuitive as possible. [5]
- A cultural shift towards blockchain and the required number of blockchain developers and experts is necessary to implement blockchain in healthcare. [26]

- A crucial challenge is the cost involved in storing a lot of medical data on the blockchain itself. It is incredibly expensive to store a lot of data on the blockchain. A solution to this, as explained in the next section, is the usage of the Interplanetary File System (IPFS) for the storage of the data and to simply use the blockchain to store the hash of the data stored on the IPFS instead of the sizable medical document itself.

The following section provides a use case of a case study of a DApp using Ethereum Blockchain and IPFS for a secure medical data management system.

11.7 Case Study: DApp for Healthcare Data Management Using Ethereum Blockchain and IPFS

In this section, a decentralized application (DApp) using Ethereum Blockchain and IPFS (Interplanetary File System) [25] for secure medical records storing and sharing is explained. Using IPFS for medical data storage and Ethereum blockchain for storing the hash addresses of this data, creates a blockchain-based health record system that can be used inexpensively compared to the unaffordable cost involved in storing large data onto the blockchain itself. Blockchain-based EHR helps ensure a secure exchange of EHR documents between patients and healthcare providers. The Ethereum blockchain public ledger enables the immutable nature of data uploaded on the blockchain along with an immutable audit trail. In this system, patients and doctors can correspond with each other without intermediaries and patients are the sole owners of their respective medical data. Every doctor must be recognized as a registered, certified doctor to have access to this medical data access facility. Figure 11.2 depicts the overall flow of the process of secure medical file storing and sharing in the DApp using Ethereum Blockchain and IPFS. [27]

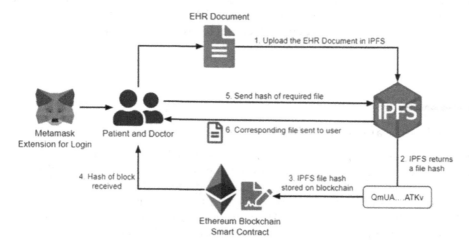

FIGURE 11.2
DApp for healthcare data management using Ethereum blockchain and IPFS.

The various tools and technologies used to implement this DApp are as follows. The Ethereum Blockchain is used in this application. Ethereum is a blockchain platform having smart contract functionality to build DApps. Ethereum blockchain facilitates the storage of smart contracts (pre-configured and deployed code blocks and agreements between stakeholders). These smart contracts contain the authorization logic, the Access Control List, and store the IPFS hashes of the records, thus ensuring security and immutability. Ethereum uses the Ether (ETH) cryptocurrency for transactions and uses the solidity programming language for building the DApp. IPFS is used for secure, distributed, decentralized file sharing and storage of medical records. IPFS is a content-addressable, peer-to-peer network protocol for the storage of files in a distributed file system. IPFS helps prevent the necessity of storing records on the expensive blockchain itself and, instead, the large medical records can be stored across nodes in the IPFS network and the unique hashes corresponding to these files help elegantly encrypt, store, and share this data. Remix IDE is a web application that can be used to write, deploy, and run smart contracts. Infura, which is a development suite, is used to provide API access to the IPFS network and Ethereum blockchain for the DApp. Metamask is an extension used to store and manage Ethereum accounts, transactions, and to help connect the Ethereum DApp via the browser securely. Metamask enables verified transactions over DApps and provides a password-less login feature via access to Ethereum smart contracts. This is performed via a user account having a unique Ethereum address provided by the Metamask extension, i.e. a SHA3 hash of public key through which the proof of ownership of the account is performed using the signing of data with the private key provided by the account. Solidity is the object-oriented programming language for writing smart contracts on the Ethereum blockchain platform. In this system, public and private key cryptography are implemented to provide secure access to patients, doctors, physicians, and hospitals to access medical health records. To upload a medical record (EHR), the medical records are encrypted using cryptography provided by the system and uploaded to the IPFS. Next, the hash address generated for this file in IPFS is stored in blocks in the Ethereum blockchain. The blockchain maintains the record of all data transactions that occur in this medical health record system. All data modifications are recorded. When a patient or a doctor (with permission from the patient) wishes to retrieve a medical record from IPFS, based on the IPFS hash address of the required document, that particular document is retrieved from IPFS and delivered to the end-user. [27, 28]

11.8 Conclusion and Future Scope

In this chapter, the complete study of blockchain in healthcare systems is described. Today's healthcare systems face several challenges related to interoperability, security, accessibility, availability, fragmented and scattered medical data, and lack of a patient-centric model. These challenges can be combated through various features of blockchain applicable to healthcare applications. The workflow of a blockchain-based healthcare system comprises of the primary medical data, the blockchain technology components, the core healthcare applications to be incorporated with blockchain, and the end-users/stakeholders benefiting from this system. The architecture of a healthcare system implementing blockchain follows a series of steps from the creation of the medical records to the storage of these documents using blockchain, database, and cloud storage, and finally the accessing of these records by the appropriate entities. Next, some use cases of blockchain in healthcare were described such as EHR, supply chain management, remote patient monitoring, supply chain, insurance claims management, and health data analytics. Some challenges that blockchain-based healthcare systems face include scalability, navigating regulations, interoperability, transaction speeds, integration of blockchain with existing healthcare systems, the accuracy of healthcare data and progress of cultural adoption of blockchain technology, and availability of blockchain developers and experts. Finally, a case study explaining the development of a DApp for securing, storing, and sharing medical records using Ethereum blockchain and IPFS is covered.

Blockchain is a relatively new technology and hence its adoption in various domains, although gaining momentum, is still comparatively slow due to skeptics of the technology and a deficit of experts and developers of blockchain. In healthcare, the transition from the traditional pre-existing healthcare systems to a blockchain-based one is gradual as the number of products providing such services is still on the low side. Furthermore, the people's trust and reliance on blockchain as a solution to the many pressing problems in the healthcare industry needs to get stronger, which will only happen through the ongoing expanding research and implementation going on in this field. Hence, although it might take some time, a blockchain revolution that impacts every sector of our lives including healthcare is already in progress and is set to have a bright future.

References

1) Zhang, Peng and Maged N. Kamel Boulos. "Chapter 50 — blockchain solutions for healthcare." *Precision Medicine for Investigators, Practitioners and Providers* (2020): 519–524.
2) Buterin, Vitalik. "Ethereum white paper: A next-generation smart contract and decentralized application platform." *White Paper*, vol. 3, no. 37 (2014).
3) Mettler, M. "Blockchain technology in healthcare: The revolution starts here." *2016 IEEE 18th International Conference on E-Health Networking, Applications and Services (Healthcom)* (2016): 1–3.
4) Azaria, A., A. Ekblaw, T. Vieira and A. Lippman. "Medrec: Using blockchain for medical data access and permission management." *2016 2nd International Conference on Open and Big Data (OBD)* (2016): 25–30.
5) Shukla, Rashmi G., Anuja Agarwal and Shekhar Shukla. "Chapter 10 — blockchain-powered smart healthcare system." *Handbook of Research on Blockchain Technology* (2020): 245–270.
6) Emanuele, J. and L. Koetter. "Workflow opportunities and challenges in healthcare." *BPM & Workflow Handbook* (2007): 157–166.
7) Zhang, P., D.C. Schmidt, J. White and G. Lenz. "Blockchain technology use cases in healthcare." *Advances in Computers*, vol. 111 (2018): 1–41.
8) Schiff, G.D., O. Hasan, S. Kim, R. Abrams, K. Cosby, B.L. Lambert, A.S. Elstein, S. Hasler, M.L. Kabongo, N. Krosnjar and R. Odwazny. "Diagnostic error in medicine: Analysis of 583 physician-reported errors." *Archives of Internal Medicine*, vol. 169, no. 20 (2009): 1881–1887.
9) 7 Major Challenges Facing the Healthcare Industry in 2021 — MailMyStatements, https://mailmystatements.com/2020/10/27/2019challenges/ (accessed 8 July 2021).
10) Hripcsak, G., M. Bloomrosen, P. FlatelyBrennan, C.G. Chute, J. Cimino, D.E. Detmer, M. Edmunds, P.J. Embi, M.M. Goldstein, W.E. Hammond and G.M. Keenan. "Health data use, stewardship, and governance: Ongoing gaps and challenges: A report from AMIA's 2012 health policy meeting." *Journal of the American Medical Informatics Association*, vol. 21, no. 2 (2014): 204–211.

11) Zhang, P., J. White and D. Schmidt. "Architectures and patterns for leveraging high-frequency, low-fidelity data in the healthcare domain." *2018 IEEE International Conference on Healthcare Informatics (ICHI)* (2018): 463–464.

12) Zhang, P., J. White, D.C. Schmidt, G. Lenz and S.T. Rosenbloom. "FHIRChain: Applying blockchain to securely and scalably share clinical data." *Computational and Structural Biotechnology Journal*, vol. 16 (2018): 267–278.

13) McCoy, A.B., A. Wright, M.G. Kahn, J.S. Shapiro, E.V. Bernstam and D.F. Sittig. "Matching identifiers in electronic health records: Implications for duplicate records and patient safety." *BMJ Quality & Safety*, vol. 22, no. 3 (2013): 219–224.

14) Kaushal, R., K.G. Shojania and D.W. Bates. "Effects of computerized physician order entry and clinical decision support systems on medication safety: A systematic review." *Archives of Internal Medicine*, vol. 163, no. 12 (2003): 1409–1416.

15) Pennic, J. *Top 10 Challenges, Issues and Opportunities for Healthcare Executives in 2019*, https://hitconsultant.net/2018/09/28/challenges-issues-opportunities-healthcare-executives/#.YOarxugzZPY (accessed 8 July 2021).

16) Rabah, K. "Challenges & opportunities for blockchain powered healthcare systems: A review." *Mara Research Journal of Medicine & Health Sciences*, vol. 1, no. 1 (2017): 45–52.

17) Das, R. "Does blockchain have a place in healthcare?." *Forbes*, www.forbes.com/sites/reenitadas/2017/05/08/does-blockchain-have-a-place-in-healthcare/ (accessed 8 July 2021).

18) Ethereum, www.ethereum.org/ (accessed 8 July 2021).

19) Hyperledger—Open Source Blockchain Technologies, www.hyperledger.org/ (accessed 8 July 2021).

20) Khezr, S., M. Moniruzzaman, A. Yassine and R. Benlamri. 2019. "Blockchain technology in healthcare: A comprehensive review and directions for future research." *Applied Sciences*, vol. 9, no. 9 (2019): 1736.

21) Dimitrov, D.V. "Blockchain applications for healthcare data management." *Healthcare Informatics Research*, vol. 25, no. 1 (2019): 51–56.

22) Panesar, A. *Machine Learning and AI for Healthcare*, 2019, pp. 1–73, https://hitai.ir/posts/288/1611463181.Arjun_Panesar_Machine_Learning_and_AI_for_Healthcare_Big_Data_for.pdf.

23) Androulaki, E., A. Barger, V. Bortnikov, C. Cachin, K. Christidis, A. De Caro, D. Enyeart, C. Ferris, G. Laventman, Y. Manevich and S. Muralidharan. "Hyperledger fabric: A distributed operating system for permissioned blockchains." *Proceedings of the Thirteenth EuroSys Conference* (2018): 1–15, Article no. 30.

24) Nugent, T., D. Upton and M. Cimpoesu. "Improving data transparency in clinical trials using blockchain smart contracts." *F1000Research*, vol. 5 (2016): 2541.

25) IPFS Powers the Distributed Web, https://ipfs.io/ (accessed 8 July 2021).

26) Yaqoob, I., K. Salah, R. Jayaraman and Y. Al-Hammadi. "Blockchain for healthcare data management: Opportunities, challenges, and future recommendations." *Neural Computing and Applications* (2021): 1–16.

27) Mandal, A., P. Dumaru, S. Bhandari, S. Shrestha and S. Shakya. "Decentralized electronic health record system." *Journal of the Institute of Engineering*, vol. 15, no. 1 (2019): 77–80.

28) Naz, M., F.A. Al-zahrani, R. Khalid, N. Javaid, A.M. Qamar, M.K. Afzal and M. Shafiq. "A secure data sharing platform using blockchain and interplanetary file system." *Sustainability*, vol. 11, no. 24 (2019): 7054.

12

Smart Microgrid-Based Energy Management Using Blockchain

Rashmi Jain, Sachin Jain and Sanchit Jain

CONTENTS

12.1 Introduction to Blockchain Technology

Blockchain was first introduced in 2009 by Satoshi Nakamoto. Bitcoin, a cryptocurrency (electronic cash), was the first and most popularly used implementation of this technology. For a successful decentralized approach, it must support the following fundamental operations.

DOI: 10.1201/9781003203933-15

12.1.1 Fundamental Operations

Blockchain Technology has the potential to replace currently used technologies in industries and to facilitate new business structures. Strategists, planners, and decision-makers across industries and businesses should focus on the ways of applying this technology to different applications. The concepts on which the Blockchain Technology works and provides a way of committing transactions are as follows:

- Peer-to-Peer Messaging: All the nodes have dedicated links to share data between them. Data transfer is secure over a dedicated link and the delay is short.
- Distributed File Sharing: The current and all previous status of transactions are available with all the nodes. In case any device fails, it will not affect the operation of the rest of the network.
- Autonomous Device Coordination: Special programs called Smart Contracts are designed to streamline communication among devices. By using these smart contracts and consensus algorithms, device coordination is done.

12.1.2 Workings of Blockchain

A Blockchain contains a sequence of blocks where each block is numbered and includes information about the new operations to be included in the block. The hash of the block is calculated by using a secure hash function and the previous block's hash. The chain of blocks is created from the first block—the genesis block—to the current block. The genesis block is generally hardcoded into the software. Figure 12.1 shows the structure of a simple Blockchain. Blocks contain a set of transactions that denote the operations to be performed or values to be transferred to other entities. The transactions from different entities are sent to the network and gathered into a block. After verification of data in a block, it is added to the existing chain. All transactions are visible to all the peers in the Blockchain, and everyone has precisely the same copy of information available in the chain. Pool or solo miners mine or validate the transactions included in a block. Mining is a resource-intensive and complex task in the Blockchain. The toughness of the mining process will decide how resistant the system is to any kind of

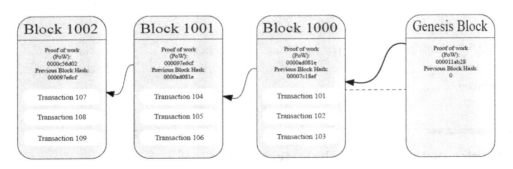

FIGURE 12.1
Blocks in blockchain.

tampering. Every block contains a challenge-response-based Proof of Work (PoW). The PoW generated by a node is verified by the rest of the miners when they receive a block. Mining ensures that the node added to the chain is secure, tamper-resistant, and attains consensus. Miners charge some fee or some coins for the validation work done. The consensus is a crucial feature in decentralized systems, which require that two or more nodes mutually reach an agreement on a proposed value needed for computational purposes. Consensus methods include Proof of Stake (PoS), PoW, Byzantine Fault Tolerance (BFT), Practical Byzantine Fault Tolerance (PBFT), and Binary Consensus. These protocols guarantee that for every block, a specific level of difficulty is attained to generate a new block [1].

12.1.3 Features of Blockchain

Blockchain Technology is not just a backup network for cryptocurrencies, but it offers a lot more. So, the key features that make it so irresistible are as follows:

- Decentralized Approach: Not a single node or entity gains control of the complete system. All the participating entities take part in controlling operation of the system.
- Distributed and Transparent Data: The status of data in a blockchain is available with all the nodes. The blocks store the set of all transactions committed up to the recent one and nodes distribute all information publicly among peers.
- Auditable Transactions: Every node can verify the operations performed by all other nodes. Each user must digitally sign the transactions to be included in a block. A digital sign verifies who had performed which transaction. The current block has a hash value computed over the hash of previous block.
- Consensus Algorithms: Every node participates in a consensus process to validate a transaction. If the majority of nodes agree on a specific operation, then only that operation can be performed.
- Security: As there is no central entity for transactions, it is very challenging to make any changes to transactions done earlier. Digital signatures are put with all the transactions, and the hash value generated in the current block is computed based on previous block hash along with current block transactions. Therefore, tampering with data is very challenging for any malicious user.

12.1.4 Types of Blockchain

Two major types of Blockchain can be used, depending upon the nature of the application: public or private. Hybrid Blockchain combines the features of public and private Blockchains according to the need of the application.

- ***Public Blockchain***

There is no need of any identity of the node available in the Blockchain and all nodes have read or modify rights for data. The most successful Bitcoin application provides write as well as read permissions to all the nodes and is the best example of a public Blockchain.

- *Private Blockchain*

This type of structure can be deployed in an organization where all the users are trusted and known to each other. Here, the rights of users may vary according to the hierarchy to identify the roles of participants.

- *Hybrid or Community Blockchain*

This type of blockchain has security and transparency features of a public Blockchain along with the data privacy feature of private Blockchains. Applications can decide which data they want to share publicly and which data to keep secret. A ledger of a hybrid Blockchain is available to all users, but access control rights are not given to all of them.

12.2 Concept of Microgrid and Smartgrid

Energy is a very essential factor that always needs optimization. Traditional energy resources gradually become insufficient with respect to time and increasing requirements by recently developed devices; so is the need of more and more resources for generating and distributing electricity. Industries and academia are designing different renewable and sustainable power generation techniques that can support the existing power supply units to suffice the current power requirements. These new resources are also taking care that the end users' need is satisfied in a more efficient way as compared to the traditional ones; this is also the purpose of the Microgrid—also called Smartgrid (SG). The share of energy from resources such as solar power and wind power used in world-wide energy generation is increasing annually, which are managed by SGs since 2007. There is huge growth in renewable energy utility [2]. India is one of the countries with a large production of energy from renewable sources. As of 27 November 2020, 38% of India's installed electricity generation capacity is from renewable sources (136 GW out of 373 GW).

12.2.1 Contributors of Microgrid (MG)

Microgrid is a small network of electricity users that has its own local source of energy supply. This network usually connects to a centralized national power grid but can function independently. Microgrid is made smart by using a protection system of the grid and central control through a Supervisory Control and Data Acquisition (SCADA) system, monitoring transmission equipment with diagnostics, and treating the whole power system as a complex adaptive power system with self-healing capability [3]. The European Commission Task Force on Smart Grid says that a SG intelligently integrates the activities of all users connected to it, like producers, consumers, and prosumers. Prosumers do both the works of producers and consumers. These SGs ensure an economically efficient and sustainable power distribution system with low losses, high quality, security of supply, and safety [4].

An SG takes care of electricity generation, transmission, distribution, and consumer technologies along with integrated information and communication applications. Figure 12.2 shows the contributors of an SG. Users can manage their usage, have different offerings, choose an economic plan for buying energy, and check for a reliable and stable power supply. These capabilities of an SG improve the throughput of the system and reduce energy

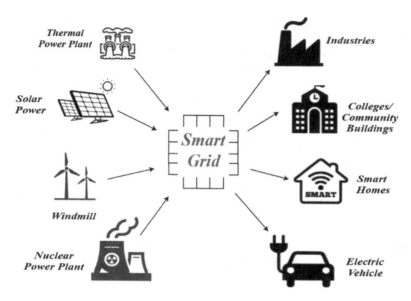

FIGURE 12.2
Smartgrid contributors.

consumption. SGs are often powered by local energy sources where transmission and distribution of power from a major centralized grid or the traditional energy source is far away and costly to execute. This type of SG is referred to as an autonomous, stand-alone, or isolated Smartgrid. [3]. These Smartgrids can operate in one of the two modes-autonomous mode or a connected mode. A Smartgrid can effectively integrate various sources of distributed generation (DG), especially renewable energy sources (RES).

12.2.2 Components of a Smartgrid

A Smartgrid generally consists of the following components to achieve all functionalities needed:

- *Local Power Generation Unit:* Smartgrids have their own power generation units so that they can operate in a standalone mode. It uses various types of generation sources that feed electricity to the user. The resources have two major groups— thermal generation sources and renewable generation sources. Microturbines, fuel cells, and photovoltaics (PV) are some of the examples of power generation units.

- *Consumers:* They are the users or customers who consume energy, also called the load. They may range from a single device to the lighting, cooling, and heating systems of buildings, commercial centers, running various gazettes, etc. In the case of controllable loads, electricity consumption can be modified according to the demands of the network.

- *Energy Store:* It stores the energy generated by power generation units. It includes all chemical, electrical, pressure, gravitational, flywheel, and heat storage technologies. It must perform various functions, like ensuring power quality, regulation of frequency and voltage, smoothing the output of renewable energy sources, and keeping backup power for the system. The process of energy storage plays an important role in cost optimization. It uses a unique supervising unit if there are multiple types of power generation units for energy management purposes.

- *Point of Common Coupling:* To be able to operate in the two specified modes, the Smartgrid gets connected to a main grid. This point of connection in an electrical circuit is known as the point of common coupling. If a Smartgrid does not have point of common coupling, then it is a standalone grid, which is generally available in remote areas where the network of the main grid is unavailable due to technical or economic issues.

- *Smart Meters:* It is a very important and unique feature in the Smartgrid for measuring power generation as well as power consumption. They have a communication system integrated with a measuring system, which allows the user to monitor energy usage in real time. Users can control their power consumption according to their budget from real time information. Suppliers of power use the smart meter to generate accurate bills for the respective users depending on their power consumption [3].

12.2.3 Features of Smartgrid

SG includes different functionalities like usage monitoring, data analysis, operation and mode control, and communication capabilities to the traditional grid system to maximize the throughput of the system and reduce cost and energy consumption. The following features help these systems perform the tasks of a Smartgrid in an efficient way [4]:

- *Smart Metering:* It measures the consumption of energy and communicate it to the consumer and supplier. It is an intelligent interaction between utility grids and end users. It also helps to achieve capital flow in bi-directional ways.

- *Self-Healing:* Different monitoring capabilities help in quick detection of malfunctioning of the system and take corrective action to resolve issues.

- *Security:* Security system of a grid can identify any cyber or physical attack, information security breaches, illegal consumption of energy, and natural disasters.

- *Dual Operation Modes:* It operates in two modes—centralized power generation mode when connected to main grid and standalone mode when it uses a distributed power generation. Energy storage capabilities make them more reliable.

- *Cost Reduction:* Due to monitored usage of power, a user can manage to use power in their budget and improve the use of assets. This results in minimization of cost and operation and maintenance cost is low.

12.2.4 Functions of a Smartgrid

The components and features of Smartgrid conclude with the following functions:

- *Self-Healing:* Ability to solve grid disturbances automatically. Has an automatic response system for grid failure that saves the system from cascading and a complete blackout.

- *Energy Storage Systems:* Manage storage and maintenance of large amounts of solar and wind power.
- *Power System Reliability:* Though the supply from the main grid is disturbed, it has its own Renewable Energy Sources (RES) to keep functioning. The self-healing feature also improves reliability.
- *Renewable Energy Integration:* It has many local RES connected to the grid which can easily trade their energies. The plug and play ability is available to connect new resources to the grid.
- *Privacy and Security:* Smart meters and secure local energy network ensure privacy and security.
- *Power Quality:* Provides better power quality as compared to a conventional grid.

The functions of new Smartgrid system need a host of supporting technologies. Figure 12.3 shows the functions of the SG.

12.3 Application of Blockchain Technology to Smartgrid

Blockchain features such as distributed ledger, transparency, tamper-proof transactions, security, and smart contracts have attracted many businesses. Blockchain's peer-to-per network can eliminate the middleman or third party in traditional energy supply and reduce transaction costs [5]. The existing grid networks have a substantial drawback that

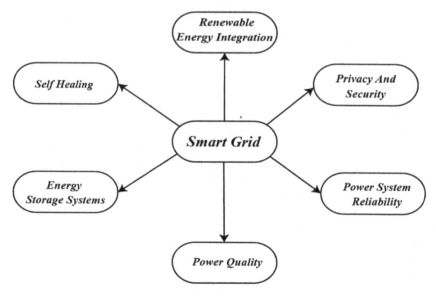

FIGURE 12.3
Functions of a Smartgrid.

is the lack of security due to the involvement of mediators, high operational costs, and low efficiency of working. On the counter- part, Blockchain's potential to bring significant benefits and innovation has inspired power distribution companies to deploy this technology for efficient distribution. Several use cases are being developed such as peer-to-peer energy trading, wholesale energy trading, vehicle-to-vehicle energy trading, security and privacy, power generation and distribution, Smartgrid equipment maintenance, and so on [6]. The most common application of Blockchain in energy sector is trading energy and currency crediting. Organizations or individuals can stimulate this technique for transactions among their own loads and resources, with other peer entities in the network, and with the main grid. The rules in the form of smart contract govern the whole transaction process. The transactions are sometimes delayed due to a validation technique that is a consensus. The following sections describe some of the use cases [7].

12.3.1 Peer-to-Peer Energy Trading

In this era of renewable energy usage, communities and individuals are also having arrangements for energy generation, which may suffice their own needs. If they have some surplus energy, they can trade it with other users. The Blockchain application in the peer-to-peer (P2P) energy exchange or energy marketplace is a very promising and exhilarating use case. Renewable Energy Source (RES), producer-cum-consumer (prosumer), consumer, finance, smart meter, and energy aggregators are the entities connected in this peer-to-peer network. Community residents with solar panels generate and sell their energy to the people without solar panels using a customized mobile app. Users have a P2P connection established and negotiate the cost of electricity directly with the seller without any intermediaries. Smart meters help to communicate with each other reliably over this P2P network [7].

The P2P energy trade in the Industrial Internet of Things (IIoT) leads to the development of microgrids for using sustainable energy. Governments are investing huge amounts in Smartgrid-based local energy markets [8]. The typical architecture and working of such a P2P network are discussed in the following section.

12.3.1.1 Network Architecture

There are various types of Blockchains available which can be used to develop the Blockchain-based network to implement this P2P energy trading network. Public Blockchains provide more flexibility, high level of transparency, and ability to participate in consensus to each node. But the delay occurs in validating a transaction and consumes more computing power in the validation process, therefore consortium Blockchains are more suitable [8]. Here only a set of pre-authorized nodes have rights to handle the transactions in a distributed ledger, thereby reducing some energy of nodes not participating in a consensus and speeding up the validation process. More computing power is provided to these special nodes to solve the power-hungry consensus algorithm. Many real applications developed call this network an energy Blockchain. The energy nodes in the network can be small-scale consumers, individual houses or buildings, industrial consumers, smart meters, finance application, electric vehicles, etc. Nodes have the flexibility to choose their roles as prosumers (sellers), buyers (consumers), or idle nodes. Any node can initiate transactions according to the requirement. A record of these transactions (that is the block) is kept and managed by Energy Aggregators (EAGs). They are a set of especially authorized nodes from the set of nodes in the network There can be one or more nodes working as an aggregator node. Figure 12.4 shows a general architecture of P2P blockchain and Figure 12.5 indicates a detailed structure of EAG. Overall components are as follows [8]:

- *Prosumer Nodes:* The energy nodes with surplus energy to sell. They have their own sources to produce energy for their usage. They trade the energy remaining after their requirement is fulfilled.
- *Consumer Nodes:* The energy nodes who need energy are consumer nodes. They are the customers in the network.

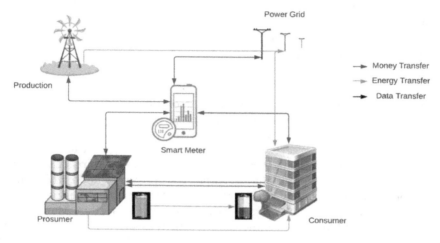

FIGURE 12.4
Architecture of P2P energy Blockchain.

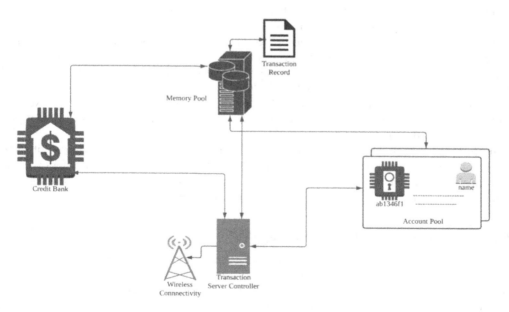

FIGURE 12.5
Energy Aggregator (EAG) structure.

- *Credit Banks:* For transactions of selling and buying a cryptocurrency or energy, coins are used. Credit banks provide energy coins to borrowers based on their credit values.
- *Borrowers:* Energy consumers who want to buy energy must pay for the energy, so they borrow energy coins from credit banks
- *Transaction Servers:* They keep information about the nodes that have energy for trading; they also collect and count energy requests and match transaction pairs of energy trading.
- *Account Pools:* These are the objects that keep a record of wallets created, and maintain the wallet addresses and accounts of energy-coin in the EAGs.
- *Memory Pools:* They are the systems which store the blocks containing transactions of all the nodes of the Blockchain.
- *Wallets:* They store energy coins.

The fields of transaction in the block contain data on the quantity of energy traded and the timestamp indicating the time of transaction for usage of energy. Further detailed information about a transaction may contain the amount of energy requested, amount of energy granted, transaction server ID, meter ID, digital signatures of seller to indicate receipt of money (energy-coin), transaction validator, timestamps of activities, and a transaction ID. A transaction is initiated by either the consumer node who wants to buy energy or the producer node who wants to inform about the surplus energy it wants to sell. Transaction servers of the supervisory nodes carry out the transaction. Many transactions can be accumulated in a block; after validating all the transactions by the predetermined supervisory nodes, the block is added to the chain. Each block contains a block ID, a block header, a hash value generated using a Secure Hash Algorithm (SHA), previous block header, timestamp, and the transactions. A buyer will transfer energy coins—the cryptocurrency—to the seller and their wallets are updated accordingly. Credit banks provide coins to buyers depending upon their credit value.

The parties involved in trading should follow the conditions mentioned in the smart contract. Smart contracts are the programs that check the conditions are satisfied and ensure security during transactions, mainly deployed on the smart meters and the validating/supervisory nodes in the blockchain [6].

A project by LO3 Energy, the Brooklyn Microgrid, is a Blockchain-based energy exchange project, where people get connected to trade electricity directly with consumers, bypassing the traditional energy utility companies.

Bangladesh has a Blockchain start-up, ME SOLShare, which connects homes with solar panels through a microgrid. A bi-directional DC electricity meter, SOLBox, offers access to community trading. The SOLBoxes have built-in wireless internet connection to get connected with each other in the network and exchange information.

12.3.2 Wholesale Energy Trading and Supply

Energy Blockchain also suits wholesale energy markets. The decentralized aspect of Blockchain promises the elimination of third parties. Distributed ledger technologies and smart contracts help producers and consumers interact directly. Demand and supply of energy can be negotiated over a time period and a best deal can be executed with the help of an agreement. The Blockchain records the agreement safely and executes the operations automatically at the stated time. Smart contracts ensure payments are done automatically and timely according to agreed conditions. Some pre-designated nodes maintain all the transaction data, which is available with different nodes, and a consensus procedure for confirming a transaction. When a transaction is validated, it is added to a block. PoS and PBFT algorithms are helpful in designing a network for wholesale energy trading. Communication among various entities is shown in Figure 12.6. It has potential to carry out transactions faster when compared to a conventional trading system. But replacing the existing energy trading mechanism with Blockchain will need a significant revision in the roles of the brokers, mediators, and energy exchanges. There are many blockages and technical challenges to realize the wholesale energy Blockchain.

Looking into the practical difficulty in complete implementation, energy markets have not yet gone for all use cases implementation. Most systems go for the development of the imbalance settlement use case [6].

PONTON has designed an energy trading platform called Enerchain 1.0 and launched it in May 2019. It provides services for trading data and energy via the platform. Enerchain is the first-ever project for a Blockchain-based wholesale energy trading worldwide. The platform is fast in comparison to traditional platforms like Bitcoin and Ethereum. The block time is 1 second for transactions on Enerchain, whereas 10 minutes and 10 to 20 seconds for Bitcoin and Ethereum, respectively [7].

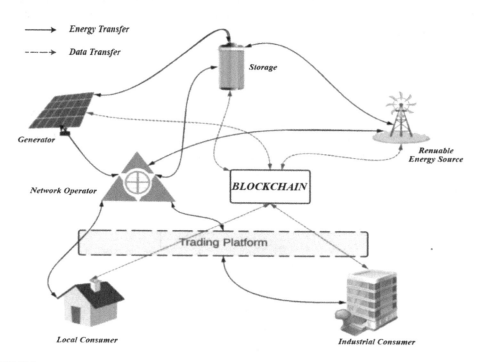

FIGURE 12.6
Wholesale energy trading.

12.3.3 Power Generation and Distribution

This is another use case where Blockchain application is beneficial. Smartgrids get an advantage from the security and immutability features of Blockchain, when traditional systems have faced many cyberattacks like Denial of Service (DoS), Data Injection Attacks (DIA), and others to get the control over the network to manipulate it. As a result, there can be stealing of energy, complete blackouts, changes in the databases, and many more. Blockchain Technology helps in the prevention of data manipulation related to various processes involved in power generation and distribution.

Various studies describe the usage of a Single Machine Infinite Bus (SMIB) system in power generation and distribution network to connect the generation unit to the Blockchain. [9]. A SIMB system consists of a synchronous generator (G) that has some measured values like current, voltage or frequency, a load switch (SL) to connect a load, a Power System Stabilizer (PSS) to grid stability, and a control switch (SC) to control the PSS in correlation with SL. The generator with these supporting components is connected to the infinite bus. Figure 12.7 shows the architecture of the system. One or more supervisory nodes can observe the states of all the switches and the generator with timestamps and record them in blocks, thereby identifying any tampering in the current state of each switch and reporting accordingly in the Blockchain network. Blocks will record the measured values, states of the switches, timestamp, and rule violation conditions. The supervisory and validating nodes then use the smart contracts designed to tackle the situation if there is any attack taking place and maintain the previous state of the system. Smart contracts are the distributed applications running on different nodes that decide how other prosumers and consumers get connected to the SIMB system as they can be the part of the network.

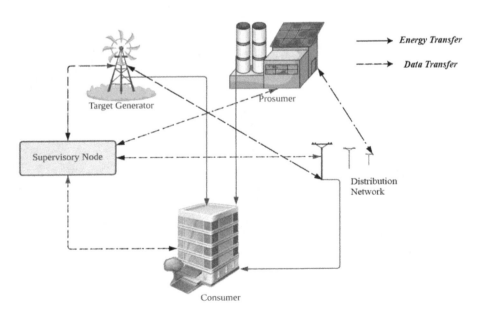

FIGURE 12.7
Power generation and distribution.

12.3.4 Financing Energy Access with Blockchain Technology

This section focuses on money transactions. Consumers pay for the energy bought in terms of energy coins according to the deal in the smart contract and validations approved by energy brokers or EAGs. Three types of transfers take place during this energy trading: energy transfer, data transfer, and money transfer. In a Blockchain-based energy network, the steps for currency transaction are as follows [8]:

i. The consumers put request for energy to the energy aggregators (EAG).

ii. Transaction server analyzes the demands received and shares them to the local resources of energy.

iii. The consumers can negotiate the rates per unit energy with the help of EAG. They work as an energy broker for energy nodes and set the charges. Smart meters help to count correct measure of energy transfer for correct bills.

iv. Energy coins or tokens are transferred from buyer's e-wallet to the seller's e-wallet. If buyers do not have sufficient coins to buy the requested energy, then they can use the credits provided by the credit banks.

v. Energy sellers verify the credits and previous transactions of buyer from the memory pool or EAG and initiate the selling event.

vi. Energy buyers can initiate energy coin or token transfer to complete the activity.

vii. The energy sellers communicate the energy traded and respond to the EAG.

viii. All transactions are done when they get approved by EAG or designated supervisory nodes and added to a block. This block is then attached to the existing Blockchain.

ix. Memory pool makes the latest copy of blockchain available to all the nodes in the network.

The energy seller with the highest contribution to energy supply is rewarded with energy coins during a certain period, which is also known as credit tokens and transferred to users' e-wallets over the grid.

Use of virtual currency was a novel payment method in Smartgrid. BASNederland was the first company to receive Bitcoin for payment of energy bills. Two more Netherlands-based companies, Spectral and Alliander, designed a token—Jouliette—for energy trading over Blockchain, where the tokens are spent from the e-wallets. Bankymoon, a South Africa-based start-up, is developing smart meters that support expenditures in Bitcoin. Australia-based start-up PowerLedger uses a smart contract-based platform, POWR, to spend tokens called Sparkz for energy trading. Many more systems are available that use a Blockchain-based P2P network and cryptocurrencies for renewable energy trading and billing purposes [11].

12.3.5 Blockchain-Based Crowd-Funding Initiatives

There are many places in the world, mostly in Africa, that do not have connections to regional conventional power grids. Communities in these regions depend on power generated by solar panels, but they do not have sufficient funds. Crowd-funding initiatives of Blockchain is a better solution here.

In Africa, it is difficult to spread national grids due to dense forests, therefore many regions and communities are not connected to the grids. These regions mostly depend on solar panel projects for electricity. Private solar projects often remain unfunded. Crowd-financing initiatives of Blockchain can close this funding gap. People can remotely purchase the photovoltaic cells needed in the solar panels on homes to construct the RES. A Blockchain-based Smartgrid can be designed to connect the RES with the community houses. The owners of the solar panel can collect rent from the users in terms of cryptocurrency.

Thus, the crowd funding feature of Blockchain enables anyone, anywhere in the world to be the part of a Smartgrid in Africa. The Sun Exchange is a finance platform for solar energy in Africa which is based on Blockchain and operates on a similar model of crowd funding [7]. This platform will allow renewable energy to expand and reach all the remote places of the world with lowered cost of energy transactions.

12.4 Advantages of Blockchain Technology in Microgrid

Blockchain Technology has plenty of advantages, but the most relevant for the energy sector is the reduced transaction cost. Some potential benefits of Blockchain in the energy sector include the following [7]:

- *Cost Reduction*: Traditional power grid is a huge infrastructure to build and maintain. Using Blockchain volatile renewable energy capacity can be integrated to the grid. It lowers the need for working capital. More information about all the RES is available to utilities and grid operators for managing energy supply in an optimal way.
- *Reduced Bills*: The cost of utility bills is reduced due to lower transaction costs in the market for electricity. Negotiation is also possible to get energy at a lower cost. There is no need of any third party or any brokerage.
- *New Opportunities for Communication*: Energy devices like electric vehicles, water heaters, batteries, solar panels, etc. can communicate with each other with the help of the grid operator (Smartgrids).
- *Secure Access*: The grid can identify any sort of tampering with energy devices with the help of monitoring and recording the status of different switches and take corrective actions using smart contracts. Stealing of power is difficult. The operations performed are immutable.
- *Affordable Energy for Underserved Communities*: The areas where the regional power grid network is not possible, Smartgrid-based renewable energy sources can fulfill the requirement of these communities through local and decentralized renewables grids.
- *Encouragement for New Developments*: People are rewarded with energy credits for more and more power supply in the Smartgrids, so more energy resources are being developed.

12.5 A Case Study: Brooklyn Microgrid (BMG)

Many projects have been developed using Blockchain Technology in IoT systems. Brooklyn Microgrid (BMG) [5] is one of the best examples. Scientists say that the BMG project is an innovative version of the energy market where people generate energy, consume it, sell it, and manage it. BMG is an energy marketplace for locally generated renewable energy. Scientists have developed this model to share energy generated by people in the community with people in the community [10].

Exergy, a permissioned data platform, is created using some innovative solutions along with the power of Blockchain Technology. It can send energy across the existing grid infrastructure, which is generated by Brooklyn residents. People participate in a simulated energy marketplace where people are willing to pay for locally generated renewable energy. The solar grid, producing electricity, can be monitored with a set of IoT systems, which will measure the electricity generated, share electricity with other users, and share the burden of maintenance. Exergy builds a reputation through its history of records and exchanges. People are producers as well as consumers, and they care for their community's energy future.

12.5.1 The Exergy Network

The Exergy platform has the potential to stimulate the future energy model, and already the possibilities are limitless. It is the network of prosumers and consumers, and there is no conventional central plant to produce and share energy as a utility [12]. The entities on the Exergy network are as follows:

- *Prosumers:* On the Exergy platform, prosumers are generating energy with their renewable resources. They can share power autonomously with consumers in near-real-time on the platform in their local marketplace. Local business prosumers and residential prosumers can be the prosumers. They take care of devices, trust that devices are recording actual solar production, and share the burden of maintenance.

- *Microgrid:* A microgrid is a network of connected prosumers and consumers. They are the energy assets of this ecosystem. These sustainable communities generate, store, and transact the energy locally, making them more efficient and resilient.

- *Distributed System Operator:* The distributed system operator has the task of managing energy usage, fulfill the demands at negotiated rates, and load balancing. It has access granted to consumer data available in the management systems.

- *Electric Vehicle Charging:* When a public or private charging station, or an electric vehicle, has a surplus of energy, it can share it and make it available for purchase on the local network. Mobile apps can be used to send alerts to consumers according to the budgets they set.

- *Consumers:* Residential users or local business organization can be the consumers. They can access the energy at a negotiated rate from various prosumers. The messaging system can be used to inform the user about the availability of energy and the requirement of the user.

12.5.2 Working of Microgrid

Figure 12.8 shows the connection of the entities of the microgrid. Prosumers generate energy and connect it with smart meters that are used to measure the amount of energy transacted with the consumers. The community solar generates energy. Smart contracts

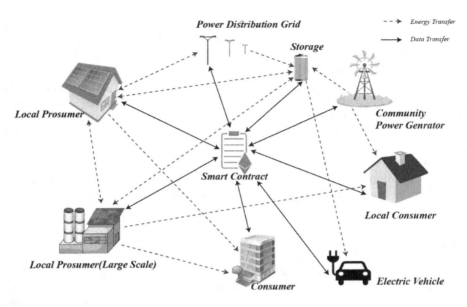

FIGURE 12.8
Entities on a Brooklyn Microgrid.

implemented govern the sharing energy between prosumers and consumers. Rate contracts are used for selling extra energy generated, which is cheaper than the energy supplied by the conventional electricity suppliers. Regional energy companies and other private companies can also access energy generated by prosumers if they have extra energy available with prosumers.

All energy trading is validated and in a new block, which is then connected to the chain. This block is tamper-proof and trusted. Thus, this project provides environmental, cost, and reliability benefits.

Because of their ability to offer sure energy supply, secure, and high-quality energy supply, microgrids have been receiving much attention recently. They are also providing sustainable, economic, and efficient energy supply. The cryptocurrency model is efficiently deployed to develop a platform for trading energy.

12.6 Conclusion

Blockchain Technology has a lot of scope in the energy sector and a significant potential to change the trading and crediting of energy. Many companies leverage this technology for energy exchanges on a distributed level, creating a virtual distribution grid. Traditionally, energy distribution requires a lot of infrastructure and capital. But through a distributed energy trading system, we can trade energy generated locally in our societies and in a more secure way, which enables us to provide energy to more people and make it accessible to the poor in form of prepaid energy, which can be done by small mobile transactions. With the help of peer-to-peer energy trading, prosumers and consumers directly communicate without any third-party involvement. Different renewable sources generate energy that is stored and shared through a Blockchain-based network to benefit small- as well as large-scale consumers. All consumers get access to energy more efficiently and at a considerably lower cost.

References

[1] Jain, Rashmi. *Blockchain Architecture for Securing the IoT, Security and Privacy in the Internet of Things*, eds. Syed Rameem Zahra Mohammad and Ahsan Chishti, CRC Press, Taylor & Francis Group, New York, 2020, pp. 51–65.

[2] Jaganmohan, Madhumitha. *Share of Renewable Power in Energy Generation Globally from 2007 to 2019*, 2021, www.statista.com/statistics/489131/share-of-renewables-in-power-generation-globally.

[3] Shuva, Paul, Rabbani Md Sajed, Kundu Ripon Kumar, et al. *A Review of Smart Technology (Smart Grid) and Its Features*. Proceedings of 2014 1st International Conference on Nonconventional Energy (ICONCE 2014), https://ieeexplore.ieee.org/document/6808719.

[4] Petinrin, J.O. and Shaaban Mohamed. "Smart power grid: Technologies and applications." *IEEE International Conference on Power and Energy (PECon)* (December 2012): 2–5.

[5] Sani, Yahaya Adamu, Javaid Nadeem, Fahad A. Alzahrani, et al. "Blockchain based sustainable local energy trading considering home energy management and demurrage mechanism." *Sustainability Journal* (2020), www.mdpi.com/journal/sustainability.

[6] Merlinda, Andoni, Robu Valentin, Flynn David, et al. "Blockchain technology in the energy sector: A systematic review of challenges and opportunities." *Renewable and Sustainable Energy Reviews, Elsevier*, vol. 100 (2019).

[7] Akash, Takyar. *Use Cases for Blockchain Energy*, CEO Leeway Hertz, 2020, https://www.leeway-hertz.com/blockchain-in-healthcare/.

[8] Li, Zhetao, Jiawen Kang, Rong Yu, et al. "Consortium blockchain for secure energy trading in industrial internet of things." *IEEE Transactions on Industrial Informatics*, vol. 99 (2017).

[9] Tejasvi, Alladi, Chamola Vinay, Joel J.P.C. Rodrigues, et al. "Blockchain in smart grids: A review on different use cases." *Sensors Journal* (2019), www.mdpi.com/journal/sensors.

[10] Lawrence, Orsini. *Brooklyn Microgrid Project*, www.brooklyn.energy.

[11] Asma, Khatoon, Verma Piyush, Southernwood Jo, et al. "Blockchain in energy efficiency: Potential applications and benefits." *Journal Energies* (2019), www.mdpi.com/journal/energies.

[12] Esther, Mangalam, Gartner Johannes, Rock Kerstin, et al. "Designing microgrid energy markets A case study: The Brooklyn Microgrid." *Applied Energy Journal, Elsevier*, vol. 210 (2017).

Index